T0305405

The Politics and Economics of Brexit

The Politics and Economics of Brexit

Edited by

Annette Bongardt

Professor of European Political Economy, INA and Universidade Fernando Pessoa, Porto and Senior Associate Researcher, CICP, Universidade de Évora, Portugal

Leila Simona Talani

Chair in International Political Economy, European and International Studies Department, King's College London, UK

Francisco Torres

Professor of European Political Economy, Católica Lisbon School of Business and Economics, Universidade Católica Portuguesa, Portugal

 Edward Elgar
PUBLISHING

Cheltenham, UK • Northampton, MA, USA

Cover Image: boschettophotography.

Published by
Edward Elgar Publishing Limited
The Lypiatts
15 Lansdown Road
Cheltenham
Glos GL50 2JA
UK

Edward Elgar Publishing, Inc.
William Pratt House
9 Dewey Court
Northampton
Massachusetts 01060
USA

A catalogue record for this book
is available from the British Library

Library of Congress Control Number: 2020938007

This book is available electronically in the **Elgar**online
Social and Political Science subject collection
http://dx.doi.org/10.4337/9781788977975

MIX
Paper from
responsible sources
FSC
www.fsc.org   FSC® C013604

ISBN 978 1 78897 796 8 (cased)
ISBN 978 1 78897 797 5 (eBook)

Printed and bound by CPI Group (UK) Ltd, Croydon, CR0 4YY

Contents

Figures

Contributors

EDITORS

Annette Bongardt is a Visiting Associate Professor at Universidade Fernando Pessoa and a Member of the Research Centre in Political Science (CICP), University of Évora. She is also a regular Visiting Professor (and National Coordinator of "Internationalization and European Integration") at the National Institute of Public Administration (INA) in Lisbon. She has been a Visiting Senior Fellow (2014–19) in European Political Economy at the London School of Economics and Political Science (LSE), and was a Visiting Fellow at the Robert Schuman Centre for Advanced Research of the European University Institute, Florence, and a Senior Member and Academic Visitor at St Antony's College, Oxford University. She holds a PhD in Economics (1990) from the European University Institute, Florence. She has authored and edited several books. Her more recent articles in academic journals have dealt with sustainable integration (*Journal of European Integration*, 2015), Brexit, the optimal size of the Union (2018) and EU comprehensive trade agreements (2017), and the EU's approach to global trade (2018, with F. Torres). She has also authored or co-authored chapters for the main handbooks on European integration (Oxford University Press, 2012; Palgrave, 2013; Routledge, 2015 and 2018) and the *Oxford Encyclopedia of EU Politics* (forthcoming). Among her recent chapters/articles on Brexit are "Trade Agreements and Regional Integration: the EU after Brexit", in *Routledge Handbook of International Trade Agreements* (Routledge, 2019), and "The Political Economy of Brexit", *Intereconomics* (2016).

Leila Simona Talani is Professor of International Political Economy in the department of European and International Studies since 2014. In 2018 she was awarded the prestigious Pierre Keller visiting Professorship at the Kennedy School of Government of the University of Harvard. She was also appointed as Jean Monnet Chair of European Political Economy by the European Commission in 2012. She was previously at the European Institute of the London School of Economics and in the department of European studies of the University of Bath since the year 2001. From November 2000 until September

2001 she held the position of Associate Expert for the United Nations Regional Office for Drug Control and Crime Prevention based in Cairo, working on irregular migration from the Middle East and Northern Africa to EU countries. In the academic year 1999–2000 she taught "The Political Economy of European Integration" at the European Institute of the London School of Economics where she had previously held a research and teaching fellowship for the academic year 1998–9. Leila Simona Talani was awarded her PhD with distinction at the European University Institute of Florence in 1998. She is the author, among other titles, of: *The Political Economy of Italy in the Euro* (Palgrave, 2017), *The Handbook of the International Political Economy of Migration* (Edward Elgar, 2014–17), *The Arab Spring in the Global Political Economy* (Palgrave, 2014), *Dirty Cities: Towards a Political Economy of Shadow Dynamics in Global Cities* (Palgrave, 2013), *European Political Economy* (Routledge, 2013), *Globalization, Migration and the Future of Europe* (Routledge, 2011), and *From Egypt to Europe* (I.B.Tauris, 2010).

Francisco Torres is Visiting Professor of European Political Economy (EPE) at Católica Lisbon SBE. He has also been an EPE Visiting Senior Fellow at the LSE (2014–19) and PEFM Associate at St Antony's College, Oxford University (2012–19). He holds a PhD in European Political Economy (Católica, Lisbon), a Master in Economics (Nova, Lisbon) and a five-year degree also in Economics (Católica, Lisbon). He also holds an MA in International Affairs from the Johns Hopkins University, SAIS, and has studied Economics at the EUI in Florence (PhD programme, 1986–9), having become the first Robert Schuman Fellow of the European Commission at the Centre for European Policy Studies in Brussels thereafter, and having returned later on to the EUI for a year as a Visiting Fellow at the Robert Schuman Centre for Advanced Studies. He held a one-year post-doctoral fellowship at the University of Oxford. Among his most recent books are *Governance of the European Monetary Union: Recasting Political, Fiscal and Financial Integration* (Routledge, 2016, co-edited with Erik Jones), and *The Political Economy of Adjustment throughout and beyond the Eurozone Crisis: What Have We Learnt?* (Routledge, 2020, co-edited with M. Chang and F. Steinberg).

CONTRIBUTORS

Stefania Baroncelli is Full Professor of Public Law at the Free University of Bolzano/Bozen, Italy, where she acts also as Pro-Rector. Her main research interests are governance, institutions, adaptation to the EU legal order, European Monetary Union, regionalism and rights of minorities, and educational rights. She is author of "Long-term vs short-term perspectives: adaptation, stability and the roles of the constitutional courts in the management of the Eurozone crisis in Germany and Italy" (*Contemporary Italian Politics*, 2018).

Rémi Bourgeot is an economist and associate fellow at the French Institute for International and Strategic Affairs. His work centres on monetary arrangements, both in Europe and emerging economies. His recent studies investigate technology, trade and monetary issues, with a particular focus on the political–economic implications of the fourth industrial revolution and the crisis of globalisation. He holds Master's degrees from the Higher Institute for Aeronautics and Space (SupAero) and the Toulouse School of Economics, and a PhD from EHESS.

Pompeo Della Posta (PhD, MA) is associate professor of Political Economy at the University of Pisa (Italy). He has published many scientific articles in journals, such as *Journal of Macroeconomics*, *Macroeconomic Dynamics*, *Journal of Policy Modeling* and *North American Journal of Economics and Finance*, among many others. He has written many chapters in books, edited several volumes and authored a book on *The Economics of Globalization* and one on European monetary integration. He is the Editor of the Scientific Journal *Scienza e Pace/Science and Peace* and the President-Elect for 2019 of the *International Trade and Finance Association*.

Emidio Diodato is Associate Professor of Political Science and International Politics at the University per Stranieri of Perugia, where he is President of the Postgraduate Course of studies in International Relations and Development Cooperation. His research interests focus on geopolitics and foreign policy analysis. He is author (with F. Niglia) of *Italy in International Relations: The Foreign Policy Conundrum* (Palgrave Macmillan, 2017) and *Berlusconi 'The Diplomat': Populism and Foreign Policy in Italy* (Palgrave Macmillan, 2017).

Roberto Di Quirico is a tenured Lecturer in Political Science and Aggregate Professor of International Relations at the University of Cagliari (Italy) and is a former Jean Monnet Module professor at the University of Florence, and visiting Lecturer at the University of Bath (UK). His research interests focus on monetary integration, EU economic governance, and democracy in Southern Europe. His principal publications are *Italy, Europe and the European Presidency of 2003* (Paris, Notre Europe, 2003, preface by Jacques Delors) and *A Europe Apart: History and Politics of European Monetary Integration* (forthcoming).

Serena Giusti is Head of the research group on the EU's Eastern neighbourhood, Russia, post-Soviet space, and Senior Lecturer in International Relations at Sant'Anna School of Advanced Studies (SSSA) Pisa. She is also a senior associate researcher at the Institute for International Political Studies (ISPI), Milan. Her main research interests are IR Theories, Foreign Policy Analysis, and the EU and Russia's Foreign Policy. She has published extensively on these topics in, among others, *The International Spectator*, *European Foreign Affairs Review*, *Journal of Balkan and Near Eastern Studies* and *International Journal of Cultural Policy*.

Scheherazade S. Rehman is an expert on international financial markets, and global economic, political, and digital technology cybersecurity risks. She is a Professor of International Finance, Director, World Executive MBA in Cybersecurity, and the Director, European Union Research Center at The George Washington University, Washington DC. She is a Senior Research Fulbright Global Scholar. Dr Rehman sits on various private bank and academic boards of directors and advises various US government agencies. She has written over 80 scholarly articles and books including *The Path to European Economic and Monetary Union, Financial Crisis Management in Regional Blocs* and *The Quest for Exchange Rate Stability in the Next Millennium*.

Monica Rosini is Assistant Professor of Public Law at the Free University of Bolzano/Bozen (Italy). She holds a PhD in Public Law from the University of Florence. In 2017 she received the National Scientific Habilitation as Associate Professor in Constitutional Law. Her main research interests are on regional law, with particular focus on regions with special autonomy, and on the implementation of EU law. She has published two books and several articles on these topics.

Acknowledgements

The editors would like to thank their institutions at the time this project was initiated and conducted and where there was ample opportunity to discuss our views on Brexit with colleagues and students: King's College London (KCL), where the specific preparation of the volume took place and where the three editors gave various classes on the topic while this volume was being prepared, and the European Institute of the London School of Economics and Political Science (LSE), where we have also given various sessions on Brexit, notably within the LSE Brexit Lectures and the Political Economy of Europe regular course. We also benefited from the comments provided on our regular contributions to the "Brexit blog" at LSE and to "The UK in a Changing Europe blog" at KCL. Annette Bongardt and Francisco Torres are also thankful to CICP-Universidade de Évora and UFP and to Católica Lisbon School of Business and Economics, respectively.

We are most grateful to several colleagues who provided feedback on our various presentations and/or on draft chapters of this volume, in particular Lorenzo Codogno, Thomas Sampson, Keith Pilbeam, Roberto Tamborini, Benedicta Marzinotto, Andrea Boitani, Waltraud Schelkle, Kevin Featherstone, Iain Begg, Guy De Vries and Michiel van Hulten. We would also like to thank Alex Pettifer, Editorial Director, and Rachel Downie, Assistant Editor, at Edward Elgar for very competent guidance in the conception and production of the volume and an anonymous reviewer for very helpful comments.

Last but not least, we would also like to acknowledge the financial support of the Jean Monnet Centre for Europe in the World of King's College London that made the organization of this volume possible.

1. Introduction: the politics and economics of Brexit

Annette Bongardt, Leila Simona Talani and Francisco Torres

1.1 BREXIT MEANS WITHDRAWAL FROM THE EU, YET THE UK WAS DITHERING

It was only after the 12 December 2019 parliamentary elections that it became clear that the United Kingdom (UK) was to finally leave the European Union (EU). By giving a clear majority to the Conservative party, which had campaigned on the slogan 'get Brexit done' and in favour of leaving with a (the renegotiated) withdrawal agreement by the end of January 2020 (ten months after the original Brexit day), Brexit looked all but assured, after the UK had been seen dithering over its departure from the EU since the referendum vote against its EU membership on 23 June 2016.

The UK had created a *fait accompli* when it invoked the Union's exit provisions (Article 50 of the Treaty on European Union, TEU) on 29 March 2017, having embarked on an EU membership referendum in June 2016, which resulted in a majority for 'leave' (52 per cent, versus 48 per cent in favour of remaining).[1] It meant that the UK set the clock ticking down towards the two-year time limit within which it had to institutionally extricate itself from and settle withdrawal issues with the EU. The UK had thus set itself on course to, by default, become a third country to the EU by 30 March 2019 at the latest. Past that time limit, the departing country's EU membership should have ended, irrespective of whether any withdrawal agreement had been reached and ratified.

However, the UK formally requested and was granted, with the unanimity of its (former) fellow EU members (EU-27), successive extensions to the withdrawal period. The first extension was until either 22 May, subject to British MPs approving the Withdrawal Treaty reached with the EU, or failing that until 12 April 2019. The second extension, after MPs had rejected the withdrawal agreement for the third time, was granted until 1 June 2019 if the UK had not held European Parliament elections, or otherwise 31 October

2019. The third Article 50 extension until 31 January 2020 was forced on the government by parliament and immediately accepted by the EU. The Court of Justice of the European Union (CJEU) clarified that, during any extension period, the UK was legally still a full EU member and as such entitled to – unilaterally and definitely – revoke its exit notification if it wished to do so.[2] In theory, the postponement of Brexit had left all outcomes still on the table – the UK could leave the EU in a disorderly fashion ('no-deal Brexit'), or leave with the agreed withdrawal treaty in an orderly way, or even revoke Article 50, but it also created uncertainty and at best pushed back difficult choices.

Note that a ratified withdrawal treaty is only a first step towards, but importantly also a pre-condition for, any successive negotiations of the post-Brexit future bilateral (trade and wider) EU–UK relationship. Although part of the withdrawal agreement, the political declaration on the future relationship, unlike the withdrawal treaty, is non-binding in nature, it affirms that the EU cannot negotiate, and even less conclude, any international treaty (other than a withdrawal treaty) with a country while it is still a member state.

It was widely anticipated that the withdrawal negotiations would be the more straightforward and the comparatively easy part of the Brexit process, including ratification of the withdrawal treaty, as they require only a qualified majority of EU member states plus European Parliament (EP) consent. The negotiations of the details of the future (trade) relationship were expected to be much more complex and very likely lengthy and drawn-out, and ratification a priori more difficult, as it requires unanimous approval in the Council as well as ratification at the national and sometimes regional level (the future trade agreement likely being a mixed agreement in terms of competences), in addition to EP consent.

However, it was for the UK that withdrawal from the EU proved tortuous, and ratification of the withdrawal treaty became blocked. To start with, somewhat surprisingly, in the withdrawal negotiations it was not a UK united by Brexit purpose and behind Brexit positions that confronted a disunited EU. Rather, the EU presented itself remarkably united behind its chief Brexit negotiator (Michel Barnier) and in its stance, with respect to the UK government's positions.[3] In fact, the EU stood firm in the defence of EU principles (although it could also be argued that it made things unnecessarily difficult for the UK government led by Theresa May, by attaching too many conditions to the withdrawal agreement that could have been dealt with at a later stage)[4] and was consistent and transparent throughout in its approach. It had to come to terms with a UK government unable to formulate and create a consensus around withdrawal negotiating positions and even less capable of making a choice on the kind of future relationship it aimed at with the Union post-Brexit. The EU side faced a UK perceived as mostly negotiating with itself. On top of that, in the House of Commons, a majority to ratify the withdrawal agreement was not forthcoming; in fact, there were no positive majorities forthcoming *for* any-thing but only *against*. The UK government attempted to let the process go to the wire time-wise, in the hope of securing last-minute majorities in parliament to achieve ratification of the negotiated withdrawal agreement in the face of an imminent no-deal scenario (also called 'cliff-edge', as without a withdrawal treaty in place there would be no transition period and departure would be abrupt).[5] As it happened, the EU (and the world) came to watch the unfolding of events (and their tweaks and turns) in the UK with incredulity and concern (and some degree of amusement).

The UK's tortuous divorce illustrated the extent to which the UK polity – in spite of the country having been a member of the club since 1973 – still failed to understand how the Union works and what motivates it. It also showed the country's failure to grasp its diminished bargaining power as a departing member vis-à-vis the EU-27 and as a soon-to-be third country to the bloc, thrown back into dealing with the rest of the world on intergovernmental terms but without the supporting weight of the EU.

It is telling that it had taken the UK government until very late in the with-drawal process (December 2018) to accept the reality set out in the withdrawal treaty, which protects EU interests while respecting the red lines that the UK government had set out in the negotiations. Drawn up by UK negotiators and the EU negotiation team from the European Commission, the withdrawal treaty settles withdrawal-relevant issues (from citizens' rights, the financial settlement, the Irish border question,[6] to governance) and, upon the UK's request, also included a 21-month transition period that would preserve the UK's status quo post-Brexit until the end of 2020.

The UK government had agreed the withdrawal treaty but had not assured sufficient backing for its ratification in the national parliament, the House of Commons. Against that background, it did a notable volte-face, disowning its own proposal (and commitment) for ensuring the continued absence of a hard border in Ireland post-Brexit (the EU had conceded a UK-wide backstop rather than a Northern Ireland-specific backstop, its preferred solution), demanding that the EU either give it a unilateral exit clause to the backstop or a time limit on it. However, this was not acceptable to the EU, as in both cases the backstop would lose its insurance function.[7] There was a stalemate in the UK parliament, which could neither muster a majority for ratifying the withdrawal treaty (referred to somewhat erroneously as the 'deal', which suggests a trade deal that by definition it is not), defeated in fact by a large margin, nor for any realistic and workable alternative.

The UK government then allowed the process to drag on as long as possible in the hope that the prospect of and damages associated with an imminent cliff-edge scenario would encourage Conservative members of parliament and a sufficient number of opposition MPs to back its withdrawal treaty. It could also still have harboured the aim of eliminating the provisions relating to the continued application of workers' rights and environmental protection legislation after Brexit, which were included in the withdrawal agreement negotiated by Theresa May. This eventually happened in the withdrawal deal renegotiated by Boris Johnson. Still, the generosity of any free trade agreement that the UK will get from the EU will depend on its alignment with EU standards.

On their part, UK MPs largely tried to postpone having to make a choice, notably proposing (i) votes against a 'no deal' (the default scenario if parliament had not made a choice that led to the ratification of the withdrawal agreement, and hence nonsensical), (ii) an extension to the Article 50 withdrawal period (requiring unanimous EU-27 agreement and thus always likely to come with conditions attached) and (iii) calling on the people to decide (a re-run of the 2016 referendum, presumably with the UK also extending its permanence in the EU). Interestingly, it was taken for granted that the EU-27, especially the EU Council presidency, would accommodate UK internal squabbles and cooperate.

As for the EU, it appeared firm in the negotiations, stating that the withdrawal treaty would not be reopened (presenting it as a take-it or leave-it decision for the UK), although the EU declared (i) that it was open to changes to the (non-binding) political declaration on the future relationship under certain circumstances (especially if it was to become more ambitious), and (ii) that without a ratified withdrawal treaty there was no transition period, but that it could (albeit reluctantly) under certain conditions contemplate a UK request for a limited extension of the withdrawal period.[8] However, in the event, that limited extension was transformed into not one but three consecutive extensions. The last extension was given for the period requested by parliament, against the will of the government (the prime minister did not even sign the request he was obliged to write) and despite the fact that there were no new facts that would justify it, except Brexit politics on the part of the EU. In fact, some prominent European actors sounded very much in tune with anti-Brexit forces in the UK, favouring the cancellation of the result of the 2016 referendum.[9]

However, a focus on the UK (or the Isles) only, understandable on the part of UK (or Irish) polity, tends to conceal the fact that the EU was putting its future at risk by allowing all successive extensions of Article 50. Some may call this position naive; others may ascribe it to a well-constructed strategy of some in the Union joining forces with 'remainers' in the UK to reverse the country's democratic decision(s) to leave the EU. (Leaving had effectively been confirmed on three occasions: the result of the 2016 referendum, the 2017 parliamentary elections and parliament's decision to invoke Article 50 and leave the EU, with or without a deal, by 29 March 2019.)

What the Brexit process did lay bare in our view are some serious mis-conceptions on the part of the UK (George, 1998). First and foremost, they concern the nature, motivations and functioning of the European Union and the UK's role in it, well-illustrated by the UK's failure to conduct the withdrawal process, even in the early stages of 2017,[10] but there is a longer history to be considered (Davies, 2007). Furthermore, in its relationship with the Union – past, present and future – the UK has faced trade-offs while a member, which will not disappear after its departure. On the contrary, the country will have to make a choice post-Brexit between available economic benefits and national sovereignty, so that a preference for sovereignty repatriation implies lower economic benefits (Bongardt and Torres, 2016). In the UK discussion, that trade-off and implications for single market access have tended to be pushed aside. Rather, reference is made rather simplistically to a 'soft' or 'hard' Brexit, translating into staying closer to the EU and its single market, which is by far the UK's largest market, or privileging trade with the rest of the world ('Global Britain').

However, underlying the form that Brexit takes is a hard choice that needs to be made, incidentally present in both the UK's attraction to, and its unease with, the European integration project since the beginning, namely, that the economic benefits that the UK has enjoyed (and became accustomed to) as an EU member came with sovereignty costs (the need to coordinate actions with other member states) and that post-Brexit, in future trade agreements, any UK preference for more sovereignty also means less benefits. The fact that the UK has enjoyed the best of 'deals' as a member of the Union – in fact having been allowed to cherry-pick EU policies and enjoying significant influence – does not help, as any alternatives that are on offer for the UK–EU relationship once it is a third country to the Union look less attractive for the UK (but not necessarily for the EU).

The UK polity attempted to not have to confront the choices that withdrawal brought with it (including refusing to recognize the differences between, and implications of, a withdrawal agreement and a future trade relationship, and also for reasons of leverage[11]) and to postpone the reckoning (e.g. by transition periods, extensions of Article 50). With the UK as an EU outsider, those hard choices, very visible in the context of the negotiations with the EU on the future bilateral relationship, are still acute and inevitable.

1.2 THE POLITICS AND ECONOMICS OF BREXIT

The above discussion of the United Kingdom's exit from the European Union illustrates that with regard to Brexit, economics and politics cannot be treated in isolation. As conveyed by the title of this volume, this book aims to contribute to the literature on Brexit doing justice to real-world complexity through an interdisciplinary perspective.

The ambition and scope of our volume is therefore to examine Brexit from more than a single angle and benefit from the additional insights to be gained from a juxtaposition of politics and economics. Chapters draw mainly on political economy and political science approaches but also resort to history and law. They shed light on key motivations and factors to thereby contribute to a better understanding of Brexit and of its likely consequences. They take a step back to try to better understand what shapes the UK's political and economic preferences and what are its fundamental motivations and issues that mould its stance, as that conditions the likely consequences for the EU.

The volume is organized in two parts, 'The Politics of Brexit' and 'The Economics of Brexit', with a final chapter that discusses and elaborates on the lessons learned and provides an outlook.

Part I on 'The Politics of Brexit', addresses Brexit-related political issues that range from the political rationality of Brexit and the reasons for an unsustainable UK position in the EU, to specific UK sovereignty concerns in the absence of a written constitution, a preference for Anglo-Saxon neo-liberalism, and the UK's standing in the world post EU exit.

Annette Bongardt and Francisco Torres adopt a political economy approach to analyse the question of the political rationality behind Brexit. The authors argue that Brexit triggered a qualitative change in the nature of European integration and discuss the resulting political ramifications for the functioning of the European Union club, notably the limits of EU differentiated integration. Roberto Di Quirico's chapter focuses on the issue of the (un-)sustainability of the UK's position in the EU. He traces the UK's road from European integration to Brexit, from joining the EEC towards the adoption of a failed strategy of what he terms "malign neglect" towards the EU, aimed at curbing further integration in Europe, in particular political integration and regulation. Stefania Baroncelli and Monica Rosini examine the control/sovereignty issue by introducing a constitutional law perspective to Brexit and by discussing the role of parliaments in the exit option. The authors elaborate on what sovereignty means for the UK in the absence of a written constitution and employ a comparative approach to insert the UK's Brexit decision in an ampler framework. Finally, the chapter by Emidio Diodato and Serena Giusti sheds light on what Brexit means for British foreign policy. The authors consider the prospective alternatives for the post-Brexit UK's role in global affairs ('Global Britain'), underpinned by role theory and evidence.

Part II focuses on 'The Economics of Brexit', including issues pertinent to the economic model. It features four chapters, which examine possible motivations for Brexit, above all EU regulation in general or of financial services in particular, but also the importance played by subjective well-being rather than economic growth, and the challenges to be confronted post-Brexit. Pompeo Della Posta and Scheherazade Rehman shed light on the puzzle of a leave vote despite a favourable environment of economic growth and low unemployment. The authors consider the role of social capital and subjective well-being, once the subjective perception of people's well-being will, together with economic growth (objective perception), and determine prosperity and sustainable development. The UK dithered for a long time over Brexit, and Annette Bongardt analyses what role the properties of the European single market cum regulatory model, with the unfettered participation that the UK enjoyed as an EU member, played therein. Her chapter discusses and contrasts the choices and trade-offs before the UK with regard to any future access to the single market once the country ceases to be an EU member. The chapter by Leila Simona Talani zooms in on regulatory issues in the context of financial sector regulation. The City of London, with its special role and weight in the British economy, benefited from a friendly regulatory environment and economic policies set up by the British government. After Brexit, the issue of escaping EU-driven financial sector regulation has moved to the limelight. Remi Bourgeot's chapter considers what the challenges are in terms of economic rebalancing that Brexit will pose for the UK and the EU.

NOTES

1. Article 50 of the Treaty on European Union (TEU) was, incidentally, inserted in the European treaties (Treaty of Lisbon, signed in 2007) only on the occasion of the latest comprehensive revision.
2. The Court of Justice of the European Union (2018) provided a legal clarification, notably that the UK is entitled to unilaterally revoke its withdrawal notification and under which conditions, namely that this requires an unequivocal and unconditional decision communicated in writing to the European Council, within the Article 50 two-year timeframe or, if applicable, its agreed extension and before the withdrawal agreement takes effect.
3. The situation is a bit more complex in broader political terms, as various high-profile EU members, namely former EU Council President Donald Tusk and European Parliament Brexit coordinator Guy Verhofstadt but also various national heads of state, constantly expressed their views very much in line with the UK internal opposition's to the government in its wish to block Brexit.
4. This EU stance was arguably unnecessary, if not counterproductive. It only served the purpose of delaying Brexit. In the end, the result of the December 2019 elections was (again) to 'get Brexit done' and the new UK government may well choose to trade on WTO terms after the end of the transition period (on 31 December 2020) and thereby ignore EU-imposed conditions.
5. Since the UK's June 2016 in–out referendum, the EU faced a UK that let almost nine months elapse before proceeding with the formal notification of Article 50, embarked on general elections shortly thereafter (effectively reducing the time left for negotiations), and which appeared ill-prepared and as dragging its feet during most of the negotiations. The EU presented itself as well-prepared and organ-

ized, implementing what can be called Asian negotiating tactics: the European Commission Brexit task force worked on a clear mandate circumscribed by guidelines from the Council, conducting the negotiations on the EU side; this approach was successfully followed through (despite UK attempts at dividing the EU-27 and appealing to member states directly, over the heads of the EU institutions). The UK, on the other hand, was perceived as not knowing what it wanted from the negotiations (apart from all the benefits of EU membership without the obligations) and negotiating more with itself than engaging with the EU. Not only did reaching a withdrawal agreement with the UK become very cumbersome from the EU's perspective but the UK minority government furthermore lacked a majority in parliament to ensure the ratification of its eventually negotiated deal or, in fact, a majority for any other outcome.

6. The included backstop solution to ensure frictionless trade if a future bilateral agreement was not Northern Ireland specific (as the EU had insisted it must be), but instead UK-wide, at the UK government's insistence. The UK Tory minority government was sensitive to the Northern Ireland Democratic Unionist Party, on whose parliamentary support it depended by means of a support and supply agreement. The EU in the end accepted the UK's preferred UK-wide backstop, which, rather than keeping only Northern Ireland in the internal market and customs union to avoid a hard border between the Republic of Ireland and the British province of Northern Ireland, would keep the entire UK in the customs union unless and until a future trade agreement would solve the matter. As the EU has pointed out, a free trade agreement (FTA) between the EU and the UK would still require a backstop.

7. Having dealt with the arguably less contentious issues first (citizens' rights, even the financial settlement), the so-called Northern Irish backstop   included to uphold the Irish Good Friday Peace Agreement after the UK's exit from the Union by notably ensuring the continued absence of a physical border and frictionless trade between the British Province of Northern Ireland and the Republic of Ireland – became contested and the major stumbling block to ratification in the UK parliament of the withdrawal agreement that had been agreed between the EU and the UK government.

8. For legal reasons, the European Parliament elections in May 2019 were a major stumbling block to any extension. Apart from that, it would also seem inconceivable that a country that had decided to leave the Union (because national interests took precedence) still participated in the European elections and would have (albeit temporary) MEPs determining EU-27 interests.

9. It is interesting to follow Tusk's declarations all through the negotiation process, constantly expressing the hope that the UK could still revoke Article 50 and its decision to leave the EU, sometimes in clear contrast to the European Commission. The content and timing of Tusk's comments were very much aligned with UK prominent anti-Brexit politicians like Tony Blair, or academic opinion makers like Timothy Garton Ash.

10. This point has been made repeatedly by the UK's former EU ambassador, Sir Ivan Rogers, who had stepped down in the beginning of the withdrawal process alleging 'muddled thinking' on the part of the UK government in its handling of Brexit.

11. A priori the UK would have more leverage in the withdrawal context than in negotiating as a third country, which also explains why it tried to bring trade issues into the withdrawal treaty.

REFERENCES

Bongardt, Annette and Francisco Torres (2016), "The political economy of Brexit: Why making it easier to leave the club can allow for a better functioning EU", *Intereconomics*, 51, 4, July/August, pp. 214–19.

Davies, Norman (2007), "Not forever England: A European history of Britain", in *Europe East and West*, London: Pimlico, pp. 83–105.

George, Stephen (1998), *An Awkward Partner: Britain and the European Community*, Oxford: Oxford University Press.

PART I

THE POLITICS OF BREXIT

2. Brexit as a question of political rationality: hard choices for the UK, lessons for EU sustainability

Annette Bongardt and Francisco Torres

2.1 INTRODUCTION

This chapter approaches the British exit from the European Union (Brexit) as a question of political rationality.[1] It departs from the idea that it did not make sense for the United Kingdom (UK) to remain in the European Union (EU). In fact, ever since the treaty of Maastricht, the UK has essentially stayed outside the EU's main institutions, opposing and blocking the very process of European integration, with the result that its membership has had very negative consequences for the EU and by extension also for the UK, and that this situation has become unsustainable. The chapter also contends that with the Euro currency being at the political core of the EU and the European integration project, those countries that do not want to be part of Economic and Monetary Union (EMU) and that are not committed to an ever-closer union should invoke Article 50 of the Treaty on European Union (TEU) – incidentally a British contribution to the Lisbon treaty – and seek some form of association with the EU rather than membership.

The clear result of the December 2019 UK election meant that Brexit could go ahead at last in January 2020 – parliament had already passed the second reading of the withdrawal agreement bill (WAB) by a majority of 124 votes on 20 December. The many attempts to reverse the UK's democratic decision on Brexit had failed. Those very political attempts to reverse Brexit were mainly channelled through a series of procedural challenges through the courts and through a British parliament seemingly disconnected from the non-binding referendum mandate to exit the EU that it had promised to honour. Brexit-blocking MPs ignored the 2016 expressed will of the people for exiting the EU and their own 2017 decision to trigger Article 50 of the TEU and implement Brexit by 29 March 2019. It is noteworthy that none of the 'remainer' MPs who tried to block Brexit, delaying it several times, and who left the Conservative and Labour parties for other parties or ran as independent candidates, managed to be re-elected.

The Conservative party's clear stance on Brexit ('get Brexit done') seems moreover to have been successful in obtaining the votes of part of the Labour 'Leave' electorate. The Labour leader, Jeremy Corbyn, unable to resist external and internal pressures, gradually conceded to the demands of external critics and to an inside Blairite minority on Brexit that Labour would promise another referendum if elected. However, the result of the December 2019 election was a resounding victory and an 80-seat majority for the Conservative Party and the end of a blocking parliament and continuous legal challenges. Labour's share of the vote fell from 40 per cent in 2017 to 32 per cent in 2019 (though still above the party's 2010 and 2015 results), apparently not because of Corbynism, which did not change between 2017 and 2019, but because of Corbyn's weakened position in the face of his internal (pro-Blair, anti-Brexit) opposition that led him to abandon his initial and successful stance of respecting the result of the 2016 referendum.

However, Brexit comes not only with hard (if protracted) choices for the UK with respect to the future relationship with the EU, but there are lessons to be learned for the Union's political sustainability. The UK became the first member state to have embarked on exiting the European Union, a club that had hence far only experienced continuous enlargement.[2] Brexit set a precedent for any permanently discontented member state to exit and thereby brought about a qualitative change in the nature of European integration (Bongardt and Torres, 2016c, 2017a). It put into sharp focus the challenges facing differentiated integration and the issue of what is the optimal size of the club, a question that the EU seems to be dodging.

The remainder of this chapter is structured as follows: Section 2.2 addresses the implications of and choices facing the UK after it triggered the EU's exit clause and its political system's incapacity to deliver between 2016 and 2019. Section 2.3 presents Brexit as a logical consequence and culmination of a UK entity – including both 'remainers' and 'leavers' – harbouring ever more divergent preferences from the EU and argues that it was with the EU's deepening of integration to EMU that the UK's blocking position in the EU became unsustainable. Section 2.4 focuses on EU differentiated integration and its limits in light of Brexit and on the related question of EMU as the club's present political core. Section 2.5 discusses Brexit in terms of an opportunity and lessons for the EU. Section 2.6 concludes with a possible outlook.

2.2 THE IMPLICATIONS OF AND CHOICES FACING THE UK AFTER THE EXIT CLAUSE FROM THE UNION WAS TRIGGERED

2.2.1 The Triggering of Article 50 TEU

When the UK invoked the EU's exit provisions (Article 50 TEU) to leave the EU – and thereby all its institutions – the country lost its bargaining power and all privileges and concessions that it had gained over more than four decades. In the notification letter to the president of the European Council, the British prime minister made it clear to the Union that post-Brexit the UK no longer wished to participate in the EU customs union or in its internal market. This included an understanding that the EU's four freedoms (that is, the free movement of goods, services, capital and persons) are indivisible so that there could be no cherry-picking, and confirmed that the UK government was fully aware of the consequences of the country's decision, notably that it meant losing its influence over the rules that affect the European economy. The few supporters of the UK remaining in the EU or in the European Economic Area (EEA), anti-Brexit but not necessarily pro-EU MPs, attempted a parliamentary vote on the UK's exit conditions or terms of the divorce, which parliament (and also the non-elected House of Lords) overwhelmingly rejected. The UK government would subsequently 'soften' its stance, in what amounted to a quest to preserve the economic benefits (frictionless trade) that the UK enjoyed as a member of the EU internal market and the customs union, despite becoming a third country to the EU, yet without the obligations. Not unsurprisingly, the EU declined.

By definition, Article 50 TEU negotiations are about withdrawal and the UK's extraction from the Union. They did not and could not contemplate agreements on any ad hoc access to EU institutions. The EU does not allow for any partial membership that would see a country select only those policies or institutions that it is interested in. On that account, while an EU member, the UK already had achieved the 'best deal' it could possibly have in line with its preferences, as it had managed to elicit ever more privileges (significant 'cherry-picking') over the course of its membership. Nonetheless, the country decided to leave and subsequently invoked the Union's exit clause with overwhelming support in parliament.

The terms of the UK's participation in the club were negotiated before its accession to the European Communities in 1973 and subsequently evolved in line with numerous revisions to the treaties and intergovernmental agreements, which involve all member states and are subject to unanimous agreement. The negotiation of UK exit was about disentangling the UK from the Union and agreeing the terms of the divorce. It included the need to settle issues such as citizens' rights, ensuring the continued absence of a hard border in Ireland (upholding the Good Friday Agreement when the border between the Republic of Ireland and the British province of Northern Ireland passes from an internal to an EU external border), and the need to settle accounts. With regard to the financial settlement, no fines or punishment were involved, merely the payment of expenses voted by the UK in the EU's current budget period (2014–20).[3] Any refusal to honour its financial obligations would predictably have serious consequences for the UK's international reputation (who would then trust the UK to honour its agreements?).

In contrast to the British government, which received a mandate from parliament to freely negotiate Brexit following approval of the decision to exit the EU (Article 50 bill), the European Commission received and had to stick to clear negotiating guidelines issued by the European Council (EU-27), limited to the exit negotiations and therefore withdrawal issues.[4] Nevertheless, the Union showed some flexibility in facilitating the transition of the UK from EU member to third country by agreeing to start conversations about the possible future post-Brexit bilateral relation (with a view to creating certainty for economic agents as to the destination) at a later moment in the withdrawal negotiations, conditional upon sufficient progress on the principal withdrawal issues. The future relationship is contemplated in the withdrawal agreement – in both Theresa May's withdrawal agreement and Boris Johnson's slightly modified withdrawal agreement – albeit only in a political declaration of a non-binding nature. By definition, the EU cannot conduct any proper negotiations and even less conclude international agreements with member states – any trade or other bilateral agreement hinges on the UK having already exited the EU. And as the significant size differences between the parties already suggest, it will not be the preferences of the UK that are likely to prevail but those of the EU (in 2016, the UK's GDP corresponded to 16 per cent of EU GDP) and its member states (note that ratification requires a unanimous vote by EU member states).

The UK kept harbouring the (illusionary) idea that it could use Article 50 TEU as a strategic bargaining tool – beyond the normal period of multilateral negotiation of treaties and political reforms – to extract additional economic advantages from, and at the expense of, the Union. The EU appeared determined throughout not to give in to what amounts to an attempt at cherry-picking club benefits by a country that is exiting, be it in the withdrawal treaty or the future bilateral relation. The UK nevertheless stuck to threatening a no-deal scenario with the aim of forcing the EU to make concessions on the already agreed Irish backstop. The EU restated its position that no part of the withdrawal treaty agreed between the EU and the UK government would be reopened, rather awaiting ratification by the UK to ensure an orderly withdrawal, and that it was at best prepared to discuss possible changes to the political declaration.

Following the change in UK government in summer 2019, it was, however, re-opened, with the notable result that the UK-wide backstop that had been agreed in the initial withdrawal agreement was replaced by a front-loaded Northern Ireland-specific backstop.[5]

Apart from the fact that any future (trade and wider) agreement was conditional on a withdrawal treaty, the EU also made clear the range of available options for the UK with regard to a future trade relation (illustrated by the so-called Barnier staircase[6]) and that it was the UK's red lines on sovereignty that would determine what the EU could offer in terms of the proximity of the economic relation and the economic benefits available (for a detailed discussion, see Bongardt and Torres, 2019).

The EU being the UK's largest market, and one to which it had frictionless access, the UK may want a closer trade relation than the one afforded by resorting to multilateral World Trade Organization (WTO) rules (the situation of the USA, Australia, New Zealand and other third countries with regard to the EU). This is because trade would be subject to tariffs, although the UK would be free to strike preferential trade agreements.[7] Other options for a post-Brexit trade relation between the EU and the UK range from a free trade agreement (like the EU's with Canada) to participation in the EEA that grants participation in the internal market (like Norway), with intermediate solutions such as the EU–Switzerland agreement (in reality not one but some 120 agreements through which Switzerland shadows single market access, albeit with exceptions like financial services) or participation in the EU customs union (like Turkey), which, however, would subject the UK to EU trade policy.[8]

Note that all of the above options imply a trade-off between sovereignty and economic benefits so that the UK's preference for repatriating sovereignty from the EU comes at the expense of potentially lower economic benefits.[9] Only participation in the internal market cum customs union would provide for the frictionless bilateral trade (without visible or invisible barriers) that the UK has enjoyed as an EU member (and which would make the Irish backstop redundant); the difference when the UK is an EU outsider, without a seat at the table, is that in that case it becomes a rule-taker rather than a rule-maker (which can hardly be equated to a de facto reaffirmation of sovereignty). The EU, respecting the UK's red lines, has offered the UK a free trade agreement (FTA) post-Brexit. For a long time, the crux for the UK government was that such an FTA could not dispense with the need for a backstop – but the new Conservative government is no longer dependent on the Northern Ireland Democratic Unionist Party for support and was able to pass the WAB (including a backstop) with a large majority.[10]

2.2.2   The UK Political System's Prolonged (2016–19) Incapacity to Deliver on the Democratic Mandate for Brexit

From 2016 to 2019, in the face of the trade-off between sovereignty and economic benefits, the UK political system became paralysed, unable to make choices. Close to Brexit day, 30 March 2019, it was still not clear whether its parliament would ratify the withdrawal treaty negotiated between the EU and the UK, allowing (or not) the UK to leave on 29 March 2019 with an agreement for an orderly withdrawal, whether the country would ask for an extension to the withdrawal period (justified or not by a general election or a second referendum to break the impasse in parliament), or even cancel Brexit altogether. The UK government opted to allow the process to drag on as long as possible in the hope that the prospect of and damages associated with an imminent 'cliff-edge' scenario would still bring Conservative MPs and a sufficient number of opposition MPs to back the withdrawal treaty. On their part, a majority of MPs (also from the Conservative Party) were opposed to respecting the 2016 referendum result to which they had previously committed and kept postponing having to make a choice, notably by proposing votes against a 'no deal' (the default consequence of not voting for the withdrawal agreement) and forcing the government to extend the Article 50 period.[11]

An initial limited extension granted by the EU gave way to three extensions, the last one for the period requested by parliament against the will of the UK government (and without the prime minister's signature) and regardless of the fact that there were no new facts justifying it, except Brexit politics on the part of the (anti-Brexit allies of the UK opposition in the) EU. The UK parliament and two different governments were incapable of delivering on their commitment to respect the result of the 2016 referendum and on their approval and triggering of Article 50 in 2017.

One may speculate that if the EU had not granted those extensions, the UK parliament, faced with the alternative of a no-deal, cliff-edge scenario, would most likely have approved Theresa May's WAB. However, the EU, notably the EU Council, entered a political game very much on the side of the UK and other anti-Brexit forces, to try to provoke another referendum and/or to call off or soften Brexit. However, as a result of the stalemate created in the UK parliament, there had to be elections, which led to a defeat of that strategy and also of the possibility of a softer Brexit.

2.2.3   Why has Brexit been Delayed and/or Blocked?

In broader political terms the situation is considerably more complex than the seemingly united stance in the negotiation process, with various prominent European actors playing different roles. This applies most notably to former

European Council President Donald Tusk, siding with the anti-Brexit forces in the UK favouring a re-run or the outright cancellation of the result of the 2016 referendum, and to European Parliament Brexit Coordinator Guy Verhofstadt, defending the maintenance of some Union citizenship privileges for UK citizens and a toughening of the conditions attached to the withdrawal agreement, some of which the UK may still decide to ignore if it chooses to trade on WTO terms after the end of the transition period.[12]

Arguably, the EU was putting its future at risk by contributing (with permanent whisperings of a possible reversal and with the insistence on conditions attached to the withdrawal agreement) to delaying Brexit and also to accommodating successive extensions of Article 50 TEU (even in spite of France's warnings, which turned out to be empty threats, that it would not allow them).[13] Some may call this position naive; others may ascribe it to an attempt of some forces (and countries) also in the Union to reverse the democratic decision of the UK to leave the EU and forge a more intergovernmental (and 'Atlanticist') EU.[14] That concerted strategy eventually backfired, not without strong reputational costs for the EU, and led, after the December 2019 elections to a clear strengthening of the UK government's position. It has also encouraged stronger pro-Brexit sentiments in various political forces across the EU, notably in Hungary and Italy. And yet, EU negotiators seem more preoccupied than UK negotiators about the costs for the latter of not reaching a trade deal.

On the part of the UK, after an initial period in 2016 where prominent 'remainers' – whom we do not classify as Europeanists but rather mostly as a group composed of Eurosceptics and Atlanticists in favour of an apolitical, non-regulatory type of EU model, without EMU at its core – seemed to abide by the decision of the British electorate, they eventually considered repeating the referendum to arrive at a different result.[15] It is obvious that not all but a large part of the attempts to reverse Brexit had little to do with a positive vision of UK participation in the process of European integration. Rather, they often reflected special interests on the part of some who harboured a critical vision of or even antagonism towards the EU (among whom were also many EU citizens living in the UK) and who now face the possibility of losing individual or collective rights. Desired selective opt-ins include access to mobility and healthcare in the EU; the financial passport and maintenance of euro-denominated financial transactions in London; the open skies aviation agreement between the EU and the US; European risk capital funds; research funding in universities and defence industries; and the internal market in general.

Geostrategic issues also played a major role. 'Remainers', like former prime ministers Tony Blair and David Cameron, expressed their preference to maintain a strong UK (and US) influence in Europe (another good example is the declarations of former prime minister John Major (Major, 2018). They have, moreover, voiced their dislike for the Eurozone at the political core of the EU, in line with Soros (2017) who proposed that the EU should transform into an organization that countries like the UK would like to join. In sum, the strongest opponents of Brexit were also the strongest opponents of an ever-closer Union and of the very process of European integration, which the UK had always opposed.

The withdrawal agreement and the negotiations and agreement on the future bilateral relation are separate matters, which the UK had tried to link in order to gain leverage (concessions). Attempts to obtain an agreement tailor-made to specific British interests surfaced ever more clearly and insistently. They involved attempts to transform a clear mandate for a 'hard Brexit' (84 per cent of the popular vote in the June 2017 'Brexit' election, held shortly after the UK had triggered Article 50 TEU, for parties that ran on a hard Brexit platform) into a 'soft Brexit' or into 'a tailor-made agreement', complemented by a longish 'implementation' (that is, transition) period post-Brexit during which access to the internal market and the customs union would be prolonged and maintained on unchanged terms (for three years). Rather predictably, the pressure exerted by special interests would always tend to increase to the extent that the potential (economic) consequences of Brexit would start to sink in or to be felt.

In any event, those attempts appeared – and so far have been – doomed to fail given that the EU has to defend the integrity of its political project in general and the internal market in particular, as well as the interests of its citizens and the remaining 27 member states. Still, in the period 2016–19 the EU sometimes appeared to be more concerned about the interests of those opposed to Brexit than with the interests of the Union as a whole. As is self-evident, it is not acceptable that a country that wants to exit the Union in order to affirm its sovereignty and does not wish to provide solidarity be allowed to extract privileges that are not available to other member states and/or that risk damaging the common good. This applies to the UK's demand to have regulatory autonomy and single market access without being subject to the jurisdiction of the Court of Justice of the EU (CJEU); to impose limits on the free movement of persons (one of the four freedoms and as such a non-negotiable precondition for unfettered access to the internal market); to have the freedom to strike trade deals with third countries (which is incompatible with being a member of the EU customs union); or to have a say in the EU customs union despite having become a third country.

On the other hand, and contrary to what most 'remainers' defended,[16] it did not appear acceptable or likely that the results of the referendum and of the June 2017 'Brexit' elections and of various votes in parliament in favour of an unequivocal exit (from all institutions) of the EU, could be ignored.

It did not seem acceptable because in a democracy one cannot simply assume that the voters erred and that the result of their choices has to be corrected if it is not to one's liking.[17] In our view, this is shown by the December 2019 election results.

It did not seem likely – although while still an EU member the UK was entitled under EU law to legally revoke Brexit before Brexit day – because a reversal of the exit process would belittle and cast doubt on the democratic processes and the institutions of the UK that repeatedly committed an exit to its citizens, the EU and the rest of the world. That said, a second referendum could not be dismissed out of hand given that the British political system was unable, at least until the 2019 general elections, to find any parliamentary majorities in favour of exit solutions (only against), and a second referendum would allow elected politicians to pass the responsibility (once again) to the voters.

If they had or were still to materialize, however, those eventualities would firstly translate into a heavy cost and (auto-inflicted) humiliation for the country, and furthermore would have as an immediate consequence the total loss of the UK's credibility and bargaining power with respect to the EU and the international community. Most likely, such a turnaround would also (quite naturally) be regarded as a betrayal of the expressed wish of the British people, with the resulting political and social consequences for a country that is deeply split on the issue. The UK's institutions would risk facing permanent internal opposition and the non-acceptance of EU membership, and any UK government would be hostage to various Eurosceptic factions that would feel betrayed, and which would in turn make the Union – even more so than in the past – hostage to the UK's special interests.

2.3 DIVERGENT AND DIVERGING PREFERENCES ON EUROPEAN INTEGRATION OVER THE YEARS

2.3.1 Extracting Economic Advantages from Participation in the EEC while Impeding further European Integration

The decision-making process that led up to the UK triggering Brexit is a logical consequence and culmination of the UK having ever more divergent preferences from the EU.

The UK had subscribed to the European integration project in spite of sovereignty reservations, first at the time of its accession treaty (1972) but also repeatedly thereafter, indeed on the occasion of all subsequent revisions to the European treaties. That commitment comprised the objective of creating 'an ever closer union among the peoples of Europe'. The UK unilaterally reneged on the latter in 2016, even before embarking on its in–out referendum on EU membership. At the European Council of 18 and 19 February 2016, the UK obtained the so-called New Framework for the UK in the EU, which, among other things, granted it an exemption from the EU club's political goal of ever-closer union. Those concessions were only possible since the Union and the Eurozone in particular were particularly fragile and vulnerable at that time and, arguably, lacked any political leadership and strategic vision. The agreement in question – rather thankfully, being arguably very complicated for the future of the EU and its political integration process – ended up losing any legal value (Fabbrini, 2017) due to the outcome (a majority for leave) in the June 2016 referendum.

However, in reality, the UK had been opposed to the very model of European integration, which is necessarily political, already since the beginning of the process of European integration. As far back as 1955 the UK left the Spaak Committee in disagreement with the proposed supranational model of integration, opting not to become a member of what would become the European Economic Community (EEC) created by the 1957 Treaty of Rome. Not wishing to join such a supranational international organization, the UK instead became the principal promoter of a rival club of European economic integration, with a lower level of integration that made do with intergovernmental coordination, the European Free Trade Association (EFTA), founded in 1960.[18]

That notwithstanding, the UK did not hesitate to abandon its new EFTA partners a very short time afterwards when applying for EEC membership in 1961, in a display of its famous and characteristic diplomatic pragmatism. The move was clearly motivated by not wanting to lose out on the economic benefits associated with access to such an important (and fast-growing) market and customs union. It was made in spite of the EEC's supranational nature, which the UK was so opposed to, relegating the previously overriding concerns with sovereignty to second rank for the sake of higher potential economic benefits.[19] As already referred to, higher levels of economic integration come with higher potential benefits but require more coordination and sovereignty sharing to deliver them. The UK joined the EEC/European Community (EC) only belatedly in 1973, in what was the EC's first enlargement (together with Denmark and the Irish Republic, but not Norway, where the referendum produced a negative result), having been refused entry in the 1960s (barred twice by France's General de Gaulle's 'non'). For the UK, the changes brought about by EEC membership delivered economic benefits, contributing significantly to the revival of the British economy and to the creation of a support base for structural reforms in the 1980s (Campos and Coricelli, 2017).

Since the beginning it has been a constant feature of the UK's membership in the European integration project that the country focused on obtaining economic advantages from the club while at the same time demanding compensation for those policies that were less favourable to it and distancing itself from participating in common objectives.[20] The fact that the UK was the only member state not to take part in the Exchange Rate Mechanism (ERM) of the European Monetary System (EMS) in 1979 serves as a case in point. The proposal to re-launch the idea of monetary union, incidentally even put forward by a Briton, Roy Jenkins, at the time President of the European Commission,[21] hardly made a secret of the political intention of thereby promoting European integration.

It is well illustrative of the UK's tormented relationship with the EEC/EU that since its 1973 accession the UK monopolized the attention of the other member states four times with respect to the terms of its relations with the club. The first time was in the mid-1970s, very shortly after having joined, with a first referendum held in 1975 on the continuation of its EEC membership (resulting in a small margin for remain, it had already evidenced a clear division within the country's two principal political parties). The second occasion was at the beginning of the 1980s, when the UK demanded and obtained from its partners the so-called 'British cheque' – a rebate on its budgetary contribution – in exchange for its vote and for letting the club function. The third time was in the middle of the 2010s, following an increasing self-distancing, which culminated in another in–out referendum on its membership being called. In February 2016, the EU Council had granted new exceptions to the UK, demanded as a precondition for the UK government to support the 'remain vote'. The fourth time, of course, followed the lost referendum in June 2016 with its majority for 'leave' (i.e. Brexit), and especially since the UK invoked Article 50 of the TEU in March 2017, in order to at last negotiate its exit from the EU.

But even and especially thereafter, during the two-year withdrawal period (at various times extended) and even though being on its way out, the UK kept systematically monopolizing the EU-27's attention to further its national interest (as witnessed by the many special Brexit summits and countless council-, ambassador- and staff-level meetings, or the taking hostage of the EU–Arab meeting in Cairo, which had been the first of its kind and an important agenda). Brexit thus has been deviating scarce EU resources away from common EU-27 concerns and problem solving, thereby risking being more than a mere distraction for the Union and damaging its very *raison d'être*.

In Hirschman's (1970) terminology, the UK has used the threat of exit (before and after the Brexit referendum of 2016) as a means to gain leverage and force the EU club to grant it additional privileges and concessions. Once Brexit had been triggered in March 2017, that threat became void. Still, the EU went on giving the UK extensions to Article 50, which were not politically innocent but showed the force of the 'remain coalition' between some British, European and other vested interests. The UK shifted to threatening to leave the

EU without settling withdrawal issues (disorderly exit), a threat that it sought to uphold up to the end of the withdrawal period in a quest to elicit further EU concessions, even with the already concluded (and subsequently the slightly revised) withdrawal treaty. A disorderly, cliff-edge Brexit would inflict large-scale self-harm on the UK, not least in light of its large dependence on the EU single market. With respect to the EU, the 'no-deal' threat has also commanded limited effectiveness in light of the sheer difference in economic size and bargaining power between the EU and the UK and given its institutions and expertise.[22] Still, that threat has been used by the 'remain coalition' as an attempt to scare EU public opinion and thus EU and national leaders in order to delay Brexit and if possible overturn it.

The UK's principal interest in and focus on economic advantages went together with a strategic objective to impede the (political) deepening of European integration.[23] De facto, each time there were revisions to the European treaties, the outcome would lead to inferior solutions in light of red lines (veto threats) imposed above all by the UK,[24] that is, to insufficient integration and treating as secondary issues the European objectives and model, in turn creating popular discontent in many countries of the EEC/EU, including the UK.[25] The Maastricht Treaty and the Treaty of Lisbon are cases in point. In the latter, the UK imposed practically everything it wanted (Brady and Barisch, 2007: 4–5), encouraging other countries like Poland and Denmark to do the same, in the process very much distorting the objectives of a treaty that had already not been very ambitious following the non-ratifications of the ill-fated Constitutional Treaty. Even after the removal of all Union symbols (flag, hymn, European law, article on the primacy of Community law, reference to a 'Europe of citizens') that had been part of the Constitutional Treaty,[26] the British prime minister Gordon Brown did not even participate in the joint signing ceremony of the Treaty of Lisbon, in a clear sign of political distancing on the part of the UK. The above suggests that by 2007, after more than 30 years of membership in the club, the UK's attitude had still not changed, resuming to extracting merely the economic advantages from the Union, obstructing the process of integration and distancing itself from political commitments and shared common objectives.[27]

2.3.2   Contributing to the Completion of the Single Market of the EU but Increasing Discomfort with the New Regulatory Model

Yet, even from the point of view of a mere extraction of the economic advantages of participating in the EEC and later on the EC/EU, the UK faced a problem that became increasingly acute, namely that the realization of economic benefits from deepened economic integration, as is the case of the single market, also requires more sovereignty sharing. The reason resides in the trade-off between a higher level of economic integration (and of corresponding potential economic benefits) and the preservation of national sovereignty (even if merely formal). The UK always sought to obtain both, which is, however, only possible at the expense of the other members of the club. When the time came for the country to make a choice, in the 2016 referendum called by its own government, the British pronounced themselves in favour of more sovereignty, even if this was liable to result in potential economic costs (Bongardt and Torres, 2017a).

It is insightful to frame the economic benefit – sovereignty trade-off in terms of preferences. While a higher level of economic integration offers higher economic benefits, it also requires more sovereignty sharing to deliver. However, increased sovereignty sharing in turn presupposes (a certain degree of) preference convergence, which is only possible between countries with relatively similar models of society (political, economic and social organization) or which, if different, are at least open to convergence towards the objectives they adhered to.

While the UK's discomfort evolved over time, having started immediately after the UK joined the EEC (George, 1998), it was (somewhat paradoxically at first glance) the very success of completing the EU's internal market in 1992, for which the British contribution (under Prime Minister Margaret Thatcher) had in fact been fundamental, which made the UK an even more reluctant member of the club. The new phase in the integration process was based progressively, starting already with the 1986 Single European Act, on decision-making in the Council passed by qualified majority voting, and with the completion of the internal market, from the initial trade-led model of integration (with tariff-free trade between the various member states) to a regulatory model (a single market, with the abolition also of non-tariff or frictional barriers to trade). With it, the Community passed to a higher level of economic and political integration with more sovereignty sharing, which the UK had always wanted to avoid. It is important to note in this context that the preferences manifested by the UK (and also Ireland) with regard to market regulation of goods and services, labour markets and financial markets, tend to be closer to North American preferences (OECD, 2015).[28] The majority (but not all) of EU member states privilege a model of society that is more in line with the continental values of a welfare state and environmental sustainability.

2.3.3   Diverging in the European Union Era

It was, however, the EU's subsequent step up on the economic integration ladder (that is, the deepening of integration to European Economic and Monetary Union (EMU) at Maastricht and the subsequent divergence of preferences concerning the nature and way to complete the economic union), which put the UK on a collision course with the integration objectives of the Union and in particular with the policies of the Eurozone (Bongardt and Torres, 2016c).

Since then, the UK opted to constantly manifest its opposition to almost all steps towards greater integration and institutional reform while limiting its participation in European common goods to a minimum. Most notably, the UK never joined the border-free Schengen Area; it did not adhere to multiple aspects of judicial and police cooperation (more precisely, it got a block opt-out with selected opt-ins, meaning that the UK chose to reject the whole policy area while selecting only those aspects of cooperation to its liking, although it still benefited from access to European databases in security matters); it obtained a special protocol (like Poland) with regard to the application of the European Charter of Fundamental Rights; obtained a derogation (along with Denmark) with respect to the adoption of the common currency of the Union, the Euro (which has in the meantime become the political and economic core of the EU club); and participated in hardly any of the economic governance institutions, having refused any (financial) solidarity with the rest of the Union and in particular with the countries that had to recur to adjustment programmes during the sovereign debt crisis.

In sum, the UK's position in the EU became characterized by its non-participation in what has become de facto the EU's core, the Euro area, and by substantial cherry-picking of EU policies. The UK's distancing, which began with the Maastricht Treaty, resulted in the UK becoming the member state with the least participation in European institutions and policies. The EU is currently characterized by differentiated integration, with the Euro area arguably being its core. Only eight countries participate in all principal institutions and reinforced cooperations, namely Austria, Belgium, France, Germany, Greece, Italy, Portugal and Slovenia (König, 2015; updated in Wolfstädter and Kreilinger, 2017). The UK today stands out as the least integrated of all member states, followed by the Czech Republic, Sweden, Denmark, Poland and Hungary. It follows that for the UK the benefits of membership in the EU club became, if not confined to then very much determined by, the economic benefits associated with the internal market (Bongardt and Torres, 2016b, 2017b). And yet, even in that domain – which is at the centre of the UK's participation in the Union – the European regulatory model and governance (the model of decision-making by qualified majority to make it function) became the subject of strong contestation in the name of (a perceived loss of) national sovereignty.[29]

Also, from the point of view of the EU and of all the other member states, the UK's non-participation in some of the Union's most important institutions and policies meant that the benefits of its membership were also relatively more confined. Conversely, for the insiders of the Union the costs associated with the UK's blocking attitude, be it with regard to a deepening of cooperation in the area of defence, the reinforcement of the economic union, or a vast range of policies in the internal market sphere, became each time larger. For all those reasons the situation became no longer sustainable for an EU that needs to continuously reform its institutions and advance with the process of European integration in order to be able to respond to the manifold challenges that it faces.

2.3.4   The UK's Incompatibility with the Euro

It was with the deepening of European integration from an internal market to EMU that the UK's preferences became incompatible with EMU's and indeed the Union's political sustainability. The reason is that with EMU, the economic union part, which includes the single market, can no longer be treated as a stand-alone and independent function, since the economic union needs to be thought of in the context of and coordinated with a view to sustaining monetary union. The UK's preference for such a stand-alone economic union ultimately put it on a collision course with EU integration (Bongardt and Torres, 2016b).

On the one hand, the very logic of the Single European Act demanded further progress. On the other hand, failure to react in political terms would have meant accepting disaggregation. In the absence of a common currency, the single market and capital liberalization had already exposed the national currencies to exchange rate speculation, with the UK's Pound Sterling the first victim. The UK was forced to abandon the exchange rate mechanism (ERM) of the European Monetary System (EMS) that it had adhered to in 1990. In contrast, the French Franc, the Irish Pound, the Portuguese Escudo, the Spanish Peseta and other national currencies resisted and the Italian Lira managed to get back into the ERM. It was thus possible to create a new common currency for Europe, which became the new core of the European integration process. In this context the Maastricht Treaty furthermore created the European Union (albeit still without a legal personality, which would be added only in the Treaty of Lisbon), broadening the range of Community competences and reinforcing the role of the European Parliament (legislative co-decision procedure) and of European citizenship, and in the process already getting closer to the idea of a political constitution of Europe (Torres, 2009: 54–74). At Maastricht, EMU was set up as an open political construct, requiring a continuous deepening of integration (Bongardt and Torres, 2017a).

Experience with the very functioning of EMU brought home the need for greater economic integration – completing the economic part of EMU so that it can sustain the common currency and realize the wider objectives of the Union – and for larger political accountability of its supranational institutions to the European Parliament.

EMU's characteristics imply that the internal market cannot be treated as static. It is hence in the legitimate interests of present (all EU member states except Denmark, which benefited from an opt-out) and future Eurozone members that the single market be deepened with regard to the requisites for EMU functioning for the monetary union to work efficiently. (Although Denmark ends up following all the decisions of the Eurozone in terms of monetary policy, it does not participate in decision-making due to auto-exclusion.) The question is obviously important for the sustainability of the monetary union but goes much beyond and to the core of the integration process. The EU needs to complete EMU in order to be sustainable, notably through more coordination of economic, fiscal and budgetary policies and a banking and capital markets union, and to be able to deliver positive (economic, environmental and social) results to the entire Union.

However, the UK's preferences and interests in this domain, highlighted by the specificity of and dependency on its financial sector, concentrated in the City of London (see Talani, Chapter 8 in this volume), became incompatible with the sustainability of EMU and the good functioning of the European institutions and their response to the challenges facing the EU. Not only did the UK opt to stay out of monetary union altogether but neither did it wish to take part in the deepening of economic union, hindering the necessary reinforcement of its institutions and governance. It did not participate in the Competitiveness (or Euro Plus) Pact but even vetoed the budgetary pact or Treaty on Stability, Coordination and Governance in Economic and Monetary Union, in turn obliging the other member states to settle for an intergovernmental pact out of the Union framework, at a time of great Eurozone fragility.

The UK also refused any solidarity with the member states of the Eurozone that were most affected by the crisis and subject to adjustment programmes. In the sovereign debt crisis, the UK did not participate in the European Financial Stability Fund or in the European Stability Mechanism (whose enactment it only accepted in exchange for the European Financial Stability Mechanism, which involves a guarantee of the EU budget for granting loans, no longer being used to support Eurozone countries), making only an exception for Ireland when its own national interest in the British financial system was at stake (Bongardt and Torres, 2016a, 2017a). At the same time, the UK continued to benefit substantially from the Eurozone, notably through the British banks' privileged access to the European Central Bank (ECB)'s liquidity operations during the 2008 global financial crisis and above all through the high proportion of financial activities denominated in Euros (the so-called Euro clearing and the negotiation of sovereign debt by investment banks) that take place on the London financial market.

It obviously did not make much sense that the financial stability of the Eurozone and especially of some countries that are more affected by market turbulences could be put at risk by financial activities in London that are denominated in Euros, taking place beyond the reach of the ECB's jurisdiction, as happened during the sovereign debt crisis.[30] One might add that the UK almost continuously maintained a non-constructive attitude throughout with respect to the problems of the Eurozone, putting at risk EMU's architecture and viability, criticizing the adjustment programmes and the so-called austerity, but refusing to contribute constructively (and financially) to fellow EU member states in need and to what it deemed to be problems that only concerned the Euro area. It furthermore opted to not participate in the European Banking Union, in spite of the European Banking Authority (EBA) being headquartered in London.

Brexit has already triggered the removal of the EBA to the EU-27 (from London to Paris) and hence into the Eurozone.[31] It also opens up the prospect for the EU to finally direct internal market financial regulation towards the common good of the Eurozone, financial stability, thereby reinforcing the economic union in a crucial area for the monetary union. It also ought to become easier to bring the intergovernmental economic agreements made at the margins of the EU (due to the UK's veto) into the Community framework and to complete the institutional architecture of EMU with a banking union, new institutions like a European monetary fund and a Eurozone budget and greater integration/budgetary coordination. For that to happen it is essential that the Eurozone be the political core of the Union that all member states come to be part of (or at least that they do not obstruct, as is the case of Denmark, which after Brexit has remained the only country that has a derogation). The Eurozone countries may then strengthen both the efficiency and the political responsiveness of the monetary and financial institutions, that is, complete EMU and advance the integration process.

All other countries that do not wish to be part of the Eurozone, despite having committed to do so upon joining the EU, are bound to conclude sooner or later that they are on the periphery of the European integration process and certain to lose their capacity to influence it.

2.4   THE LIMITS OF DIFFERENTIATED INTEGRATION IN AN EU WHOSE POLITICAL CORE IS EMU

In its successive enlargements the initial EEC (later EC/EU) came to include countries harbouring different views on supranational governance and European economic integration as a political project. It integrated countries as diverse on a variety of accounts (not only living standards) as EFTA members (and here notably the UK, which had been the free trade area's chief promoter), former non-aligned countries and former Council for Mutual Economic

Assistance (COMECON) members. The UK was possibly also the main promoter of the successive EU enlargements with the objective of impeding the
club's deepening. In 2004 it was the UK (Blair government) that anticipated
the free movement of workers from the new EU member states (with a negative
impact on European public opinion and possibly the outcome of the French
and Dutch referendums on the ill-fated Treaty establishing a Constitution for
Europe in 2005),[32] about which it would later come to complain (Cameron
government), trying to undo the principle of free movement of persons in the
EU (rather than making use of the instruments at the disposal of all member
states and used by the other EU members to control EU immigration).

The necessary completion of EMU was rendered more difficult due to the
fact that the Euro area remained smaller than the EU club. This is not only due
to the derogations for the UK and Denmark granted at Maastricht, but above
all due to the UK's insistence on institutionalizing this difference in a permanent way, with the support of other member states like Sweden and Poland.
According to some authors, writing before Brexit, the division between the
Euro area members and the other EU countries made the crisis response and
the attempts to reinforce EMU difficult, putting at risk EMU's sustainability as
well as that of the EU as such.[33]

Fortunately, in this regard, Brexit came to solve that pending issue since
the artificial divide is bound to disappear with the UK's exit from the EU.[34]
Denmark follows the Euro area's monetary policy and all other member states
(including Sweden and Poland) committed in their accession treaties to adopt
the Euro as their currency. It will, therefore, be up to countries like Sweden
and Poland to decide whether they want to comply with the objectives to which
they committed at the time of accession to the Union, or whether they intend to
invoke Article 50 to exit the EU.

Once EMU became the core of the Union and of the European integration
process, it is the Euro area and no longer the internal market (the predominant
view in the 1990s) on which to anchor EU differentiated integration. If the
countries that committed to join EMU at the time of their accession no longer
wish to do so (e.g. Sweden and Poland) and only want to be part of the internal
market, it could make sense for them to exit the Union in order to only be
part of the EEA.[35] A similar reasoning applies to another EU core institution,
Schengen and harmonized asylum policies cum burden sharing, where some
countries refuse to receive a share of refugees on the grounds that they are or
want to be different.

It therefore does not seem compatible that countries want to have at the
same time a Europe without differentiation (in which a group of countries
is not able to progress faster on integration than laggards) and different
objectives and trajectories. It is obvious that upon exiting the Union, those
countries exclude themselves from other policies in the domains of cohesion,

agriculture, defence, and so on, but by not wanting to be part of the political core of the Union and not providing solidarity with it they convey the wish to follow another path. Those countries may always – as is the case of Norway or Switzerland or even of non-European countries – cooperate with the EU in various domains. For that reason it appears important that there are explicit provisions for exiting the EU, as is the case of Article 50 TEU (Spolaore, 2015). Especially with Brexit as a precedent, the door has become open for any permanently discontented member to exit and to redefine its trade (and wider) relationship with the EU in line with its preferences on integration.[36]

2.5 BREXIT: AN OPPORTUNITY FOR THE EU?

One implication of the UK's decision to exit the EU – backed up by the June 2016 referendum, overwhelming parliamentary majorities in 2017 and the very clear results of the June 2017 and December 2019 general elections – is the fact that it has made the exit of any other member state (permanently in disagreement with the objectives of the Union) politically easier. In consequence, member states will now have to redouble their efforts – be it with respect to their electorates or their partners in the EU – to ensure that their participation in the EU continues to make sense. In our opinion this is a very positive development rather than a danger for the EU and for the European integration process. EU membership ceases to be a given, as participation of each member state demands constant attention to the common good. This is in the interests of any discontented member state that no longer intends to contribute to the club's public goods, but above all of the remaining EU members.

A higher level of integration also requires more sovereignty sharing. For that reason it does not make much sense that countries with electorates that are very divided on participation in the EU and the objectives of ever-closer union between its people stay in the Union. In the event of permanently divergent or even irreconcilable preferences it is preferable for those countries to exit the Union and strike more or less deep trade (and other) agreements with the EU (typified by the ones that the EU has with Norway,[37] Switzerland, Canada, Ukraine, and Turkey).

It also follows that member states need to correct their narratives, in the sense of ceasing to blame the EU for domestic failures (a well-known UK practice,[38] but also, maybe to a lesser extent, of the other member states). That attitude has doubtless contributed to weakening the EU (Buti and Lacoure-Labarthe, 2016). Yet, it also weakens the countries that use it more systematically, given that without noticing they also weaken, above all, their own institutions. The latter seems to be the case of the UK and also of Greece.

Notably, the UK today finds itself in a situation of great fragility in light of its large dependence on European institutions with which it never wanted to have great affinity. That dependence explains the apparent unpreparedness and panic which the government, opposition parties and various sectors of society have exhibited over Brexit at least until the end of 2019. Time will tell, but British institutions nowadays seem, to a certain extent, incapable of responding to the challenges facing the country.[39] The UK's constant dissatisfaction with the EU's alleged democratic deficit has masked, in our opinion, the inadequacy of British institutions with regard to the new times, both from the viewpoint of efficacy and democratic legitimacy.[40]

Apart from the qualitative change referred to above (that is, the fact that the EU's exit door is now open for any member, which limits any member state's blocking capacity), the exit of the UK from the Union in particular also provides the EU with an opportunity to re-start the integration process and focus on providing responses to the concerns of its citizens. It involves in the first place the reinforcement and deepening of integration by those countries that share a currency and external border.

With the exit of the UK, the primary blocking force to major progress in certain areas will disappear: (i) a common defence and security policy (that according to the UK should only function within the context of NATO), (ii) the creation of a genuine area of freedom, security and justice (even with its chief emphasis on combatting terrorism, the UK showed little willingness to collaborate with the EU and even less to become part of Schengen), and (iii) openness towards refugees. On the other hand, as emphasized above, the EU will finally be free to complete EMU and improve its economic governance mechanisms without opposition from the UK and its (less regulated and potentially more destabilizing) London financial sector, the City. Last, but not least, the EU will be able to augment the democratic legitimacy of its supranational institutions (in particular in the financial area) that should be accountable to the European Parliament. Those advances, which are of course conditional on the very often non-constructive stance of various if not all other member states, would contribute to raising European citizens' trust in the EU's institutions and to strengthening the shared identity and destiny between all member states committed to the objectives of the Union.

2.6 CONCLUDING REMARKS: A POSSIBLE OUTLOOK

This chapter has argued that Brexit is a question of political rationality, which has obliged the UK (including both leavers and remainers) to confront some (protracted) hard choices that regard the trade-off between economic benefit and sovereignty in its relation with the Union. For the EU, Brexit has offered some lessons with regard to its political sustainability.

European integration is a dynamic political process, with the goals of sovereignty sharing and ever-closer union, and not a set of intergovernmental agreements in the area of trade and investment or even defence and internal affairs. As such, it requires solidarity from all its members and a constructive stance with openness towards building a shared destiny. The UK, and possibly other member states, will therefore be better off out of the Union's political project.

The continuation and worsening of a UK attitude of systematic non-constructive opposition from within the Union would have impeded the good functioning of the institutions and obstructed the capacity of problem solving, likely fuelling discontentment and populism throughout Europe and thereby contributing to the end of the EU. Therefore, it was neither in the interest of the EU nor in the interest of the UK to delay Brexit, as happened several times (rather irresponsibly, we would argue) mainly at the expense of the EU's capacity to deal with other more urgent problems, but rather to deliver on the mandate of the 2016 referendum and on the 2017 parliamentary decision to leave the EU.

In truth, the EU entertains excellent and more or less close relations with third countries like Norway (which does not block the process of integration, accepts the rules established by the EU and contributes to its budget), Iceland (that again opted to stay in the EEA and not adhere to the EU; after having presented an accession request in 2009, it revoked it in 2015) and with Switzerland (based on a set of some 120 bilateral agreements with the EU) and even with non-European countries. The same will apply to the UK after its exit from the EU, with the degree of proximity to the EU (and the available benefits) being a question of the UK's choice (red lines), which can evolve over time.

Of course, in the future – in particular taking into account that there is already a precedent – the UK might reconsider the benefit–sovereignty trade-off should it find that it were no longer in its interests to stay out of the "ever closer union between the peoples of Europe" process. It could decide to once again ask for accession (through Article 49 TEU) to the Union and its political project. Back into a world of pure intergovernmental interests, the UK will have the occasion to consider with more distance how close it feels to the EU or to its apparently preferred allies (e.g. the USA, Australia, New Zealand, Canada) – it could adopt a constructive role in EU governance, as it had done most notably in the completion of the single market. However, the UK would have to be prepared to re-join the EU fully committed to the project of an ever-closer Union, as a member of its main institutions, notably EMU and Schengen. Above all, the UK would have to converge towards the main values and objectives of the EU.

NOTES

1. The chapter builds on the authors' previous work on Brexit and on the political rationality argument developed mostly in Bongardt and Torres (2017b).
2. Although there were exits of territories before, notably of Algeria (upon its independence from France in 1962) and Greenland (from Denmark), the UK was the first member state to embark on this path.
3. Added up are other responsibilities like pension liabilities for British EU staff (that could hardly be expected to be assumed, say, by Bulgarian, Greek or Irish taxpayers), responsibilities for loans that the EU provided (until those are paid back), and costs associated with Brexit, like the need to transfer EU agencies into the Union (the case of the European Banking Authority and the European Medicines Agency, which were both headquartered in London). There will also be payments by the EU to the UK (for example, its share in the capital of the European Investment Bank). The UK had asked for a transition period post-Brexit, which the EU granted in principle, conditional on a withdrawal treaty being in place. Shorter than what the UK had wished for, it would run until the end of the budgetary period (end of 2020). One extension of up to 1 or 2 years was possible if the UK requested so before 30 June 2020. The UK legislated not to do so.
4. The set-up gave rise to an 'Asian' negotiating situation, in which the EU negotiation team, headed by Michel Barnier, had limited room for concessions (having to operate within the limits set by the EU-27 Council), putting pressure on the UK side, which had no such constraints and was represented by ministers with competences to take decisions (represented by successive Brexit secretaries and/ or the UK negotiator operating in liaison with the Prime Minister).
5. The EU had always favoured a Northern Ireland-specific backstop but had reluctantly conceded a UK-wide fall-back solution. The revised withdrawal agreement not only instituted a Northern Ireland-specific backstop but front-loaded it.
6. See https://ec.europa.eu/commission/sites/beta-political/files/slide_presented_by _barnier_at_euco_15-12-2017.pdf.
7. There is no single country in the world that trades on WTO rules alone. By exiting from the EU the UK loses access to all EU's preferential trade agreements (including the recent comprehensive trade agreements with Canada, Singapore and Japan) and is hence under great pressure to strike preferential trade agreements on its own. The mixture of urgency and diminished bargaining power once out of the bloc was always likely to make it difficult for the UK to do so on advantageous terms, even more so before the UK has settled its future relationship with the Union.
8. For an analysis of the options for a post-Brexit trade relationship, see Bongardt and Torres (2017a and 2019).
9. An interesting YouGov opinion poll, conducted shortly after the June 2017 Brexit elections on 1 August 2017, indicated that 60 per cent of pro-Brexit voters thought that it was worthwhile to exit the EU even if that option carried high economic costs.
10. For a discussion, see Bongardt and Torres (2019).
11. At the same time, another group of Tory MPs (the so-called European Research Group) opposed the Brexit deal negotiated by Theresa May and defended leaving the EU without a withdrawal agreement, knowing, however, that they would never command a majority in parliament and therefore would only contribute to

postponing or blocking Brexit. Eventually they managed to achieve another objective: to replace the prime minister, provoke new elections and obtain an absolute majority for the Conservative Party in parliament.

12. Former EU Council president Donald Tusk was openly in favour of reversing Brexit, with 'well-timed' interventions with that very objective, in our view much more in tune with UK (and global, EU and non-EU) anti-Brexit interests and actors than with a EU position (see Tusk, 2019).

13. At the same time the EU has even maintained the UK access to the Schengen Information System, also in the transition period when the UK is already an EU outsider. There has been strong criticism on how the UK has used that facility by a group of MEPs in the European Parliament's civil liberties committee demanding that the UK sever all ties to the EU police database. See https://euobserver.com/justice/147084.

14. Leaving had effectively been confirmed on three occasions: the result of the 2016 referendum, the 2017 parliamentary elections and parliament's decision to invoke Article 50 and leave the EU, with or without a deal, by 29 March 2019.

15. Immediately after the 2016 referendum Timothy Garton Ash (2016), a leading European historian and intellectual, warned against any hasty actions: "If we on the remain side of the British argument had won this referendum, we would expect the Brexiteers to respect the result. We can't just say: we lost, so retrospectively change the rules of the game. (Then England's soccer team would beat Iceland after all.) There would be a justified outcry." He was later to change his stance, favouring a second referendum (Garton Ash, 2018) and asking the EU for an extension to Article 50, much in line with Tony Blair's diplomatic offensive, and apparently very much listened to by former EU Council president Donald Tusk.

16. This line of argument materializes in the anti-Brexit political stance led by former UK prime minister Tony Blair, the Liberal Democrats, some conservative and labour MPs who in the meantime left their parties, some influential financial groups and think tanks and part of the British press, trying to influence the attitude of Labour against Brexit. They managed to do so, and the Labour Party suffered heavy losses in the 2019 elections. In 2019, the Liberal Democrats, with their new leader Jo Swinson, even defended simply revoking Article 50 and cancelling Brexit without a second referendum. She was not re-elected.

17. For a pro-European view, accepting the outcome of the democratic process that led to the UK's decision to trigger its exit from the EU, see Hix (2017).

18. In Zurich in 1946 Churchill had set out his vision for a kind of United States of Europe post-Second World War, although it is less clear what place, if any, the UK was to have in it.

19. On the Balassa scale, the UK expressed its preference for the lowest economic integration level (a free trade area), whereas the EEC staked out a high ambition with a customs union plus a common market. The latter offer higher benefits but require substantial sovereignty sharing.

20. See also Di Quirico (Chapter 3 in this volume), who likens the UK's attitude while a member of the club to a malign neglect strategy, which reached its limits with EMU. Another line of reasoning is given in Della Posta and Rehman (Chapter 6 in this volume), who focus on the role of UK social capital.

21. In his Jean Monnet lecture at the European University Institute in Florence on 27 October 1977, he argued that: "It is the straight political argument that monetary union stands on offer as a vehicle for European integration."

22. The term 'no-deal scenario' is somewhat misleading, as it does not mean that things remain equal for a country should a deal not materialize. The UK would find itself overnight out of the EU and of all its institutions, on which it has come to depend heavily.

23. This UK stance is illustrated in many political declarations. One case in point are the above-referred to remarks of former British prime minister John Major (2018) who argued that Britain's interest is best served as a member of the EU: "For centuries, our state schemed and plotted to prevent all Europe uniting against us. Yet very soon – on our current course – we will no longer be able to argue from within the EU for Anglo-American beliefs in free trade, open markets and strong defence" (*The Guardian*, 16 October 2018).

24. See Davies (2007), according to whom the attitude of the UK, or rather of England, towards Europe can be attributed to erroneous conceptions of its history (Anglo-centrism and neglect of the many interactions with Europe).

25. With some countries having a preference for less integration (more national sovereignty, if illusionary in a globalized world) and others for more sovereignty-sharing in order to effectively tackle common challenges, the risk becomes that the blame is put on the EU club, albeit for different motives.

26. EU symbols were not part of the Treaty of Lisbon of 2007. However, in a declaration 16 Member States (declaration 16), namely Belgium, Bulgaria, Germany, Greece, Spain, Italy, Cyprus, Lithuania, Luxembourg, Hungary, Malta, Austria, Portugal, Romania, Slovenia and the Slovak Republic, state that the flag, the anthem, the motto, the currency and Europe Day would "for them continue as symbols to express the sense of community of the people in the European Union and their allegiance to it". France endorsed it only in 2017.

27. This is still the UK stance at the end of 2019, both in the 'leave' camp and, especially, we would argue, in the 'remain' camp, which gathers basically around David Cameron's and Tony Blair's 'remainer' but Eurosceptic views on what the EU should be: a common market without EMU at its centre stage and no longer an ever-closer Union.

28. Ireland has benefited from the unconditional solidarity of the other 26 EU-27 member states throughout the entire Brexit negotiations but maintains a less than fully committed relation with the EU, as exemplified by its stance on taxation, data protection, EU symbols, exclusion from Schengen or the Eurozone budget (siding with the non-euro new Hanseatic-league countries).

29. For a discussion, see Bongardt (Chapter 7 in this volume). The notion of sovereignty is of course often illusionary in an interdependent world where solutions to transnational problems require international cooperation and sovereignty sharing. See Jones (2018) for a discussion of why the UK's notion of sovereignty is fraught in its dealings with the EU.

30. It is interesting to note the convergence of views between some British and American media and the populist anti-European parties and movements (in Greece, France, Italy, Spain, and the Netherlands) against the Euro and the EU throughout the crisis (Bongardt and Torres, 2016a).

31. It made little sense to have the EBA located outside the Eurozone. Following the triggering of Article 50 TEU by the UK, the European Medicines Agency (EMA) was also relocated from London to Amsterdam.

32. See Sternberg (2015). Already in 2017, President Macron had drawn attention to the negative effects of the British choice for the European social model in the context of the posted worker directive.

33. See Zielonka (2014).
34. The Eurogroup could function as a formation of the Council (see European Commission, 2017).
35. As the UK's participation in the EU is already essentially limited to the internal market, it follows that the UK's exit from the EU implies exiting the single market, which corresponds to the UK government's stated intentions, supported by parliament, in its notification letter to the European Council of its decision to invoke Article 50 TEU for the UK to exit the EU, and corresponds to the official position of the two principal parties that obtained more than 80 per cent of the vote in the 2017 (Brexit) elections (see also Bongardt and Torres, 2017a).
36. For a discussion of what should be the EU's approach to global trade, see Bongardt and Torres (2018).
37. Norway, Iceland and Liechtenstein are members of the EEA and as such are obliged to respect the four freedoms and the jurisdiction of the CJEU, as well as to contribute to the EU budget.
38. As illustrated by the European Commission's efforts to correct untruths that are in circulation and put the facts straight (See https://blogs.ec.europa.eu/ECintheUK/category/euromyths/, consulted on 5 March 2019). Many of its efforts were directed towards the UK.
39. As witnessed by the apparent unpreparedness of the British government, administration, diplomacy and the business (including the financial) sector to deal with the process of its exit from the EU and to negotiate agreements with other countries or regions, which led the UK to ask for exceptions, transition periods, etc. (Rachman, 2017). The UK's limited capacity cum international clout is also evidenced by its difficulty to simply roll over EU trade agreements (https://www.wto.org/english/thewto_e/countries_e/united_kingdom_e.htm, consulted on 5 March 2019).
40. Even in areas such as combatting terrorism, the UK is totally dependent on the EU's Schengen Information System (to which it has been granted free access by the Union, arguably at the cost of EU citizens' rights). The same holds true for its financial system without a European passport and without transactions in Euros (even the successful risk capital operations in the UK were strongly based on the European Investment Fund), for the certification of nuclear safety, the operation of international flights, not to mention trade, the environment, food safety and scientific research, among many other areas.

REFERENCES

Bongardt, Annette and Francisco Torres (2016a), "EMU and structural reform", in Leila Simona Talani (ed.), *Europe in Crisis: A Structural Analysis*, Basingstoke: Palgrave, pp. 37–64.

Bongardt, Annette and Francisco Torres (2016b), "EMU reform and resilience in a re-dimensioned EU", *Journal of Economic Policy*, 32, 3, December, pp. 575–96.

Bongardt, Annette and Francisco Torres (2016c), "The political economy of Brexit: why making it easier to leave the club can allow for a better functioning EU", *Intereconomics*, 51, 4, July/August, pp. 214–19.

Bongardt, Annette and Francisco Torres (2017a), "Brexit: a qualitative change in the process of European integration", in N. Cabral, J. Gonçalves and N. Rodrigues (eds), *After Brexit: Consequences for the EU*, Basingstoke: Palgrave, pp. 101–27.

Bongardt, Annette and Francisco Torres (2017b), *Brexit: Uma questão de racionalidade política*, Lisbon: Universidade Católica Editora.

Bongardt, Annette and Francisco Torres (2018), "What should be the EU's approach to global trade?", Forum, *Intereconomics*, pp. 245–9.

Bongardt, Annette and Francisco Torres (2019), "Trade agreements and regional integration: the European Union after Brexit", in Robert Looney (ed.), *Routledge Handbook of International Trade Agreements*, London and New York: Routledge, pp. 296–306.

Brady, Hugo and Katinka Barisch (2007), "The CEPR guide to the Reform Treaty", briefing note, London: Centre for European Reform, pp. 4–5.

Buti, Marco and Muriel Lacoue-Labarthe (2016), "Europe's incompatible political trinities", VoxEU.org, 7 September.

Campos, Nauro and Fabrizio Coricelli (2017), "EU membership or Thatcher's structural reforms: what drove the great British reversal?", Centre for Economic Policy Research, DP 11856.

Davies, Norman (2007), "Not forever England: a European history of Britain", in *Europe East and West*, London: Pimlico, pp. 83–105.

European Commission (2017), Reflection paper on the deepening of EMU, Brussels: European Commission, 31 May.

Fabbrini, Federico (2017), "Brexit and a multi-speed Europe: a lawyer's perspective", Jacques Delors Institut and Bertelsmann Foundation, 16 March.

Garton Ash, Timothy (2016), "If you think Britain is angry and divided, look at the continent", *The Guardian*, 1 July.

Garton Ash, Timothy (2018), "Europe's door is still open – but Britain will have to move fast", *The Guardian*, 17 November.

George, Stephen (1998), *An Awkward Partner: Britain and the European Community*, Oxford: Oxford University Press.

Hirschman, Albert O. (1970), *Exit, Voice, and Loyalty: Responses to Decline in Firms, Organizations, and States*, Cambridge, MA: Harvard University Press.

Hix, Simon (2017), "What would a pro-European hard Brexit look like?", LSE blog, 6 April.

Jones, Harold (2018), "Winter is coming to the UK", Project Syndicate, 1 November.

König, Nicole (2015), "A differentiated view of differentiated integration", Policy paper 140, Berlin, Jacques Delors Institut.

Major, John (2018), "I have made no false promises on Brexit – I can tell you the truth", *The Guardian*, 16 October (consulted 5 February 2019).

OECD (2015), *Economic Policy Reforms: Going for Growth*, Paris: OECD.

Rachman, Gideon (2017), "Brexit and the prospect of national humiliation", *Financial Times*, 10 July.

Soros, George (2017), "Standing up for Europe", *Project Syndicate*, 1 June.

Spolaore, Enrico (2015), "Monnet's chain reaction and the future of Europe", VoxEU. org, 25 July.

Sternberg, Claudia (2015), "What were the French telling us by voting down the 'EU constitution'? A case for interpretive research on referendum debates", *Comparative European Politics*, 56.

Torres, Francisco (2009), "The role of preferences and the sustainability of EMU", in Leila Simona Talani (ed.), *The Future of EMU*, Basingstoke: Palgrave Macmillan, pp. 54–74.

Tusk, Donald (2019), "Keynote speech by President Donald Tusk", opening ceremony of the 2019/20 academic year at the College of Europe, 13 November.

Wolfstädter, Laura and Valentin Kreilinger (2017), "European integration via flexibility tools: the cases of EPPO and PESCO", Policy Paper 209, Berlin: Jacques Delors Institut.
Zielonka, Jan (2014), *Is the EU doomed?*, Cambridge: Polity Press.

3. The road to Brexit: European integration, the UK and the failure of the "malign neglect" strategy toward the EU

Roberto Di Quirico

3.1 INTRODUCTION

Many observers have interpreted Brexit as the unfortunate and unexpected consequence of a referendum where propaganda, inadequate knowledge of EU affairs, and limited participation by the younger and most pro-European citizens, permitted the exit supporters to prevail. In appearance, one of the most critical decisions in recent UK history thus resulted from an erratic event, and the political naivety of the Cameron government in calling the referendum ruined the British integration process.

In this chapter, we will demonstrate that the referendum simply acted as a catalyst for choices that had to be taken anyway. In other words, the UK government had to decide between full integration in the EU or Brexit, independently of the referendum result. In fact, the UK's approach to further integration with Europe since the Thatcher years, here called "malign neglect",[1] had become less and less sustainable. In particular, deeper European economic and financial integration since the introduction of the euro and the adoption of the New European Economic Governance made the UK's position in the EU, and its influence in European decisions so marginal as to endanger the global role of the country.[2] This marginalisation happened because the UK had not adopted the common currency and was not part of the EU core and its decisional arena. This core was primarily focused on the Economic and Monetary Union (EMU) and economic governance.

Meanwhile, the UK continues to face the problem of its special relationship with the USA and the diverging priorities of the EU and the American allies, in economic, military and foreign policy. The progressive detachment and marginalisation of the UK in EU governance has also reduced British influence and its role as the "American referee" in the EU.[3]

This chapter is structured as follows. Section 3.2 shows that a long-term perspective is required to understand the cumulative process that led to Brexit. Section 3.3 emphasises the prevalence of economic reasons for the UK application for membership and the poor interest shown in political integration from the early days in the European Economic Community (EEC). Section 3.4 explains how the British and the EEC/EU routes diverged almost irremediably since the Maastricht Treaty, in particular on the issue of monetary integration and its political consequences. Section 3.5 shows the consequences of the UK's relationship with the rest of the EU, as determined by the growing importance of monetary and economic governance issues following the international economic crisis. Section 3.6 concludes.

3.2 THE RATIONALE FOR A LONG-TERM ANALYSIS OF BRITISH INVOLVEMENT IN EUROPEAN INTEGRATION

The analysis proposed in this chapter shows that there is a logic for Brexit and that it had been a potential outcome since the early years of the UK membership in the EEC. It also demonstrates that the political and economic costs of remaining in the EU were not neutral as supposed by anti-Brexit supporters. Both full integration and marginalisation imply costs.

This chapter combines a historical and political science approach to show that UK integration in the EEC/EU was based on other reasons than Europeanism. The UK application for, and membership of, the EEC will be explained as a "third-best solution" taken to face the consequences of decolonisation and the crises of the UK's international position, in particular in the economic and financial sectors. The initially poor results of that strategy and the rise in power of Thatcher changed UK European policy. They led to the adoption of a "malign neglect" strategy that aimed to curb or delay further integration with Europe, in particular, political integration, and strict regulation in sectors that are crucial for the UK economy, such as banking and finance, as well as foreign policy. British resistance to further integration and regulation emerged in fields that the "Thatcher revolution" shaped more deeply, such as welfare, job markets and public services. This approach survived in the Tory government's approach to EU politics until Cameron's call for the referendum, notwithstanding the more conciliatory attitude adopted by Labour governments. Since the introduction of the euro, however, and particularly after the 2008 crisis and the subsequent rise of the New European Economic Governance, the malign neglect strategy lost effectiveness because fundamental transformations in the EU, which shaped more EU politics, arose in fields in which the UK had minimal influence.

At the end of the Cameron era, it was evident that the UK had to choose from full integration, Brexit or suffer complete marginalisation in European affairs, so Brexit was a real political option, and not an accident resulting from the unexpected outcome of a populist referendum.

Brexit can thus be understood in all its aspects only by adopting a long-term perspective; however, the long-term approach to analysing political events adopted in this chapter is unusual in EU studies. Usually, scholars use history to introduce the recent events that they want to study and explain. Sometimes, historical events support diachronically comparative analysis or suggest the influence of past experiences in shaping today's decisions.

Brexit is different. In fact, since the early days of UK membership in the EEC, Brexit was a credible option for the future. We can thus see Brexit as a process that started with the UK's membership, remained latent for decades, and finally became the preferred policy choice. As a consequence, we need to trace the whole process in order to understand Brexit, and identify the elements and the turning points that shaped the "road to Brexit".

The UK's relationship with the European Communities (the EU included) could be divided into four periods: the inconvertible sterling period (from 1945 to 1956–57), the non-adhesion period (1957–61), the adhesion and membership period (1961–2016), and Brexit. This timeline matches the different strategies adopted by the UK toward Continental Europe and European integration. During the inconvertible sterling period, British strategy toward Continental Europe complemented the broader ambitions of the UK in international politics, and mainly referred to the sterling problem. In the non-adhesion period, the UK instead searched for an alternative solution to integration with Continental Europe. More specifically, the UK searched for a "softer" integration that was entirely concentrated on free trade, such as the British-led European Free Trade Area (EFTA).[4] The adhesion and membership period saw a progressive convergence between the UK and Continental partners, halted by the EEC founders' ambitions for greater economic and political integration. A mix of British scepticism about the ability of Continental partners to effectively realise political objectives, and the hope that they would fail in the fields that the UK was not interested in following, generated the attitude of malign neglect that we identify as the main characteristic of British policy toward European integration, from Thatcher to Cameron.

The timeline proposed above also fits well with the historical analysis of the UK–Western Europe relationship since 1945, and in particular the European integration issue. One of the most widespread interpretations of the genesis and path dependence effects of the early two periods described above sees that period as the years in which the UK missed the "European train" and the opportunity to take leadership of the European communities (Gowland 2017, p. 15; Wall 2008, p. 215). This lost opportunity shaped the future of the UK–

EEC/EU relationship, encouraged Euroscepticism and created the divergence of interests between the UK and its Continental partners. An alternative interpretation saw the two first periods as the years of a "failed national strategy" to solve the problems generated by the war, and to reinsert the UK into the international economic system (Milward 2002).[5] Today, a mix of these two approaches seems acceptable. It suggests that the UK missed the train in the 1950s because the European integration train was not capable of solving the post-war problems of the UK and the Commonwealth (Baker and Schnapper 2015, p. 45), and because there were no certainties about the success of the European solution and the impossibility of retaining the British Empire. The British government understood that the UK had emerged from the war with short-term advantages to be used as soon as possible (Milward 2002, p. 2). They tried to use these advantages to realise a national strategy and to gain a position in the post-war world coherent with the British status as a victorious West European power. When it became evident that they had failed, EEC membership became a crucial element in pursuing a new strategy (Milward 2002, p. 7).

The analytical perspective adopted in this chapter is not just historical. Instead, utilising a long-term approach means focusing on a specific event and seeing it as the result of interactions between different processes, in particular, long-term cycles that shape each other, and turning points that create path dependence. This approach overcomes the limits of short-term causality analysis that suggest Brexit is just the result of a series of unfortunate events.

In the following sections, we will debate the consequences of path dependence in UK European policy, stressing how the UK arrived at European integration following a different path than the founding members. These differences depend on two elements. The first is the cyclical economic desynchronisation between Continental Europe and the UK since the end of the Second World War. This made European integration a last resort policy for the UK, after other solutions had failed, and Europeanisation a poorly fitting process for the UK.[6] The second element is the heritage of the imperial era. This element profoundly influenced UK foreign policy due to its status as an international power, the role of sterling and the Commonwealth in British international economic relations, and the particular relationship with the USA. The cultural heritage of the empire also contributed to limiting the support for European integration, an element that favoured Euroscepticism and hostility toward further integration, and that, in the end, created the conditions for the Brexiteers' victory.

All these elements fed a multiphase process of UK marginalisation, mainly due to the UK European policy itself. The early phases of UK marginalisation (the UK's hostility to the European Payment Union and the refusal to join the European Coal and Steel Community (ECSC) and the EEC from the beginning) happened during the pre-accession period and were (apparently) overcome due to the UK's membership in the EEC. Other choices, such as opting-out from the EMU, in particular, had irreversible consequences for the UK's role in the EU and can be considered the final turning point toward Brexit.

We can trace a process in which turning points resulted from systemic interactions. Cyclical economic desynchronisation played a fundamental role in shaping the UK's relationship with Continental Europe and the rising EEC, as well as in explaining the reasons for the UK application for EEC membership and the new divergent UK path that followed the failure of the membership strategy carried out by the pre-Thatcher governments. The heritage of the empire in its various forms, as well as the privileged Anglo-American partnership, later pushed the UK gradually to the margins of Europe. Finally, the 2008 international financial crisis acted as a catalyst, creating the opportunity for the UK to embrace entirely, or refuse definitively, European integration. The final choice is well known.

3.3   THE ECONOMIC REASONS FOR UK MEMBERSHIP APPLICATIONS

Economic issues were preponderant in shaping the UK–Continental Europe relationship since the early post-Second World War period and, again, when the UK started to consider EEC membership as a desirable objective. At that time, the main political integration initiatives in Western Europe had already failed, and the founder countries also saw the EEC mainly as a tool for economic coordination, although they continued to herald political integration objectives for the long term. The UK could thus approach European integration without problems of excessively surrendering sovereignty.

Desynchronisation between British and Continental European economies was one of the leading economic outcomes of the early post-Second World War period. Although the war destroyed or dramatically weakened the economic structure of Continental countries (colonial systems included), and meant that they had to rebuild both the economic structures and the economic relationships between Western European countries from scratch, the UK emerged from the war with the same structure as in the pre-war period, just much more troubled. The UK was still the core of an empire economically and financially connected by the Commonwealth and the sterling area respectively.[7] However, in many of their parts, both these structures were crumbling. As a victorious country that aimed to restore its international status, the UK also had to respect its obligations, in particular paying its debts for war imports. These obligations required managing the massive amount of "blocked sterling" in the hands of UK suppliers and sterling area countries.[8] While the only option for Continental European countries was redefining their economic structures, the UK had to choose between restoring the old system or creating something new.

Restoring the imperial economic system was much more attractive than dismissing it to create something new and undefined. As the leading Western European victorious country, the UK reasonably aimed to re-establish its role as the core connection between Continental Europe and the rest of the world or, at least, the "British World" connected as the Commonwealth. This ambition was coherent with two pillars of British foreign policy; its traditional opposition to the rise of a European political unit and its new Atlantic partnership that was now indispensable in granting the military security of the empire and commercial routes.

From the early post-war years, however, the terms of UK victory appeared much more fragile than expected by the British government. Early warnings about the unsoundness of the UK's optimism emerged in the Bretton Woods conferences. There, the British delegation, led by Keynes, discovered the poor attitude of the USA toward UK ambition to recreate a post-war world inspired by its colonial past. Anti-colonialism and trade liberalisation emerged as the pillars of the USA's international economic policy for the post-war period. The expected compensations for the UK's early war efforts and resistance against the Axis forces before the USA joined the war were revealed as ephemeral (Steil 2013). Instead, an "American World" emerged from Bretton Woods, in which the UK had to fight hard to survive.

During the 1946–61 period, the UK fought its battle on three different fronts and lost on all of them. The independence of India started the rapid decay of the British Empire that culminated in decolonisation in the 1960s. Notwithstanding military victory in the Second World War, the UK had no money to repress anticolonial forces in many parts of the empire and concentrated its limited resources to keep control of those regions that produced vital raw materials indispensable to keep the UK economy at work (Bell 1956). On the financial front, sophisticated management of the sterling area made decolonisation less traumatic and delayed repayment of sterling balances, simply moving them from the now independent countries to those countries still under British control (Krozewski 1993; Hinds 2001). This strategy was only a temporary solution, however, and its effectiveness declined inexorably with the advancing decay of the British Empire. Meanwhile, the Treasury proposed plans for managing sterling outside the sterling area and regaining a central position in world trade. These plans evolved from the ROBOT plan to the so-called Collective Approach, in which Continental Europe had to play a relevant role.[9]

The UK's attempt to regain centrality and to reconnect Continental European economies to the British economic sphere failed when the founding countries created the European Economic Community and the UK did not join.[10] This attempt was the ultimate step in a series of tensions between the UK and the leading Western European members of the European Payments Union (EPU).[11] While the EEC founding countries benefited from the EPU facilities for intra-European trade, the EPU represented an obstacle for UK plans to regain centrality in the European economic system and to use this gain to compensate for the loss of economic opportunities in the imperial area.[12] When the EPU had to be dismissed due to its members' return to currency convertibility (Kaplan and Schleiminger 1989), some countries, led by France, reacted to the loss of the non-tariff barrier granted by the EPU system, creating the customs union we know as the EEC. This step was irreconcilable with the UK's plans to enlarge its area of economic influence. As a counter-reaction, the UK promoted the creation of the EFTA, which joined some of the UK's leading commercial partners.

The 1961 UK application for EEC membership revealed the final failure of the UK post-war strategy to rebuild its status as an international power. The combined effects of growing decolonisation, the scarce effectiveness of the EFTA, and the difficulties of supporting the UK's balance of payments, worsened by the decline of the sterling area and the problem of the blocked sterling balances, induced the British government to see the EEC as an alternative to the empire for restructuring the crumbling UK economy. Admission to the EEC, however, proved problematic.

In the 1960s, the UK applied for EEC membership twice, and in both cases the application was rejected (Schenk 2010). Many authors explain these rejections via the opposition of De Gaulle to UK membership, because UK admission could endanger the political leadership of France in the EEC, where it found a valid alternative to its colonial empire irremediably under demission since the mid-1950s. UK membership also appeared to De Gaulle to be an American Trojan horse (Schenk 2010, p. 136). The UK's economic problems also played a role in the rejection of the UK's applications, as demonstrated by the 1967 sterling crisis.[13] Britain also remained uncertain about the best way to face the sterling problem and its impact on the British balance of payments. While the Collective Approach became mainly a European approach to sterling, Britain continued to practise "sterling-dollar diplomacy" (Gardner 1980; Hirowatari 2015, pp. 2, 19), a strategy that was poorly effective and politically embarrassing due to French hostility to the American "exorbitant privilege" and the US-led international monetary system.[14]

The departure of De Gaulle from the French presidency in the late 1960s was only one of the elements that changed the EEC's attitude toward the UK. In fact, the EEC members had started to plan a monetary union as a reaction to the instability of the Bretton Woods system since 1969.[15] Including sterling in this monetary union appeared to be an advantage for three reasons. Having sterling merged into the new European currency could make it an international currency from its early days. The British currency was still internationally relevant, and sterling circulated the world and was part of central bank reserves. Second, the British crisis that followed the 1967 sterling devaluation destabilised the whole European economy, and required it to be faced collectively. Finally, both the UK and the EEC member countries aimed to avoid International Monetary Fund (IMF) intervention in the UK. EEC intervention after the UK's admission (possibly using the European Monetary Fund then under planning) could thus be a solution to the British crisis with acceptable costs for the European partners, when considering the gains from sterling inclusion in the new European currency.

The UK's entry to the EEC in 1973 was not the result of a new "Europeanist" attitude by the UK, nor the result of an enthusiastic invitation from EEC members. Instead, it was a "third best solution" after the failure to consolidate the empire, and the poor results of the "softer international integration" solutions such as the EFTA. This third best solution arrived too late to save the UK from IMF intervention, however, and the dismantling of the British post-war economic system that opened the door to the Thatcher government.

3.4   THE UK POLICY OF "MALIGN NEGLECT" TOWARD EUROPEAN INTEGRATION

The end of the transitory period of UK membership, which included a confirmatory referendum that none of the founding countries had undertaken before,[16] almost coincided with the rise to power of Margaret Thatcher and a historical turn in British history. The so-called "Iron Lady" changed the societal and economic structure of the UK, dismantling pillars of the post-war domestic arrangement. She also re-established a strong relationship with the USA and President Reagan through a converging attitude in favour of neo-liberal economic policies and NATO. Both these attitudes collided with the preferences of the other European partners, France in particular. Since De Gaulle's presidency, France had claimed autonomy from NATO and the Americans, both in international politics as well as in the international economic and financial system. The French "dirigiste" tradition also collided with neo-liberal policies and the massive privatisation dogma that characterised them. Finally, Thatcher's pragmatic attitude to the EEC and her background in the private sector, did not allow her to perceive or understand the idealistic component of the founders' participation in the European integration process. They believed in political integration as the main result of that process, and were ready to pay for it by surrendering part of their countries' sovereignty, a price that Thatcher abhorred.

Meanwhile, the UK's membership unbalanced the existing financial structure of the EEC, originally adapted to the needs of countries, France in particular, that required the EEC to protect and support their agricultural sectors. At that time, the Communitarian Agricultural Policy absorbed the largest quota of the EEC budget. The latter was partly funded with customs duties that sustained the prices of agricultural products. The UK thus had to pay much as a food importer and gained little because of the limited number of big farmers in the country (Wall 2008; Backer and Schnapper 2015). This situation generated tensions between the UK and the other EEC members, and prompted Thatcher to ask for "her money back".[17] Finally, Thatcher's economic policy made the UK membership in the rising European Monetary System unsustainable, at least during the early years. In fact, the risk of deflation as a consequence of the EMS constraints appeared to the Tories to be "political suicide" (Needham 2014, p. 130).[18]

In the 1980s and early 1990s, economic desynchronisation was once more crucial in making the national interest of the UK divergent from the interests of the other EEC members. The discovery of the North Sea oil fields made the UK an oil exporter, changed the structure of its balance of payments, and transformed sterling into a "petrocurrency"; this meant something different (again) to the other EEC currencies (Schenk 2010, p. 398). The rising financialisation of the international economy and the enlargement of the Eurodollar market centred in London thanks to petrodollar flows increased the relevance of financial matters and the influence of the City in addressing the UK's preferences in European politics (Eichengreen 2008; Helleiner 1994; Solomon 1999). These preferences were keeping sterling and acting as an intra-EU offshore financial centre (Talani 2000). New elements thus converged in feeding Thatcher's and Major's hostility toward advanced monetary integration and financial regulation.

The image of the UK as a poorly Europeanist country rocking the boat of European integration consolidated during the Thatcher years, and Thatcher's European policy contributed to the "self-marginalisation" that generated the progressive alienation of the UK from the EU's decision-making centres and the European integration process, and later culminated in Brexit.[19] Thatcher's aggressive style and resistance to the surrender of sovereignty were repeatedly outflanked by the other EEC members who were increasingly committed to monetary integration.[20] Meanwhile, internal conflict in the UK Parliament over the UK's European policy determined the fall of the Thatcher government and the rise to power of Major, who had no alternative but to accept the EEC and decisively follow "the road to Maastricht", a road the UK finally decided to abandon.

The Maastricht Treaty and the refusal of the UK to join the euro caused "the first Brexit", and probably the most important one. This was an internal distancing by the other member states and resulted in an option to opt out from the EMU, and not in a real Brexit. However, that choice generated progressive UK marginalisation and the loss of influence in European affairs later emphasised by the central role gained by EU economic governance in European affairs. This first Brexit also modified UK policy toward European integration from confrontational resistance to obstructionism: a policy that aimed to obstruct further integration because the UK was no more capable of stopping it.

From a short-term perspective, Maastricht was a success for Major. He excluded elements from the Maastricht Treaty that were in contrast to British preferences (the Social Chapter in particular), and opted out of the EMU. The Social Chapter involved a welfare and labour market that was an economic sector in which the UK and Continental Europe models collided. The Major governments also avoided restrictions for the financial sector that would be imposed by monetary integration thanks to opting out. Finally, Major avoided the "Communitarisation" of both the foreign and security policy, and the justice and home affairs policy keeping them in the intergovernmental cooperation sphere (Backer and Schnapper 2015, p. 44). It seemed that the UK had won at Maastricht.

Despite this almost Pyrrhic victory, it soon became clear that exclusion from the EMU and the political nature of the choice about monetary integration had isolated the UK and diminished its influence in European politics. When Tony Blair gained power, the new European policy was addressed in order to regain influence in other fields, mainly EU international politics (Wall 2008, p. 169). There, Blair aimed to make the UK the fulcrum of the European–American alliance, acting to settle divergences in the attitudes of the EU and the USA toward European integration and the role of NATO. Again, it raised the problem of the UK's dual loyalty toward the EU and the USA, perceived in the 1960s by De Gaulle and still under suspicion by the EU French–German leadership. The ambiguous European position of the UK emerged dramatically in 2003 when the EU members split between supporters and opponents of the US invasion of Iraq. The UK led the USA supporter group (the so-called New Europe), while France and Germany refused to support the American allies. Blair's attempt to regain centrality in EU politics thus resulted in further hostility from the EU core.

Blair's EU policy was a different kind of malign neglect strategy, only slightly less malign and neglectful than the policies of his predecessors. While Thatcher openly opposed monetary and political integration and Major simply tried to make it slower, hoping for the failure of French and German plans for monetary and political union, Blair tried to turn the EU toward a different path. This path was strictly dependent on the USA and the Anglo-American partnership, and also proposed UK leadership over those new Eastern European member countries fiercely asserting their NATO loyalty. Meanwhile, UK membership in the EMU lost attraction due to the good results of the post-EMU British economy and the low growth rate in the euro area.

Blair's plan for calling a referendum to join the EMU thus had to be dismissed (Wall 2008).

The failed stabilisation of occupied Iraq and the discrediting of the USA and the UK due to the chemical weapons affair, as well as the financial crises, struck both pillars of the UK European policy. The American policy in the Middle East had resulted in the complete destabilisation of the area and lost every kind of attraction for EU members. Meanwhile, the financial crises thoroughly discredited the neo-liberal attitudes toward financialisation; it meant the core of British reinsertion in the European economy. At the end of the 2000s, plans for UK membership in the EMU as a strategy to face the financial crises seemed a reiteration of the 1960s strategy to face the imminent collapse of the empire; however, in the late 2000s and the early 2010s, the EU financial system was crumbling more than the British system. The last opportunity that the UK had to rejoin the core of the European Union thus vanished.

3.5   THE INTERNATIONAL FINANCIAL CRISIS AND THE OBSOLESCENCE OF UK POLICY TOWARD THE EUROPEAN UNION

Notwithstanding that the tensions raised inside the EU and the NATO in 2003 represented a crucial element in UK marginalisation, it was the international financial crisis and its effects on EU governance and politics that made the UK attitude toward the EU unsustainable (Bongardt and Torres 2016). The reaction of the member states to the crisis was mainly concentrated in the EMU channel where new rules were introduced, and the role of the European Central Bank (ECB) became crucial in shaping intra-EMU politics. Unfortunately, the UK was out of the EMU and had minimal influence in the ECB.

In the early phase of the crisis, the EU proved incapable of managing the difficulties of its member states. The European institutions had not been created to face such a dramatic crisis and changing European treaties is a long and painful process, so, national governments moved first and more incisively than the Commission. They were capable of managing the early interventions to support creaking banks or giants "too big to fail",[21] sometimes alone and in other cases cooperating with a few other governments touched by the same risk. Each member state also adopted decisions and financial rules to face the paralysis of inter-bank and inter-state financial flows; however, when the crisis worsened and a collective effort became indispensable in avoiding a systemic crisis in the whole EU, individual or poorly coordinated interventions worked no more.

It was the Greek crisis and the following sovereign debt crises that accelerated the collective approach to the mounting systemic crisis of the EMU. Rescue plans, specific funding schemes to face mounting crises in member states, and finally new agencies and financial institutions, had to be implemented or created. Meanwhile, the need to manage such a complicated network of activities required new rules and coercive tools that the EU lacked.

The absence of rules was gradually solved by the introduction of the pillars of the New Economic Governance (NEG) of the European Union. The "six-pack" and the "two pack" rules reinforced the poorly implemented Stability and Growth Pact, while new agencies and financial institutions monitored, addressed and supported banks and the more troubled governments. New and more restrictive procedures and parameters also reinforced EU governance potentialities in the EMU. Finally, the EU institutional structure was reinforced with new actors, mainly focused on economic governance such as the Euro Group and the Council of the Eurozone.[22]

The lack of coercive tools to enforce the NEG was a complicated problem to solve. The only channel of influence that demonstrated enough power to impose financial discipline and the respect of the new rules was the informal power of the ECB. The latter has broad discretion in granting loans, emergency liquidity, and support for member state bonds on the secondary market. Discretion made the ECB a powerful political actor, capable of influencing and addressing the economic policy national governments toward a cooperative attitude and the compliance of EU rules. What happened in the EMU also affected those member states that were not members of the EMU; however, the crisis and the solutions adopted to face it strengthened the role of the EMU area as the EU core. The EMU arena thus became the crucial arena in EU politics, including in EU influence on national policies and politics.

The financial crisis and the rise of the NEG influenced politics in the EU, also changing the attitudes of member states voters toward the EU and its policies. Impatience toward economic constraints, austerity policy, and the political intrusiveness of the Commission in the internal politics of member states fed anti-Europeanism and distrust for further integration, as well as rooting hostility against the euro, now suggested as the main reasons for the recession in EMU countries. New political parties arose and gained electoral consensus, targeting the EU and its policies to catalyse support, and creating a new ideology in which anti-European issues merged with traditional populist beliefs. The British UKIP party, led by Nigel Farage, was one of these parties, and successfully led the campaign for Brexit won in the 2016 referendum.

Both the introduction of the NEG and the rise of anti-Europeanist parties shaped UK faith in Europe. Although joining the EMU was an option debated in the early phase of the crisis, both the pervasiveness of EU institutions in the financial sector and public finances, and the diffusion of anti-EU feelings in Great Britain made UK membership in the EMU the last lost opportunity to regain centrality in the European Union. Renouncing deeper integration with the EU inexorably condemned the UK to marginality, and its influence on EU affairs was confined to obstructionism in order to gain concessions and preferential treatment, which the European partners were bored with facing.[23] Malign neglect under Cameron thus resulted in a growing hostility against British EU policy. This hostility contributed to isolate the UK further, and to make it more marginal than ever.

3.6   CONCLUSION

The political detachment between the UK and the so-called "old Europe" emerged in 2003, the restraining influence of the UK on deeper integration in the EU, and the impact of the international financial crisis on EU governance made UK marginality an unavoidable issue to solve. As regards political and economic influence, the UK became "a watchdog that bites no more". Its marginality meant the UK was unable to influence EU choices regarding Anglo-American priorities and the UK neo-liberal economic model. Meanwhile, the economic crisis and popular discontent with UK membership in the EU was a hot issue in internal political debate and revamped the never dismissed Euroscepticism of the political heirs of Thatcher, while new and influential populist forces made the EU their preferred target.

Brexit was thus derived from long-term dynamics and was finally catalysed by the recent consequences of the economic crisis. However, Brexit had been a potential outcome of UK membership since the 1970s, and the UK walked a parallel path to the "road to Brexit" for decades before joining it. There were many opportunities to converge toward a "European road", mainly offered by the monetary integration process. The UK refused or lost all of these opportunities. This made the UK's position in the EU unsustainable and the need to choose between full integration or exit unavoidable.

From a long-term perspective, Brexit can also be explained as the failure of the imperial era exit strategy adopted in the 1960s, rather than the simple failure of UK integration with the European Union. That strategy permitted the UK to survive the British Empire dissolution but failed in creating a perpetual link between the UK and Continental Europe. The UK also joined the EEC and the integration process too late to shape the European institutional framework and the political objectives of the Community in a different way. The founder countries shaped the European institutions and their objectives according to their national interests and economic needs, the French in particular. When the UK joined the EEC, institutional structure, informal agreements and objectives had been already defined, and the UK could no longer change them. In the 1980s and early 1990s the aggressive attitude of Thatcher, and her opposition to the enhancement and reinforcement of communitarian initiatives in the political, social and monetary fields, isolated Britain from the EEC core and favoured the consolidation of the French–German partnership. Meanwhile,

UK leaders (the Tories in particular) continued in their strategy of malign neglect, hoping for the failure of those advanced integrative initiatives they were incapable of blocking and unwilling to join.

Nevertheless, there is rationality in the Brexit choice as well as in the first refusal to join the European community in the 1950s. A systemic incongruence between British and continental economies, as well as diverging trajectories regarding their post-Second World War international role, made the UK poorly compatible with an integrated Europe from the start, and cultural barriers played a role in Britons who were "belonging without believing" in the EEC for the whole membership period (Gowland 2017, p. 80). Again, in the 1990s, the economic interests of the City and the poor attitude to sovereignty surrender made the refusal to join the EMU a coherent choice, at least in the short term. Brexit is a long-term consequence of these choices, and so it is a rational choice from a long-term perspective, although nothing guarantees that it is the better choice for the UK.

NOTES

1. The expression "malign neglect" derives from the definition adopted for the US attitude toward European monetary affairs in the 1970s, the so-called benign neglect. In this chapter "malign neglect" means a malevolent attitude that cannot be implemented because of a lack of opportunity. Insulation and the hope of failure for unwelcome initiatives remain as the only options on the table.
2. The New (European) Economic Governance (NEG) is the sum of new rules, procedures and entities created since the late 2000s for combatting the effects of the international crisis and the sovereign debts crisis that endangered the survivance of the euro. It integrates the previous rules and procedures mainly included in the Stability and Growth Pact (Degryse 2012; Kunstein and Wessels 2013; Sadeleer 2012; Salines, Glöckler and Truchlewski 2012, pp. 669–70).
3. The strict relationship between the UK and the USA, firm UK support for NATO, and the so-called sterling–dollar diplomacy fed suspicions and accusations that the UK was to be the "American watchdog" since the De Gaulle presidency (Schenk 2010, pp. 124, 136; Hirowatari 2015, p. 19; Gardner 1980).
4. The European Free Trade Area (EFTA) was created in 1960 and joined as founding members by the UK, Austria, Denmark, Norway, Portugal, Sweden and Switzerland. Finland joined in 1961 and Iceland in 1970. In 1972 the UK and Denmark left the EFTA to join the EEC (Troitiño et al. 2018, pp. 68–9).
5. Milward suggests this failed national strategy rose and fell in the 1945–63 period, and so he considers the first British attempt to join the EEC as the end of the strategy and not the start of a new British attitude toward European integration (Milward 2002).
6. The fit–misfit paradigm has been widely applied in Europeanisation studies to explain why certain countries do better than others in adopting EU rules and implementing EU policies (Cowles, Caporaso and Risse 2001).
7. The sterling area was derived from the sterling bloc created in the 1930s by the Commonwealth members after the British abandonment of gold convertibility.

It appeared when British authorities decided to centralise the management of the gold reserves of the Commonwealth in London. The sterling area survived to the end of the war and was a crucial arrangement to permit managing the so-called blocked sterling accounts. The latter were, in practice, commercial debts accumulated by Britain during the war and that Britain was incapable of repaying (Bell 1956; Fodor 1986; Schenk 1994 and 2010).

8.　Sterling balances were initially managed using agreements with British dependent and former-dependent countries, which agreed to keep blocked sterling in their reserves. Later, mainly in the 1967 sterling crisis, international organisations absorbed huge amounts of sterling. On blocked sterling balances, see Schenk (1994 and 2010).

9.　The ROBOT plan proposed in 1952 aimed at the sterling return to convertibility at flexible exchange rates, and blocking a large part of non-resident sterling balances. It was a unilateral initiative to discharge the burden of economic adjustment instead of draining UK reserves on the exchange rate. However, the ROBOT plan could create many problems inside the country (inflation and excessive costs of imported goods mainly) and outside, in particular with some sterling area countries and the European Payment Union. After the ROBOT plan rejection, a new plan for sterling flexible convertibility emerged, the so-called Collective Approach. This plan was based on the return to convertibility of the sterling and the European currencies together (Schenk 1994, pp. 114–22; Burnham 2003).

10.　The UK did not join the ECSC; however, there were obvious reasons for refusing to share British control of coal and steel industries, in particular after their nationalisation by the Atlee government (Troitiño et al. 2018, pp. 61–2). The UK's non-participation in the first created European community is thus not considered as important as the refusal to join the EEC in determining the future of UK European integration.

11.　The European Payment Union was a multilateral clearing agreement created in 1950 and funded by the Marshall Plan. Its function was to reactivate intra-European trade. It joined many countries that are today members of the European Union (Austria, Belgium, Denmark, France, German Federal Republic, Greece, Ireland, Italy, Luxembourg, Netherlands, Portugal, Sweden and the UK) and a few others (Iceland, Switzerland and Turkey). Its dismissal coincided with the creation of the European Economic Community by a limited group of former EPU members (Milward 1984; Kaplan and Schleiminger 1989).

12.　British hostility to the EPU and its consolidation as a "permanent EPU" depended on two main reasons. First, the EPU was an obstacle to the Collective Approach carried out by the UK, and also the EPU hindered the accumulation of sterling as a reserve currency by the EPU central banks. Second, in British eyes, the EPU favoured the international relevance of the Deutschemark as an alternative reserve currency to sterling (Hirowatari 2015, pp. 11–12).

13.　Susan Strange suggests that two main issues that hindered British membership involved the risk for the UK of a sudden capital liberalisation of UK payments to Continental Europe and the need for a transition period to adapt British agricultural policy to the Common Agricultural Policy. She argues that both these problems derive from the weakness and vulnerability of sterling (Strange 1967, p. 48).

14.　De Gaulle used the expression "exorbitant privilege", referring to the advantage granted by the US dollar to the USA in the world economic system. In the 1960s, De Gaulle challenged this "privilege" by converting part of the French dollar reserves into gold and accelerating the decay of the Bretton Woods system (Gardner 1980; Eichengreen 2008).

15. A committee chaired by Pierre Werner was created at the Hague European Summit in 1969 to prepare a plan for monetary integration in Europe. That plan, named the Werner Plan, was presented in 1970 and designed as a three-phase integration process for monetary unification to be accomplished in 1980 (Dyson and Featherstone 1999; Mourlon-Druol 2012).

16. In 1975 Harold Wilson called for a referendum to ask if the UK should remain in the EEC (Troitiño et al. 2018, pp. 121–2). See also Bongardt and Torres (Chapter 2 in this volume).

17. "I want my money back" was the famous expression used by Margaret Thatcher and sometimes considered a sign of Thatcher's aversion to the EEC; however, the British refund issue was one of the main problems in EEC negotiation and a sign of the economic asymmetries that hindered UK integration in the EEC.

18. Britain refused to join the European Monetary System at its start under Prime Minister Callaghan, and remained outside the EMS until 1989 (Campos and Coricelli 2017, p. 86). The reasons for opting out of the EMS are complicated and connected to the UK economy and sterling international problems at the end of the 1970s (Dell 1994). It was therefore not Thatcher's choice, but it was coherent with Thatcher's policy of economic restructuring that contributed again to de-synchronising the UK and the other EEC members' priorities.

19. Secretary of State Howe used the expression "self-marginalisation" to describe the British attitude toward those initiatives the UK could not block and would not participate in (Wall 2008, p. 76).

20. A famous case was the "Craxi's ambush" at the Milan European Meeting in 1988 (Dyson and Featherstone 1999; Wall 2008).

21. Some of those banks most affected by the liquidity reduction and the inter-bank market blockage during the early phases of the international crisis had balances comparable or more significant than the government budget of the countries where they had their centre, so some EU member states had to join to create consortia capable of supporting these banks in order to avoid a systemic crisis of the national economy.

22. The Euro Group joins the finance ministers of the euro area countries, the ECB governor and representatives of the EU Commission. The Council of the Euro Area joins the heads of state and governments of the euro area countries, organises two informal meetings each year and elects a president with a two-and-a-half-year mandate (Sadeleer 2012, pp. 354–83).

23. The Cameron government opposed the Fiscal Compact agreement in 2011, as well as the election of Juncker as the President of the European Commission in 2014. Both initiatives relied on extensive support among the other EU member states and were successfully carried out, despite British opposition. The Cameron government also hindered the approval of the new EU budget in 2013 (Baker and Schnapper 2015).

REFERENCES

Baker, David and Pauline Schnapper (2015), *Britain and the Crisis of the European Union*, Basingstoke: Palgrave Macmillan.

Bell, Philip W. (1956), *The Sterling Area in the Post-war World: Internal Mechanism and Cohesion 1946–1952*, Oxford: Oxford University Press.

Bongardt, A. and F. Torres (2016), "EMU reform and resilience in a re-dimensioned EU", *Journal of Economic Policy*, 32, 3, December, pp. 575–96.

Burnham, Peter (2003), *Remaking the Postwar World Economy: ROBOT and the British Policy in the 1950s*, Basingstoke: Palgrave Macmillan.

Campos, Nauro F. and Fabrizio Coricelli (eds) (2017), *The Economics of UK–EU Relations: From the Treaty of Rome to the Vote for Brexit*, Basingstoke: Palgrave Macmillan.

Cowles, Maria G., James A. Caporaso and Thomas Risse (eds) (2001), *Transforming Europe: Europeanization and Domestic Change*, Ithaca, NY: Cornell University Press.

Degryse, Christophe (2012), *The New European Economic Governance*, working paper 2012.14, Brussels: European Trade Union Institute.

Dell, Edmund (1994), "Britain and the origins of the European Monetary System", *Contemporary European History*, 3, 1, pp. 1–60.

Dyson, Kenneth and Kevin Featherstone (1999), *The Road to Maastricht: Negotiating Economic and Monetary Union*, Oxford: Oxford University Press.

Eichengreen, Barry (2008), *Globalizing Capital: A History of the International Monetary System*, Princeton, NJ: Princeton University Press.

Fodor, Giorgio (1986), "The origin of Argentina's sterling balances 1939–43", in Guido Di Tella and D. Christopher M. Platt (eds), *The Political Economy of Argentina 1880–1946*, Basingstoke: Macmillan.

Gardner, Richard N. (1980), *Sterling-Dollar Diplomacy in Current Perspective: The Origins and Prospects of Our International Economic Order*, New York: Columbia University Press.

Gowland, David (2017), *Britain and the European Union*, Abingdon: Routledge.

Helleiner, Eric (1994), *States and the Reemergence of Global Finance: From Bretton Woods to the 1990s*, Ithaca, NY: Cornell University Press.

Hinds, Allister (2001), *Britain's Sterling Colonial Policy and Decolonization, 1939–1958*, Westport, CT: Greenwood Press.

Hirowatari, Kiyoshi (2015), *Britain and European Monetary Cooperation, 1964–1979*, Basingstoke: Palgrave Macmillan.

Kaplan, Jacob J. and Gunther Schleiminger (1989), *The European Payments Union: Financial Diplomacy in the 1950s*, Oxford: Oxford University Press.

Krozewski, G. (1993), "Sterling, the 'minor' territories, and the end of formal empire, 1939–1958", *Economic History Review*, 46, 2, pp. 239–65.

Kunstein, Tobias and Wolfgang Wessels (2013), *The New Governance of the Economic and Monetary Union: Adapted Institutions and Innovative Instruments*, Rome: Istituto Affari Internazionali.

Milward, Alan S. (1984), *The Reconstruction of Western Europe, 1945–51*, London: Routledge.

Milward, Alan S. (2002), *The Rise and Fall of a National Strategy 1945–1963*, London: Frank Cass Publishers.

Mourlon-Druol, Emmanuel (2012), *A Europe Made of Money: The Emergence of the European Monetary System*, Ithaca, NY: Cornell University Press.

Needham, Duncan (2014), *UK Monetary Policy from Devaluation to Thatcher, 1967–82*, Basingstoke: Palgrave Macmillan.

Sadeleer, N. De (2012), *The New Architecture of the European Economic Governance: A Leviathan or a Flat-Footed Colossus?* in, *Maastricht Journal of Comparative and EU Law*, 19, 3, pp. 354–83.

Salines, M., G. Glöckler and Z. Truchlewski (2012), "Existential crisis, incremental response: the Eurozone's dual institutional evolution 2007–2011", *Journal of European Public Policy*, 19, 5, pp. 665–81.

Schenk, Catherine R. (1994), *Britain and the Sterling Area: From Devaluation to Convertibility in the 1950s*, London: Routledge.

Schenk, Catherine R. (2010), *The Decline of Sterling: Managing the Retreat of an International Currency, 1945–1992*, Cambridge: Cambridge University Press.

Solomon, Robert (1999), *Money on the Move: The Revolution in International Finance since the 1980s*, Princeton, NJ: Princeton University Press.

Steil, Benn (2013), *The Battle of Bretton Woods: John Maynard Keynes, Harry Dexter White, and the Making of a New World Order*, Princeton, NJ: Princeton University Press.

Strange, Susan (1967), *The Sterling Problem and the Six*, London: Chatham House.

Talani, Leila S. (2000), *Betting for and against EMU: Who Wins and Who Loses in Italy and in the UK from the Process of European Monetary Integration*, Aldershot: Ashgate.

Troitiño, David Ramiro, Tanel Kerikmäe and Archil Chochia (2018), *Brexit: History, Reasoning and Perspectives*, New York: Springer International Publishing.

Wall, Stephen (2008), *A Stranger in Europe: Britain and the EU from Thatcher to Blair*, Oxford: Oxford University Press.

4. Brexit, sovereignty and devolution: the view of constitutional law

Stefania Baroncelli and Monica Rosini[1]

4.1 INTRODUCTION

Debate over the UK's membership of the European Union has centred principally on the notion of "vote leave, take control", i.e. that control should be taken from the EU by leaving it and re-asserting sovereignty (Nicolaïdis 2017, 25).

After the referendum of 23 June 2016, the debate also involved the concept of sovereignty in its legal meaning. The process of withdrawal from the European Union has challenged, and still challenges, this *Grundnorm* of the British constitutional system in a number of ways.

A first challenge to the traditional principle of parliamentary sovereignty emerged in the use of the referendum to decide on the UK membership of the European Union. Even though it was merely advisory, the UK Parliament politically considered itself bound to the result and called upon to act on the will of the people.[2]

A second challenge of the Brexit process relates to executive–legislative relations. Notwithstanding Brexit's main aim is for Parliament to take back control of UK legislation and policies, the complexity of the withdrawal from the EU and the dominant position of the executive in leading the negotiations with Brussels cast doubts on Parliament's capacity to effectively take back control (Baldini et al. 2019).

A third challenge brought by the Brexit process to sovereignty of the UK Parliament is raised by the territorial distribution of powers and the existence of devolved legislatures in Scotland, Wales and Northern Ireland. This question was not taken into account by the 2015 *European Union Referendum Act*, which entrusted the decision on Brexit to a simple UK-wide referendum, without paying attention to the result of each constituent nation of the United Kingdom. However, the referendum results showed the political importance of this dimension: England and Wales voted, narrowly, to leave the EU, while Scotland and Northern Ireland voted to remain.

We intend to address these key challenges by looking in particular at the judgements of the courts, especially of the Supreme Court, which now, more than ever, seem to be of decisive importance in guiding the evolution of the UK form of State and government. Thus, we will consider the *Miller* judgements, where the High Court, and later the Supreme Court, reached the conclusion that an Act of Parliament is needed in order to trigger Brexit, and that the law does not enable devolved legislatures to block Brexit. Furthermore, we will analyse the Supreme Court's judgement of 13 December 2018 on *The UK Withdrawal from the European Union (Legal Continuity) (Scotland) Bill*, which dealt with several sensitive issues relating to devolved matters.

In conclusion, we reflect on what sovereignty means in the UK, on the basis of the most recent judgements of the Supreme Court.

4.2   PARLIAMENT *VS* THE PEOPLE? THE REFERENDUM ON THE EU

4.2.1   The Rising Use of Referendums in the UK

The 2016 referendum on leaving the EU was not the first organised in the UK regarding membership of the European Union. The first was held shortly after accession to the then EEC in 1975. This first referendum left an indelible mark on the English institutional system, since it led to the presumption that an exit from the European Union was only possible through an act of a similar legal form, i.e. through a referendum. Hence, following the commitment taken in the 2015 general election manifesto, Prime Minister David Cameron decided to hold a referendum on the permanence of the UK in the EU.[3] The result, as is well known, was in favour of Brexit, against the government's expectations.

Referendums in the UK have recently been used in constitutional cases of great importance, especially in connection with the major decisions related to the transfer of powers and competences of the Westminster Parliament to the EU or to the devolved parliaments. The use of the referendum is thus becoming a constitutionally accepted practice in the UK to resolve important and highly politically controversial constitutional matters, including issues of sovereignty and the scope of the UK Parliament's powers (HL 2010).

4.2.2   The Non-Binding Force of the Brexit Referendum

The question of whether a referendum is binding or not is resolved by the will of Parliament itself, which decides whether the electoral result should have binding or merely consultative force. For instance, Parliament decided that the outcome of the 2011 Alternative Vote Referendum was legally binding.

This was not, however, the case with the Brexit Referendum, as the *European Union Referendum Act 2015* recognised that it be consultative.[4]

While there was never any doubt about the fact that the referendum was not legally binding, the government and Parliament itself have maintained that they cannot overlook the referendum result from a political point of view.[5] Moreover, the situation has a precedent in the 1975 referendum, which was also advisory, but in that case there was no conflict between the people and Parliament, as the result was that the UK should stay in the EU.

Today, the paradoxical situation has emerged where Parliament and government find themselves voting for Brexit on the basis of a popular vote against their will. The first political consequence of the referendum was the resignation of Prime Minister David Cameron, who had promoted his position in favour of 'Remain'.

The second political consequence of the referendum has been the conflict between and within the parties, in the legislative chambers, because of members of parliament (MP)'s different positions on Brexit. The conflict was complicated further by the presence in Westminster of Scottish and Northern Irish MPs, whose electorate had voted by a majority to remain in the European Union.

The referendums on the EU have had an impact on how the principle of parliamentary sovereignty is conceived. Some authors have argued that the European Union is responsible for introducing a new principle into the English Constitution, i.e. popular sovereignty. This criterion would go beyond the doctrine of parliamentary sovereignty, since, at least on the question of remaining in the EU, the decision of the people would take precedence over that of their representatives (Bogdanor 2016, 314).

The Supreme Court in the *Miller* case has dealt with the issue of the legal force of the Brexit referendum. In its arguments, the government had stated that there would be no need for a pronouncement of Parliament, since the decision to leave the EU had already been taken based on the act establishing the referendum and its result.[6] According to the government, Parliament, by referring the matter to the voters, had stripped itself of the power to decide; it could not, in fact, have resolved to ask for a referendum assuming that it could express itself again on the same issue.

The Supreme Court clearly rejected this position. Not only does it violate the principle that the referendum is purely consultative, but it is also contrary to existing legislation on the relationship with the EU.[7] The Court makes reference to the *European Union Act 2011*, which requires legislative approval and in many cases also a referendum, to block government action in the event that the latter is in favour of expanding the powers of the EU institutions or reducing the value of UK voting rights in the EU, on the basis of the EU treaties.[8] "Where, as in this case, implementation of a referendum result requires a change in the law of the land, and statute has not provided for that change", concludes the Supreme Court, "the change in the law must be made in the only way in which the UK constitution permits, namely through Parliamentary legislation" (*Miller* [121]).

The Justices were thus clear that the referendum is a creature of Parliament. Without any legislative provision saying the contrary, its result is thus political and not legally binding. The outcome of the referendum remains thus regulated by the normal constitutional principles of the UK legal order, and especially that of the supremacy of Parliament.

4.2.3 The Consequence of a Lack of a Written Constitution

The lack of a written constitution has other consequences for the way a referendum works in the UK. As already said, a referendum is a creature of Parliament, which has the power to initiate it. It is not possible, unless a law is passed to the contrary, to give citizens the power to demand a referendum; only Parliament, at the government's request, can do this.

The lack of definite constitutional rules on the issue, the implications of which are not clear and unequivocal, added to the complexity of the institutional system, can generate strong feelings among voters as to how they view and come to terms with how the referendum results are implemented. In democratic systems with a written constitution, the referendum is a useful corrective to the imperfections inherent in the representative democratic process. In such systems, as in Switzerland, Italy, Australia and New Zealand, the constitution sets out how to request a referendum, giving voters the opportunity to decide sensitive issues of the day. Sometimes, participation quorums are established to guarantee the representativeness of the result obtained. These systems do not solve all the questions, but they certainly simplify the institutional system, contributing to better defining the rights of individuals' participation and strengthening the principle of legal certainty.

One issue left unresolved by the elastic British system concerns the duration of the validity of the referendum result. How long will it be valid for? Will it bind future generations? While a law can always be repealed by a subsequent Parliament or by shifts in the relative power of the parties in Parliament, the outcome of a referendum has a substantially eternal duration as another referendum is politically needed to reverse the first outcome.

However, in the English system, this can only happen with the approval of Parliament and at the request of the government. There is, therefore, an imbalance of powers: the electorate can decide an issue by referendum, but it has no power to express itself again on the same issue and, possibly, reverse the previous result if conditions have changed. We can call it a case of inter-temporal entrenchment: the referendum has the effect of strengthening certain principles (the decision to leave the EU) without giving the legal instruments to modulate the implementation phase of the decision itself or to change the decision. The referendum outcome will then be 'constitutionalised' or entrenched, since it cannot be modified either by Parliament (at least from the political point of view) or by voters' initiative. This 'take it or leave it' attitude does not fit in particularly well with an EU negotiation-based system.

4.3   BREXIT AND THE PRINCIPLE OF PARLIAMENTARY SOVEREIGNTY

The concept of parliamentary sovereignty is usually described by textbooks on UK constitutional and administrative law with reference to the classical definition of A. V. Dicey: "the power of law-making unrestricted by any legal limit" (1885, 39). The Parliament that has this unfettered decision-making power comprises the Queen, the House of Commons (HC), and the House of Lords (HL). Together, they form the constitutional phenomenon which is usually indicated with the expression 'the Queen in Parliament', which relates to the legislative process through which a Bill, having been voted and approved by the two Chambers of Parliament, receives royal assent and becomes an Act of Parliament or a Statute.

The centrality of Parliament is an essential feature of the UK institutional system, so much so that every new constitutional development is interpreted in terms of its impact on the doctrine of parliamentary supremacy. This was so once the UK decided to adopt the European Communities Act in 1972.

The legislative supremacy of Parliament means that this institution has unlimited legislative power. Consequently, the courts should obey all statutes approved by Parliament for whatever purpose they have been approved. This is the positive side of the principle of legislative supremacy. There is, however, a negative side, which forbids other institutions, bodies or legal persons to abrogate, amend or frustrate a statute of Parliament: "no person or body is recognised by the law of England as having a right to override or set aside the legislation of Parliament" (1885, 40). This statement from Dicey holds true today, even though the concept of 'England' should be adapted to the current structure of the United Kingdom, including Wales, Scotland, and Northern Ireland. In sum, the principle of parliamentary supremacy means that the legislative body can approve laws in any matter whatsoever and that no competing body exists capable to legislate or to put limits on the UK Parliament.

Such a principle is particularly significant due to the absence of a codified constitution in the UK. In continental Europe and the USA, countries have a written constitution that imposes limits upon the legislature and entrusts ordinary judges or a Constitutional Court with the power to set aside pieces of legislation that are not in accordance with the foundational principles of the State.

In the UK, on the other hand, parliamentary supremacy is the fundamental rule of Constitutional Law, and comprises also the power to decide in constitutional matters. Authors therefore name it as 'the ultimate rule of recognition', i.e., the fundamental rule upon which all the other norms are based and find their justification (Hart 2012; Parpworth 2018, 54).

The constitutional implications of EU membership sit uneasily with this tradition of political constitutionalism, if we consider that the doctrine of the supremacy of EU law implies its priority also over Acts of the UK Parliament. This effect has been upheld consistently by the European Court of Justice (ECJ) in a series of landmark cases, where it made clear that "No provisions of municipal law, of whatever nature they may be, may prevail over Community Law . . . lest it be deprived of its character as Community law and its very legal foundation be endangered."[9]

4.4 THE 'CONSTITUTIONAL REQUIREMENTS' TO WITHDRAW FROM THE EU: THE BRITISH CONSTITUTION AND THE *MILLER* CASES

4.4.1 The Procedure to Exit from the EU on the Basis of Article 50 TEU

The constitutional concepts of parliamentary and State sovereignty are at the core of the *Miller* cases. The issue revolved around a question of competence internal to the UK institutional framework for the triggering of Article 50 of the Treaty on the European Union (TEU). This provision regulates the case of withdrawal of States from the EU. The rule dates back to the Constitutional Treaty, which for the first time provided for the inclusion of an article authorising States to leave the EU. Given the failure of the Constitutional Treaty, the principle of withdrawal was introduced by the Treaty of Lisbon. It is now to be found at the end of the TEU, along with the rules governing the acquisition and loss of membership of States. These provisions are inspired by a traditional intergovernmental configuration, which takes the utmost account of the sovereignty of states. Moreover, they must also be interpreted on the basis of the constitutional specificities of the European legal order. The case of Brexit, in fact, shows how difficult it is to treat withdrawal from the EU as withdrawal from a simple international organisation as one that had not created rights and obligations for individuals and businesses.

Article 50 is a rule of rather indefinite content. It states that any member State may withdraw from the Union "in accordance with its own constitutional requirements", thus placing Article 50 between EU Law and national law. The right of initiative is recognised to the State, as it should notify the European Council of its intention to withdraw. From the moment of notification, a period of two years begins. After that period, the EU Treaties will no longer apply to the State in question. It is possible, however, that the period will end earlier if the outgoing State has reached an agreement with the EU. Finally, it is also provided that the two-year period can be extended by the European Council by a unanimous vote. Until recently, it was not clear whether the State could revoke unilaterally the notification of its decision to withdraw from the Union. The issue was recently solved by the Court of Justice of the EU in favour of the right of the UK to revoke unilaterally its decision. In the case of withdrawal of the notification, the UK remains a full member of the EU, without any impact on its status.[10]

4.4.2   The *Miller* Cases: The Issues at Stakes

The central issue in *Miller* concerned the UK's '*own constitutional requirements*' to trigger Article 50 TEU: who has the power to give notice to the European Council pursuant to Article 50 TEU for the UK to withdraw from the EU? Has the UK government the power to notify using its foreign affairs prerogative or is an act of Parliament necessary to authorise this notification? The ensuing litigation proved not only to be a decisive case for the interpretation of the withdrawal procedure, but also enabled the courts to investigate the meaning and scope of important constitutional principles of English law also in relation to the European Union.

The *European Union Referendum Act 2015*, establishing the Brexit referendum, gave no indication on deciding jurisdiction, as it was silent on the consequences of Brexit's victory. Not only that, but the referendum was merely consultative, so it could not be considered the decision-making source on which Article 50 could be triggered.

Gina Miller and the other litigants in the *Miller* case considered that the government did not have the power to notify the decision to withdraw from the EU to the European Council, as legislative authorisation was required. There were several reasons for their request. By asserting the competence of Parliament, they saw the possibility of delaying or even annulling the decision on Brexit, as MPs could vote in favour of remaining in the Union. The affirmation of parliamentary competence could have affected the content of the notification to the EU, to include conditions that improved the protection of rights deriving from the European system. In any case, the complainants proceeded from the conviction that Parliament was at the heart of the English constitutional system and that, consequently, the government should be subject to parliamentary control (Elliott et al. 2018, 3).

The case was first submitted to the *Divisional Court* in July 2016.[11] The claimants' argument, as described above, was based on a metaphor: the notification of the decision to withdraw was equivalent to pulling the trigger of a gun. Once the trigger was pulled, the bullet would achieve its objective of rendering the application of the EU Treaties to the UK null and void after two years. This would have resulted in the elimination of a significant number of rights arising from the European order, with considerable damage to individuals. The British government, the claimants believed, could not use the Crown's prerogative to reduce and limit these rights, because this was contrary to the English Constitution.

The British government, for its part, considered that the decision to leave the EU had already been taken and that for that reason no authorisation from Parliament was necessary for the notification, which was considered a mere administrative matter. In the government's opinion, the result of the referendum sufficed.

The decision of the Divisional Court was unanimously in favour of the claimants. The Court was clear in affirming that "subordination of the rule of the Crown (i.e. the executive Government) to law is the foundation of the rule of law in the United Kingdom".[12]

The issue was subsequently addressed by the *UK Supreme Court*, on the Secretary of State's appeal.[13] The importance of the event was witnessed by the composition of the Court: in fact, all 11 judges of the Court participated so as to avoid accusations of favouritism, given the high political profile the judgement had.

The main issue to be decided was whether the government could trigger Article 50 TEU without prior authorisation by Parliament. A second issue related to devolution issues.[14] It dealt with the obligation of the UK government to consult the legislatures in Wales, Scotland and Northern Ireland on the basis of the devolution legislation before triggering Article 50 TEU.

As for the first issue, the Supreme Court started from the assumption that the government has the prerogative power to withdraw from international treaties if it thinks it advisable. However, it cannot change UK law rules, unless it is authorised by Parliament. The arguments of the parties were very similar to those presented before the Divisional Court. Gina Miller and the other defendants argued that withdrawal from the EU has the effect of changing domestic legislation, and also the legal rights of people resident in the UK. As a consequence, the government cannot use its prerogative power to trigger Article 50. The appellant, on the other hand, argued that the European Communities Act [ECA] 1972 does not exclude the government's power to withdraw from EU Treaties and that section 2 of the Act even provides for such a power.

The Supreme Court held by eight judges to three that the government cannot use its prerogative power to trigger Article 50 TEU, thereby upholding the decision of the Divisional Court. In addition, all the judges decided unanimously that neither the *Northern Ireland Act 1998* and the *Good Friday Agreement* nor the *Sewel Convention* required the UK government to receive the consent of the UK devolved legislatures in Scotland, Northern Ireland and Wales.

4.4.3 The Decision of the UK Supreme Court: Parliamentary Sovereignty and the Executive's Prerogative Powers

The Supreme Court, before dealing with the opposing positions of the two parties, clarified the constitutional principles on which the judgement is based, from a historical perspective. Starting from the fundamental studies of A.V. Dicey, the court traces the evolution of the principle of sovereignty, highlighting how initially this was concentrated in the Crown. Over the centuries, however, following the expansion of the principle of parliamentary democracy, the prerogative powers, called Royal Prerogative, passed into the hands of Parliament, the executive and the judiciary.

As a result of these developments, the role of the English Parliament emerged strengthened, so that the legislative power that once belonged to the Crown can now only be exercised by the two Houses of Parliament, with the Queen's consent. The administrative powers of the Crown are exercised by the Executive, i.e. the ministers, who are accountable to Parliament. However, governmental powers must be exercised in accordance with the legislation in force and common law. The prerogative powers, in short, constitute a residual power for cases not governed by the law whose content may be modified or abrogated by Parliament, either expressly or implicitly.

The Supreme Court then focused on the Royal Prerogative and its content in the field of foreign affairs. The contenders did not dispute that the Royal Prerogative extends to foreign affairs and includes the specific power to withdraw from an international treaty. Although there is limited jurisprudence on the subject, the Supreme Court considered that the attribution to the government of the "power to terminate or withdraw from treaties" is for "both logical and practical necessity".[15] The fact that it is up to the government to sign and withdraw from the treaties is a consequence of the dualist theory that international and domestic law operate in two separate and independent spheres. In fact, in order to be applicable in the domestic sphere, treaty law needs to be incorporated into the internal order by law.

4.4.4 The ECA 1972 and the Executive's Prerogative Powers

The decision relating to the case depended on the correct interpretation of the 1972 ECA. This provision, considered as the vehicle that sees EU legislative acts flow into UK law from EU institutions, does not provide for the government's power to withdraw from the EU. This was interpreted by the government as meaning that there were no laws governing either the prerogative power to withdraw from treaties in general or the specific power to withdraw from the EU. But this, according to the government, could only mean that this power had not been regulated by Parliament and therefore remained, in a residual way, in the hands of the government.[16]

The position of Gina Miller and the other respondents was based, instead, on the fact that the EU Treaties had created positive legal positions for individuals who, according to the *Bill of Rights* and other fundamental acts of the English Constitution, could not be removed by an act of the government. In fact, this would have required a specific legislative amendment. From this perspective, it did not matter whether the 1972 ECA conferred a power of withdrawal from the EU, but whether that 1972 ECA was modified by the exit of the UK from the EU and, in addition, that it did not delegate to the government the power to modify it. If this was not the case, it was clear from the respondents that Parliament had retained the power to repeal the 1972 ECA, by withdrawing from the EU.

The Supreme Court pays particular attention to the interpretation of section 2 of the ECA 1972. This provision operates as a "conduit pipe": it triggered a "dynamic process" through which the European institutions issue new rules which then become part of the UK system (*Miller* [60, 65]). A partial transfer of legislative powers to the European institutions is therefore made. This legal situation can only be changed by a parliamentary decision to the contrary.

At this point, the Court makes a digression of fundamental importance and, referring to the analysis previously carried out by the Divisional Court to reject the government's claim to have jurisdiction to trigger Article 50, points out how withdrawal from the EU leads to the loss of many individual rights transposed into UK law ("rights capable of replication in UK Law") (*Miller* [69–70]). These include, for example, the four fundamental freedoms, the protections established in employment matters, the right to equal treatment and the rights arising from competition law.

It is precisely the loss of these domestic rights that would result from withdrawal from the Union that, according to the Court, requires prior parliamentary authorisation. The judges, on the other hand, reject the positions of the Secretary of State. The latter did not deny that the withdrawal from the EU Treaties resulted in the loss of fundamental rights but considered that this was provided for in the wording of section 2 of the 1972 ECA. Such provision recognises that "All such rights, powers, liabilities, obligations and restrictions from time to time created or arising by or under the Treaties, [. . .] shall be recognised and available in law, and be enforced, allowed and followed accordingly." According to the Secretary of State, section 2 of the 1972 ECA is "ambulatory", i.e. its effectiveness is achieved "from time to time" therefore when the EU Treaties require it (*Miller* [74]).

This position, the Court emphasises, is not sustainable. In fact, the rules of the new EU Treaties are not automatically incorporated into national law by means of section 2; this only happens by legislative means, amending the 1972 ECA. But above all, there is a "vital difference" between ordinary changes in domestic law due to changes in the content of EU law following the adoption of new EU legislation and more radical changes in domestic law due to withdrawal from the EU. This "involves a unilateral action by the relevant constitutional bodies which effects a fundamental change in the constitutional arrangements of the United Kingdom" (*Miller* [78]). Withdrawal from the EU Treaties, concludes the Court, is a modification not only in degree, but "in kind" and should be treated differently from a mere abrogation of rights and duties deriving from changes in EU Law (*Miller* [81]).

The Court thus concluded that the prerogative could not be invoked by the government to justify its triggering of Article 50 TEU, as it needs an act of legislation before serving notice of withdrawal to the European Council. The conclusion was not reached unanimously, however, as three judges dissociated themselves, writing their own dissenting opinions.[17] The dissenters' argument is based on the fact that the application of EU law in the UK depends on the continued application of the EU Treaties in the UK and, moreover, on the belief that Parliament has not imposed any limit on the government for the procedure for leaving the EU.

### 4.4.5	Implications of the *Miller* Case for the Government–Parliament Relationship

The *Miller* case has spurred much reflection about the role of government and Parliament vis-à-vis the EU. Many authors have supported the majority thesis (Williams 2018, 39) while some have followed and emphasised some of the dissenters' arguments or have highlighted the critical implications of *Miller* (Barczentewicz 2017, 10; Twomey 2018, 69) or have simply suggested other types of interpretation (Elliott et al. 2018). Certainly, the arguments of the majority of judges respond better to a view of the EU as a special entity, which is difficult to interpret through the lenses of classical international law. This concept is the result of the case law of the Court of Justice of the EU on the relationship with the Member States, such as the *Costa* judgement.

The objective of the Brexit referendum was for the UK Parliament to take back control. The process of European integration has led to a loss of parliamentary sovereignty and its transfer to EU institutions. In theory, therefore, Brexit implies a return of decision-making powers to the English legislative body. However, this process is not so immediate because the integration process has changed the English institutional system, as well as that of the other Member States. In particular, executive power has been strengthened at the expense of legislative power so as to improve the government's negotiating position with the European institutions. This process, combined with the complexity of the process of detachment from the EU, cast a shadow over the real possibility of Parliament's regaining its lost power.

Miller has given Parliament the power to authorise withdrawal from the EU. The *Miller* judgement's more immediate merit is to be appreciated in terms of constitutional procedure, as it had the effect of subjecting government decisions on leaving the EU to parliamentary debate (Leyland 2016, 41).

The government–Parliament relationship, however, proved to be full of tensions. This is the case of the enactment of the *EU Withdrawal Bill 2017–19*, that delegated to the government the decision-making power in many areas. It is also the case of the dispute over the 'meaningful vote' on the Brexit agreement which was negotiated with the EU. A final cause of tension is to be found in the decision by Prime Minister Boris Johnson to prorogate Parliament, in order to exclude discussion and force it into a no-deal Brexit (Stewart and Mason 2019, 1; Craig 2019b). Again, the conflict was resolved by the Supreme Court, which in its *R. (on the application of Miller) v The Prime Minister; Cherry and others v. Advocate General for Scotland* stated that the advice given by the prime minister to the Queen to prorogate Parliament is illegal.[18] In fact, such prorogation had the effect of preventing or frustrating Parliament in performing its constitutional function.

The long-term merit of the *Miller* judgement lies in its having strengthened the role of Parliament in the event of withdrawal from international treaties that have created individual rights. The Court in *Miller* emphasises the special status of EU Law for its supremacy over domestic law and the kind of rights and obligations that it entails. This leads us to ask whether the *Miller* principles can be applied to similar cases and, in particular, what scale of constitutional change and level of protection of rights would be necessary. For example, if the UK decides to withdraw from the European Convention on Human Rights using the Royal Prerogative instead of repealing the Human Rights Act 1998, would such use of the prerogative be prohibited by the *Miller* judgement? (Elliott 2017, 257). In addition, the *Miller* decision could have a negative impact on treaty-making power resulting from the increased political scrutiny on the use of prerogative power in international law that it entails (Twomey 2018, 69).

4.5 BREXIT AND DEVOLUTION MATTERS: DEVOLVED LEGISLATURES AND THEIR NO ROLE IN UK WITHDRAWAL FROM THE EU

Since 1998, the United Kingdom has been a decentralised state (Burrows 2000). As is well known, the enactment of the three devolution acts[19] has given rise to a profound process of 'rewriting' the UK constitutional system, opening up several breaches in the principle of parliamentary sovereignty (Jowell and Oliver 2000).

The Brexit process is a new and ongoing challenge to such a fundamental principle. The existence of devolved legislatures in Scotland, Wales and Northern Ireland makes the withdrawal of the United Kingdom from the European Union more complex. The reasons can be easily understood when one considers that EU membership cuts across the territorial distribution of powers between UK and devolved competences. Furthermore, the devolution settlements were designed on the assumption that the UK was, and would have continued to be, a member of the EU. This is reflected in the provisions of each devolution act which states that devolved legislatures and executive bodies cannot legislate or act incompatibly with EU law. Furthermore, the devolution statutes enable devolved institutions to implement EU law, including by way of delegated legislation, in devolved matters. Thus, Brexit necessarily requires amendments to the devolution legislation and a certain degree of cooperation between the UK and the devolved institutions in order to adjust rules and policies currently governed by European law.

This territorial dimension was not taken into account by the *European Union Referendum Act 2015*, which entrusted the decision on Brexit to a simple UK-wide referendum, without paying attention to the voting in each constituent nation of the United Kingdom. Indeed, during the parliamentary debate, the Scottish National Party (SNP), with the support of Plaid Cymru, proposed an amendment, which provided a double majority vote, both of total votes cast in the referendum in the United Kingdom and in each nation of the UK.[20] However, it was rejected by the House of Commons on the basis that relationships with the EU, including the decision to withdraw from it, were reserved to the UK level.

Importantly, the referendum of 23 June 2016 revealed noticeable territorial differences on the question of EU membership: England and Wales voted narrowly to leave the EU, whilst Scotland and Northern Ireland voted to remain (Henderson et al. 2017).[21] The demographically dominant position of England and its higher turnout were decisive in determining the UK referendum result and dragged Scotland and Northern Ireland into Brexit against their will.

The territorially divided result obtained at the referendum had immediate serious political fallout (BBC News 2016; Smith and Young 2017; Tierney 2017),[22] but with implications from a constitutional law perspective overshadowed. Nevertheless, such territorial differences soon turned into questions of constitutional significance: does Brexit require legislative consent from the devolved Parliaments? Which issues should such consent relate to? To the Brexit process as a whole or to only some aspects of it?

These issues were first raised before the Northern Irish High Court in the *McCord* case.[23] The Court rejected the argument that the Northern Ireland constitutional landscape expressly altered the prerogative power of the UK executive in the context of notification under Article 50 TEU. The salient features of this constitutional landscape were set out in the Good Friday Agreement of 10 April 1998,[24] and in the Northern Ireland Act 1998, which – enacted to implement the former – has been described as "in effect a constitution".[25] The constitutional status of Northern Ireland, as established by the above mentioned documents, is not modified by the mere triggering of Article 50(2) TEU, which "is the beginning of a process which ultimately will probably lead to changes" in United Kingdom law. "This is not to say that the United Kingdom leaving the EU will not have effects at all but it is to say at the least it is an over-statement to suggest, as the applicants do, that a constitutional bulwark, central to the 1998 Act arrangements, would be breached by notification" (*McCord and Agnew* [106]). Anyway, even if legislation were required to trigger Article 50 TEU, it would not require the consent of the Northern Ireland Assembly. In the Northern Irish High Court's view, it would not be legislation "with regards to devolved matters", even adopting a broad approach to the meaning of this phrase. Thus, the practice (the so-called Sewel Convention: see *infra*), which requires the consent of the Northern Ireland legislature for the approval of UK legislation in transferred fields, had no application to the scenario of withdrawal from the EU.

Devolution questions were also raised in the *Miller* case. The applicants assumed that legislation authorising the UK's withdrawal from the EU would have required the consent of the devolved legislatures. According to their assumption, the impact of EU withdrawal on devolution legislation would be an additional reason why notification of withdrawal could not be given under the foreign affairs prerogative. The approval of a bill, authorising the triggering of Article 50 TEU, would have required the application of the Sewel Convention. Thus, regional Parliaments' consent would have been essential to authorise the UK's departure from the EU.

Whilst the High Court did not find it necessary to address this issue,[26] the Supreme Court did.[27] However, the argument for devolved consent was unsuccessful. The Supreme Court unanimously refused to decide the issue, arguing that the Sewel Convention did not give rise to legally enforceable obligations, nor could the courts give rulings on its operation or scope. Statutory recognition of the convention by the Scotland Act 2016[28] also did not convert the Sewel Convention into a rule enforceable before the courts.

To come to this conclusion, the Court analysed the birth and the evolving nature of the Sewel Convention, which was adopted in 1998 as an instrument for establishing cooperative and harmonious relationships between the UK

Parliament and the devolved legislatures, in case of overlapping legislative competences.

Each devolution act has conferred on devolved legislatures the power to make laws on certain matters. In parallel, the UK Parliament has preserved its right to legislate on matters which are within the competence of the devolved legislatures.[29] These legislative powers are therefore concurrent. Unlike other states with a federal or regional structure, the constitutional sphere of competence of sub-state entities is not protected by a written constitution. Thus, legal constraints are not imposed on the powers of the central legislature to make laws in certain areas. The supreme principle of the UK constitutional system, that Parliament is sovereign and may make or unmake any law whatsoever, is incompatible with the common approach of federal and regional states to protect sub-state constitutional powers. In this legal framework, the Sewel Convention is a fundamental mechanism for attempting to overcome the lack of legal protection of the powers of the devolved legislatures and the weakness of instruments for shared rules (McHarg 2018, 159). It aims at achieving harmony between legislatures in areas of competing competences, enabling the UK Parliament to make UK-wide legislation where appropriate, and avoiding any risk of legal challenge by the devolved legislatures.

The terms of this convention were notably first expressed in a statement of intent by Lord Sewel, the then Scottish Office Minister, during the parliamentary debate on the Scotland Bill. In July 1998, during the debate on section 28(7), which maintained UK Parliament power to make law for Scotland, he said: "however, as happened in Northern Ireland earlier in the century, we would expect a convention to be established that Westminster would not normally legislate in Scotland without the consent of the Scottish parliament."[30]

That expectation has been fulfilled. The UK Parliament does not normally legislate in devolved areas without the prior agreement of the devolved legislatures. The consent is given by a legislative consent motion, which the devolved government introduces into the respective legislature. Such a consent motion is approved according to the Standing Orders of the devolved Parliament and after the devolved administration has expressed its opinion on the legislation in a memorandum (HC 2018).

Lord Sewel's original statement did not offer precise indications as to the scope of application of the legislative consent. Its scope has therefore been shaped and expanded by both practice and other instruments, such as Memorandums of Understanding (MoU) and Devolved Guidance Notes (DGNs).

In December 2001, the Sewel Convention was embodied in a Memorandum of Understanding, amended and integrated several times. It basically served, and still serves, as a political commitment to respect the 'consent rule' proposed by Lord Sewel. The current text of the MoU, published in October

2013, provides that the UK government has to proceed in accordance with the convention that the UK Parliament would not normally legislate with regard to devolved matters except with the agreement of the devolved legislature. On the other hand, the devolved administrations are responsible "for seeking such agreement as may be required for this purpose on an approach from the UK Government".[31] Paragraph 2 of the MoU states that the Sewel Convention is a statement of political intent and that it does not create legal obligations.

Since 1999, the UK Cabinet Office has drafted several DGNs in order to support civil servants in dealing with devolved matters. These DGNs have opted for an extension of the scope of the convention. For instance DGN 10 provides that a bill which "contains provisions applying to Scotland and which are for devolved purposes, or which alter the legislative competence of the Parliament or the executive competence of the Scottish Ministers . . . are subject to the convention requiring the consent of the Scottish Parliament".[32] This DGN has no legal effects, but establishes how UK government departments legislating for Scotland meet the terms of the convention.

According to the *Miller* judgement, the origins and evolution of the Sewel Convention clarify its nature. It has a mere political nature and does not create legally enforceable obligations. Judges are neither the parents nor the guardians of political conventions; they are merely observers. As such, they can recognise the operation of a political convention in the context of deciding a legal question, but they cannot give legal rulings on its operation or scope, because these are left to politics.

The Supreme Court adopted a self-restraint approach (McHarg 2018, 173). The fear of being involved in the political arena led the court to emphasise in several parts of the *Miller* judgement that its role was confined to issues of law. For instance, in the introduction, it said that:

> it is . . .worth emphasising that this case has nothing to do with issues such as the wisdom of the decision to withdraw from the European Union, the terms of withdrawal, the timetable or arrangements for withdrawal, or the details of any future relationship with the European Union. Those are all political issues which are matters for Ministers and Parliament to resolve. They are not issues which are appropriate for resolution by judges, whose duty is to decide issues which are appropriate for resolution by judges, whose duty is to decide issues of law which are brought before them by individuals and entities exercising their rights of access to the courts in a democratic society. [3]

The political dimension of the Sewel Convention's scope and the manner of its operation "does not lie within the constitutional remit of the judiciary, which is to protect the rule of law" (*Miller* [151]).

This perspective allowed the court not to rule on the merits of the issue, leaving the maximum room for political decision and accommodation, reducing the risk of being accused of political interference. This perspective remained, surprisingly, unchanged even in the face of the statutory 'recognition' of the Sewel Convention in the Scotland Act.

Lord Sewel's words have been inserted in the most recent version of the Scotland Act and of the Government of Wales Act, as amended in 2016 and 2017, respectively. Immediately after the provision preserving the power of the Westminster Parliament to make laws for devolved administrations, such acts now read: ". . . the Parliament of the United Kingdom will not normally legislate with regard to devolved matters without the consent of the [devolved legislature]".[33]

In the Court's reasoning, the decision of the UK Parliament to make reference to the Sewel Convention within devolution acts had no legal effect on the relationship between the UK Parliament and the devolved institutions of Scotland and Wales. The UK Parliament did not seek to convert the Sewel Convention into a rule which can be interpreted and enforced by the courts; rather, it recognised the convention for what it is, namely a political convention, and declared that it is a permanent feature of the devolution settlement. Such an outcome followed from the nature of the content, as proved by the words used ("it is recognised" and "will not normally legislate") in the two subsections. The UK Parliament would have used other words if it were seeking to convert a convention into a legal rule justiciable by the courts. In brief, "the purpose of the legislative recognition of the convention was to entrench it as a convention" (*Miller* [149]).

This is the less understandable part of the *Miller* judgement, especially for a civil law scholar, who is usually moved by the assumption that every legal provision is intended to create legal effects. Such an assumption is not absolute, but it requires to be refuted with convincing arguments. On this point, instead, the court's reasoning was rather poor. It considered as almost self-evident that statutory recognition of the Sewel Convention was not sufficient to confer legislative status on it and to permit the Court to rule on its meaning and application. It is worth noting that recognition of legal status to the Sewel Convention would represent the recognition of legal limits to the legislative power of the UK Parliament when it legislates for Scotland or Wales. This consequence seems to be in clear contrast with the principle of parliamentary sovereignty.

On the basis of these premises, the Supreme Court ruled that the Scottish Parliament and the Welsh and Northern Ireland Assemblies do not have a legal veto on the United Kingdom's withdrawal from the EU. Their consent was not a legal requirement for the approval of the Withdrawal Bill by the UK Parliament.

The Supreme Court's judgement makes it clear that only the Westminster Parliament has the power to decide whether to remain in or leave the European

Union. It clearly upholds a traditional vision of the UK as a unitary state, without acknowledging shared-rule powers or veto powers for the devolved administrations.

Even if the intention of the Court was to remain neutral with regard to the political dispute, its judgement de facto supported the UK government's position. In fact, after the *Miller* judgement, the UK Parliament approved the *European Union (Notification of Withdrawal) Act 2017* without securing the agreement of the devolved legislatures. Consequently, on 29 March 2017 the UK government notified the European Council of its decision on the UK withdrawal from the EU in accordance with Article 50 TEU (*supra* par. 4).

However, the issue of the involvement of devolved legislatures in the Brexit process cannot be said to be resolved. The reason is readily understandable, looking at the legal framework. Article 50, par. 3, TEU states that after the expiry date of a certain time period the European Treaties "shall cease to apply to the State in question". This is not enough to remove the impact of EU law in the UK. It necessarily implies repeal or amendment of the *1972 European Communities Act*, which gave effect to EU law in the domestic context. Furthermore, Brexit made, and still makes, it necessary to amend relevant parts of devolution legislation, since EU law is incorporated into the devolution acts (Douglas-Scott 2016).

Brexit is, therefore, a very complex process, which poses more than one challenge to the devolution constitutional arrangements, as evidenced by subsequent legal events.

4.6   THE *SCOTTISH CONTINUITY BILL* CASE: PARLIAMENTARY SOVEREIGNTY *VS* DEVOLUTION

The *Miller* judgement did not solve, but only postponed the issue of devolved consent to the UK withdrawal process from the EU. After Article 50 was triggered, the UK government faced a second demanding challenge, relating to the post-Brexit 'destiny' of matters falling within European competences, which at national level fell within the sphere of the competence of devolved legislatures. So long as the UK remains a member of the EU, European law governs certain matters, producing legal effects in each of the UK nations without differentiation, and the power to amend EU rights and obligations resides with EU institutions. After the UK withdrawal, EU law will cease to bind the UK and its nations, creating serious problems of legal continuity and certainty. In order to avoid such problems it was considered necessary to incorporate EU regulations into domestic law and to preserve the effects of EU-derived domestic legislation.

Thus, on 13 July 2017 the UK government introduced in the HC the *European Union (Withdrawal) Bill* (hereinafter: UK Withdrawal Bill) to repeal the *1972 European Communities Act* and to achieve legal continuity within each of the jurisdictions of the UK after withdrawal from the EU (Craig 2019a, 319). For this purpose, the bill provided significant amendments to the devolution legislation, inspired by a centralist and hierarchical conception of the UK constitution.[34] Before and during the passage through Parliament of the bill, the UK government discussed its content with representatives of devolved institutions. But in early 2018 these negotiations were blocked when the UK government's will became clear to withhold powers over many policy areas (so-called repatriated areas) that would pertain to devolved competences.

After some amendments to the UK Withdrawal Bill supported by the Scottish government were defeated in the House of Commons, the Scottish executive introduced its own *UK Withdrawal from the European Union (Legal Continuity) (Scotland) Bill* (hereinafter: Scottish Continuity Bill) in the Scottish Parliament on 27 February 2018. It was approved on 21 March 2018, despite the Holyrood's Presiding Officer having expressed the opinion that the bill was outside the legislative competence of the Scottish Parliament.[35]

Like the UK Withdrawal Bill, the Scottish Continuity Bill made provisions concerning the applicability of EU law and EU-derived law in Scotland, after the UK withdrawal. Even though the two pieces of legislation had a similar purpose, they differed in significant points. In simple terms, the UK Bill sought to repatriate powers held by the EU to UK authorities; in contrast, the Scottish Bill retained for Scotland EU law in devolved areas and created power for Scottish ministers to amend the law.

Given the state of affairs, a reference lodged by the UK Law Officers before the Supreme Court was almost taken for granted. According to the Scotland Act 1998 the Supreme Court has jurisdiction on "the question of whether a [Scottish] Bill or any provision of a [Scottish] Bill would be within the legislative competence of the [Scottish] Parliament" (Section 31(1)).

Indeed, the Scottish Parliament was not the only devolved legislature that approved legislation to provide for domestic legal continuity after the UK's withdrawal from the EU on exit day. The Welsh Assembly also approved an act – the *Law Derived from the European Union (Wales) Act 2018* – with identical scope and effects, after the UK Parliament had rejected amendments to the UK Bill that the First Minister of Wales supported. The Welsh Bill was referred to the Supreme Court as well, but, after an agreement was reached between the Welsh and the UK governments on 24 April 2018, which resulted in amendments to clause 11 of the UK Withdrawal Bill[36] and the Welsh Assembly's giving legislative consent to the UK Bill, the Attorney General withdrew that reference. Consequently, the Welsh Act was quickly repealed by the devolved Assembly.

In contrast, Scottish institutions stood by their positions and in May 2018 the Scottish Parliament voted a denial consent to the UK Withdrawal Bill, which nevertheless became law in June 2018. It was the first time that Westminster had adopted legislation in devolved areas without the Scottish Parliament's legislative consent. These events mark an unprecedented development for the British territorial constitutional system that we may term as a type of 'uncooperative devolution' (Rawlings 2017, 28).

The Supreme Court in its judgement of 13 December 2018 considered only *The UK Withdrawal from the European Union (Legal Continuity) (Scotland) Bill*.[37] Two key issues were addressed by the court, both relating to the Scottish devolution settlements. The first concerned the existence of the Scottish Parliament's power to legislate for the continuity of laws relating to devolved matters, which are now the subject of EU law but which will cease to have effect after the UK withdrawal. The second questioned whether the Scottish Parliament had acted within its legal powers by enacting the Continuity Bill, bearing in mind the limits that the Scotland Act 1998 places on that Parliament's authority. These issues had implications not only for the Scottish Parliament but also for the other devolved legislatures, which supported the case before the Supreme Court. The judgement offers, in fact, an accurate picture of the fundamental constitutional features governing the entire UK devolution arrangements.

In short, the Supreme Court ruled unanimously that only one section of the Scottish Continuity Bill was outside the Scottish Parliament's legislative competence. The remaining sections were valid when the Bill was approved. However, additional parts of the Bill could not become law due to the subsequent passing, by the UK Parliament, of the UK Withdrawal Act,[38] which amended the devolution settlement, so rendering several parts of the Scottish Bill incompatible with it (Moffat and Hardy 2018). To reach these conclusions, the Court developed a detailed and technically complex reasoning, which sheds light on some fundamental aspects of the devolution system.

The UK government had two main lines of attack. The first challenged the entire Scottish Continuity Bill, assuming it was outside the Scottish Parliament's legislative competence, because: (i) it was contrary to the constitutional framework underpinning the devolution settlement; (ii) it related to the reserved matter of "relations with . . . the European Union", set out in the Scotland Act; and (iii) it was contrary to the rule of law principles of legal certainty and legality (*Scottish Continuity Bill*, UKSC [23]).

For the court, the most relevant issue was whether the Scottish Bill "relate[d] to reserved matters", such as the relations with the EU.[39] Consistency with the rule of law or the constitutional framework underpinning the devolution settlement was considered relevant only so far as it assisted in resolving this main issue.

The Scotland Act 1998 distinguishes between international relations, including relations with the EU, which are reserved to the UK institutions, and the observation and implementation of international obligations and obligations under the Human Rights Convention (HRC) and EU law, which are not reserved.[40] The observation and implementation of EU law are accordingly within the domestic competence of the Scottish Parliament and the Scottish ministers unless they fall within another reserved matter.

In the court's opinion, the Scottish Bill was "not within the carve-out from the reserved matter for the observation or implementation of those obligations under EU law" (*Scottish Continuity Bill* [31]). The Bill had nothing to do with the observation or implementation of those obligations, but it was concerned with the domestic rules of law which, after withdrawal, would have replaced EU law. As the Court pointed out "the fact that those domestic rules may be substantially the same as the rules which previously applied as a matter of EU law does not make them obligations under EU law. Their juridical source is purely domestic" (*Scottish Continuity Bill* [31]).

The Scottish Bill also did not fall within the general reservation for relations with the EU.

In the Court's opinion, other aspects of relations with the EU are in practice likely to be relevant mainly to acts of Scottish ministers: "There is relatively little scope for Scottish legislation to 'relate to' international relations other than by the way of implementation of international obligations, unless such legislation were to purport to deal with the power of Ministers of the Crown to exercise its prerogative in foreign affairs, or to create a state of law in Scotland which affected the effectual exercise of that power" (*Scottish Continuity Bill* [32]). It is particularly difficult to envisage Scottish legislation relating to relations with the EU other than by way of implementations of EU law obligations.

Accordingly, in the court's judgement, the Scottish Bill did not 'relate to' relations with the EU, as it would have effect at a time when there will be no legal relations with the EU unless a further treaty is made with the EU. The bill did not claim to deal with any legal rule affecting the power of Ministers of the Crown to negotiate a treaty or to conduct the UK's relation with the EU. It did not aim to affect the way in which negotiations between the UK and the EU were conducted. It simply regulated "the legal consequences in Scotland of the cessation of EU law as a source of domestic law relating to devolved matters, which will result from the withdrawal from the EU already authorised by the UK Parliament" (*Scottish Continuity Bill* [33]). This is something that the Scottish Parliament was competent to do, as it concerned only domestic legal implications of the UK's conduct of international relations.

The general attack on the validity of the Scottish Bill thus failed. There was nothing legally uncertain or otherwise contrary to the rule of law about the enactment of legislation governing the domestic legal implications of withdrawal at both the UK and the Scottish level, provided that they did not conflict with the Scotland Act settlement. According to the Supreme Court's interpretation, the Scottish Parliament was allowed to make laws to ensure there was continuity in Scottish law after Brexit. The only condition was that these rules did not conflict with the provisions of the Scotland Act 1998.

The court then went on to address challenges to specific rules of the Bill, assessing the compatibility of a number of its provisions with those of the Scotland Act. The discussion on section 17 of the Scottish Bill, headed "Requirement for Scottish Ministers' consent to certain subordinate legislation", was the most controversial. It provided that, after exit day, subordinate legislation made by ministers of the UK government on matters of retained EU law, relating to devolved competences, would have first required the consent of the Scottish ministers. The UK Law Officers complained that this section was outside the legislative competence of the Scottish Parliament.[41]

In the Court's view, section 17 made UK subordinate legislation conditional on previous approval by the Scottish ministers, breaching section 28(7) of the Scotland Act, which expressly preserves the power of the Westminster Parliament to make laws for Scotland. The Scotland Act makes it clear that, "notwithstanding the conferral of legislative authority on the Scottish Parliament, the UK Parliament remains sovereign and its legislative power in relation to Scotland is undiminished" (*Scottish Continuity Bill* [41]). This provision reflects the essence of devolution, which in contrast to a federal model, preserves the powers of the central legislature of the State in relation to all matters, whether devolved or reserved. In other words, the mechanism provided by section 17 of the Scottish Bill was inconsistent with the sovereign power of the UK Parliament to legislate for Scotland, which includes the power to approve laws authorising the making of subordinate legislation by ministers or other persons. Such a mechanism clearly conflicted with the principle of parliamentary sovereignty vested to the Westminster Parliament.

The court also considered the subsequent effect of the UK Withdrawal Act on the legislative competence of the Scottish Parliament in relation to the Scottish Bill. As said, by the time the Supreme Court ruled its judgement, the UK legislation had been passed by the Westminster Parliament, without a legislative consent motion by the Scottish Parliament. The UK Withdrawal Act amended the terms of the Scotland Act 1998, adding itself to the list of provisions, which are protected against modifications by the Scottish legislature.[42] As a result, the legal framework had significantly changed since the approval of the Scottish legislation. This new normative scenario was not neglected by the Court, which in its judgement took into account the UK Withdrawal Act and amendments introduced by it into the Scotland Act.

However, the Supreme Court rejected the UK Law Officers' radical argument that the aim of the UK Parliament, with the approval of the UK

Withdrawal Act, was to create a unique *corpus* of retained EU law across the UK on withdrawal from the EU. In such a case, Parliament would have included the UK Withdrawal Act among the reserved matters, so that the Scottish legislature was not permitted to create its own version of the same regime. Instead, by adding the UK Withdrawal Act to the list of provisions which are protected against modification (Schedule 4), the UK Parliament chose simply to protect this Act against subsequent enactments under devolved powers which would alter a rule in the UK Act or conflict with it. Thus, the Scottish Continuity Bill could not be ruled invalid on the grounds that it related to a UK reserved legislation.

Consequently, an accurate analysis was needed of a set of provisions of the Scottish Bill in order to check whether they breached the UK Withdrawal Act. Adopting this approach, the Court identified a number of provisions of the Scottish Bill, which, involving modifications of the UK Act, were invalid. For instance, section 5 of the Scottish Bill provided that the Charter of Fundamental Rights of the European Union was part of Scots law after the UK's exit from the EU; in contrast, section 5 of the UK Withdrawal Act provides that the Charter is not part of domestic law. This inconsistency "clearly amounts to a modification and section 5 therefore would not be law" (*Scottish Continuity Bill* [102]). Again, the UK Act provides that, after Brexit, there will be no right in domestic law to damages in accordance with the rule in the *Francovich* case;[43] section 8 of the Scottish Bill provided that, in limited circumstances, there was such a right. This modified the UK legislation and was therefore invalid.

In short, the UK Withdrawal Act takes precedence over the Scottish Bill. This result underscores that the UK Parliament has supreme sovereignty on matters of UK law and maintains undiminished power to legislate for Scotland, notwithstanding the existence of the Scottish Parliament (Boffey 2019). The United Kingdom has not become a federal state with a written constitution regulating the relationships between the federal centre and its constituent parts, but the UK Parliament remains sovereign, and its legislative power in relation to devolved administrations is undiminished. As the Supreme Court emphatically affirms, "it reflects the essence of devolution". As in the previous *Miller* judgement, the Supreme Court judge reaffirms that the UK's territorial constitutional settlement continues to be a devolved model, in which parliamentary sovereignty is still a cardinal milestone.

The constant application of the 'consent rule' of the Sewel Convention has not changed the nature of the devolution system, as proved by this unusual phase of conflict between UK and Scottish administrations which has determined the re-affirmation of the main features of such a system. However, the *Scottish Continuity Bill* judgement cannot be read as a full victory for the UK government's position. As mentioned above, the Supreme Court ruled that the

Scottish Bill as a whole was not outside the Scottish Parliament's legislative competence and that several provisions of it were within the legislative sphere of the Scottish legislature. The significant role of the Scottish Parliament was emphasised in several parts of the judgement: it is defined as "a democratically elected legislature with a mandate to make laws for people in Scotland", which has "plenary" legislative powers, even if "within the limits of its legislative competence" (*Scottish Continuity Bill* [12]). In addition, it is described as "a legislature of unlimited legislative competence subject to the limitations in section 28 and 29 of the Scotland Act" (*Scottish Continuity Bill* [25]). Such statements, even if they do not fail to make reference also to the relative limits, underline the extent of the powers granted to the Scottish Parliament and the importance of the constitutional position occupied by devolved institutions.

This importance is confirmed by two amendments to the Scotland Act, enacted in 2016, which entrench the role of the Scottish institutions in the UK constitutional settlement. The first provides that "the Scottish Parliament and the Scottish Government are a permanent part of the United Kingdom's constitutional arrangements". The purpose of this provision is "with due regard to the other provisions of this Act" "to signify the commitment" of the UK Parliament and government to the Scottish institutions. In view of such a commitment, it is declared that "the Scottish Parliament and the Scottish Government are not to be abolished except on the basis of a decision of the people of Scotland voting in a referendum."[44]

The Supreme Court made mere reference to this new section, but did not analyse its possible legal implications with regard to the principle of parliamentary sovereignty.[45] The reasons for this silence seem clear, especially for a civil law scholar. This new section could be interpreted as a constraint to the legislative power of the UK Parliament, which could no longer discretionarily decide on the abolition of Scotland's institutions. It appears to be a rule of a constitutional nature, subordinating the Parliament's power to the popular will of the Scottish people as expressed in a referendum. The difficulty of reconciling the meaning of this new provision with the traditional principle of parliamentary sovereignty has, therefore, led the Court to assume apodictically this principle as prevailing, avoiding any in-depth and problematic analysis.

A similar approach was carried out with reference to a second amendment of the Scotland Act, which, in 2016, gave statutory recognition to the Sewel Convention.[46] According to the Supreme Court, this convention is an important instrument to facilitate harmonious relations between the UK Parliament and the devolved legislatures and its legislative recognition entrenches the role of the Scottish Parliament, without challenging the sovereignty of the UK Parliament. It is unsurprising that in the *Scottish Continuity Bill* case the Court merely made reference to the conclusions of the *Miller* judgement on the legal irrelevance of this new provision. If the UK Parliament remains sovereign, there is no room for any argument claiming legal constraints to its legislative powers (Elliott 2018).

In the Court's view, the new normative scenario described above has not, therefore, reduced the predominance of the principle of parliamentary sovereignty. However, in some points of the *Scottish Continuity Bill* judgement, the Court assumed a more ambiguous perspective, which tried to combine this traditional supreme principle with the constitutional role of the devolved administrations. This effort can be seen in the rejection of the most radical arguments submitted by the UK Law Officers.

Firstly, as already said, the Court rejected the argument that the entire Scottish Bill was invalid because it was outside the Scottish Parliament's legislative competence, recognising the power of the Scottish Parliament to regulate the legal consequences in Scotland of the cessation of EU law relating to devolved matters.

Secondly, the Court concluded that section 17 of the Scottish Bill was outside the legislative competence of the Scottish Parliament because it modified section 28(7) of the Scotland Act, which acknowledged the power of the UK Parliament to make laws for Scotland. However, the Supreme Court refused the UK Law Officers' submission that section 17 of the Scottish Bill was invalid on the additional ground of relating to the reserved matter of "the Parliament of the United Kingdom".[47] In the Court's view, such reservation includes, amongst other matters, "the sovereignty of Parliament, since that is an attribute of Parliament which is relevant indeed, fundamental to the constitution" (*Scottish Continuity Bill* [61]). Nevertheless, this reservation cannot be intended to protect legislation passed by the UK Parliament from the effects of legislation enacted by the Scottish Parliament, since that scope is pursued by other provisions of the Scotland Act. It follows that, if the Scottish Parliament makes laws in order to give effect in Scotland to a policy which has been rejected by the UK Parliament, it does not infringe the mentioned reservation. Neither the purpose nor the effect of such legislation impinges upon the constitutional functions and powers of Parliament. In the light of the above interpretation, section 17 of the Scottish Bill "does not purport to alter the fundamental constitutional principle that the Crown in Parliament is the ultimate source of legal authority" (*Scottish Continuity Bill* [62]). Thus, if it became law, "it would not affect parliamentary sovereignty". Nevertheless, section 17 of the Scottish Continuity Bill would have imposed a condition on certain laws approved by the UK Parliament for Scotland, until the Parliament exercised its sovereignty to disapply or repeal it. It would have therefore "affect[ed] the power of the Parliament of the United Kingdom to make laws for Scotland" (*Scottish Continuity Bill* [64]), modifying section 28(7) of the Scotland Act.

In short, section 17 affected the power of the UK Parliament to legislate, but it did not affect parliamentary sovereignty. Reconciling these two seemingly conflicting ideas is complex. As some authors have pointed out, the implication seems to be that the exercise of legislative powers by the Westminster Parliament could be subject to the type of condition entailed by section 17 without compromising its sovereignty (Elliott 2018). The principle of parliamentary sovereignty could be capable of coexisting with certain forms of conditional limits upon Parliament's legislative power. Perhaps this apparent contradiction in the court's reasoning can be read as a vague and ambiguous starting point towards a new reconsideration of the principle of parliamentary sovereignty, which is capable of adapting itself to the needs arising from the devolution constitutional system.

To conclude, the Brexit process represents an ongoing test for the UK's territorial constitution, the outcomes of which are difficult to predict. The mixed conclusions of the *Scottish Continuity Bill* case have opened a new phase of this test. Probably Brexit will offer additional chances to analyse the development of the complex relationship between the devolution settlement and the principle of parliamentary sovereignty.

4.7 CONCLUSION

Exit from the EU requires notification of the State to be approved under its internal constitutional system (Article 50 TEU). This requirement has put the English institutional system to the test, due to the complexity of the challenges to be faced and the uncertainty as to who is competent to complete the notification procedure with the EU. This has triggered an institutional conflict between Parliament and government, which has highlighted the operational difficulties of a system which, by historical tradition, is based on the sovereignty of Parliament and which has not yet acquired full legal awareness of the value of the referendum. Unlike legal systems with a rigid constitution, in fact, the referendum in the UK is not governed by higher-ranking rules of general application but must be regulated from time to time by the law establishing the referendum itself. The law establishing the referendum on Brexit, however, was issued on the basis of the assumption (later proved wrong) that the result would be positive and is extremely vague on the positions to be adopted. This silence also implies that the result of the referendum has a consultative effect from the legal viewpoint. The importance of the outcome of the referendum lies, however, in its political strength.

Given the ambiguity of the constitutional principles, the conflict took on the character of an appeal to the High Court, and then to the Supreme Court. In the *Miller* case, the UK Supreme Court made it clear that the direct sovereignty exercised by means of the referendum does not replace the competence of Parliament, since the latter remains sovereign and it is to decide on the value to be attributed to the referendum. It is also up to Parliament to decide by law whether to authorise notification to the European Council of the exit from the Union, given that many EU rights will be lost as a result of the withdrawal, and that there is a 'vital difference' between changes in domestic law resulting from accession to new treaties (for which the government is responsible) and the loss of rights resulting from the withdrawal from the EU.

The government–Parliament relationship, however, has proved to be full of tensions. This is not only the case of the enactment of the *EU Withdrawal Bill 2017–19* and the dispute over the 'meaningful vote' on the final Brexit agreement. It is also the case of the decision made by Prime Minister Boris Johnson to prorogate Parliament in order to exclude discussion and force Parliament into a no-deal Brexit. In seeking a way out, the legal principles set out in the *Miller* judgement are of crucial importance.

The principle of parliamentary sovereignty seems to resist also in relations with devolved legislatures. Devolved administrations have basically lost two legal battles before the Supreme Court. The first – the already cited *Miller* case – has denied them the power to block Brexit. In the Court's view, the withdrawal from the EU is, in fact, not conditional on the consent of the regional parliaments. The second – the *Scottish Continuity Bill* case – has considerably limited the devolved administration's power to control the effects of Brexit. This case-law clearly states a dominant role of the UK institutions in the decision of withdrawal from the EU as well as in the management of repatriated functions and competences, including those falling in devolved areas.

However, the analysis of the two judgements has revealed some significant differences. The *Miller* judgement stands out for a clear closure against the claims of the devolved administrations, which are completely excluded from the decision to leave the EU. The *Scottish Continuity Bill* judgement ruled that only some parts of the Scottish Bill were not within the Scottish Parliament's competence. This latter decision delivered a mixed result, which serves as a reaffirmation of the sovereignty of the UK Parliament and, at the same time, leaves some room for normative power by the devolved legislatures in the Brexit process. It also seems to pave the way for further consideration on the principle of parliamentary sovereignty, which allows it to evolve and adapt to new situations and constitutional claims.

The Brexit process can be described as a 'constitutional moment' (Simson Caird 2019), potentially capable of rewriting fundamental aspects of the form of State and government of the United Kingdom. Very likely, the decision to leave the EU will shape the UK constitution over the coming years.

NOTES

1. Both authors contributed to the chapter's conception. Stefania Baroncelli drafted Sections 4.2, 4.3 and 4.4 while Monica Rosini drafted Sections 4.5 and 4.6. Introduction and Conclusions were drafted together.
2. On 7 December 2016, following a debate, the House of Commons resolved "[to recognise] . . . that this House should respect the wishes of the United Kingdom as expressed in the referendum on 23 June; and further [to call] on the Government to invoke Article 50 by 31 March 2017". Cfr. *R (Miller) v Secretary of State for Exiting the European Union* [2017] UKSC 5, 33.
3. The referendum was aimed at deciding "whether the United Kingdom should remain a member of the European Union".
4. Section 1 of the *European Union Referendum Act 2015* provided that "[a] referendum is to be held" on a date no later than 31 December 2017 "on whether the United Kingdom should remain a member of the European Union".
5. See note 2.
6. *R (Miller) (Respondents) -v- Secretary of State for Exiting the European Union (Appellant)*, 24.1.17, Supreme Court, [38, 120].
7. Ibid., [111, 120].
8. See sections 2, 3 and 6 of the *European Union Act 2011*, and the Explanatory Notes.
9. *Internationale Handelgesellschaft*, 1972, 11 C.M.L.R. 255, 283, followed by the *Simmenthal* case, 1978, 3 C.M.L.R. 263, 121.
10. Court of Justice of the EU, *Wightman and Others v Secretary of State for Exiting the European Union*, 10.12.2018, C-621/18.
11. *R (Miller) v. Secretary of State for Exiting the European Union*, 3.11.16, Divisional Court.
12. *R (Miller) v. Secretary of State for Exiting the European Union*, 3.11.16, Divisional Court, [26].
13. *R (Miller) (Respondents) v. Secretary of State for Exiting the European Union (Appellant)*, 24.1.17, Supreme Court.
14. On this case, see following sections in this chapter.
15. *Miller*, Supreme Court, [54]. The reference is *JH Rayner (Mincing Lane) Ltd v Department of Trade and Industry* [1990] 2 AC 418, 476, "[t]he Government may negotiate, conclude, construe, observe, breach, repudiate or terminate a treaty".
16. *Attorney General v. De Keyser's Royal Hotel Ltd.* [1920] AC 508.
17. Namely, Lord Reed, Lord Carnwath and Lord Hughes.
18. *R (on the application of Miller) (Appellant) v. The Prime Minister (Respondent) Cherry and others (Respondents) v. Advocate General for Scotland (Appellant) (Scotland)*, 24.9.19, Supreme Court.
19. In 1998, the UK Parliament enacted the three key Acts of the devolution process: the Scotland Act, the Government of Wales Act and the Northern Ireland Act.
20. HC, Parliamentary Debates, 16 June 2015, vol. 597, n. 17, cols 186, 189, 190 and 231.
21. The United Kingdom as a whole chose to leave the EU by a narrow margin: 51.9%–48.1% of those who voted. The margin in favour of Leave was more consistent in England (53.4%–46.6%) and Wales (52.5%–47.5%). In contrast, remain majorities were in Scotland (62.0%–38.0%) and Northern Ireland (55.8%–44.2%).

22. Furthermore, in March 2017 the Scottish First Minister, Nicola Sturgeon, announced the Scottish government's intention to hold a second referendum on independence. This intention was already indicated in its white paper, *Consultation on a Draft Referendum Bill*, published in October 2016.
23. *McCord and Agnew* [2016] NIQB 85.
24. The Good Friday Agreement (officially referred to as the Belfast Agreement) was published in April 1998 in a command paper presented to Parliament. It was a peace agreement between the British and Irish governments, and most of the political parties in Northern Ireland, on how Northern Ireland should be governed. In particular, it contained provisions for the establishment of democratic institutions in Northern Ireland in order to achieve "reconciliation, tolerance and mutual trust and . . . the protection and vindication of human rights".
25. See Lord Bingham in *Robinson v Secretary of State for Northern Ireland and Others* [2002] NI 390 at 398 paragraph [11] and *McCord and Agnew* [43].
26. *Miller*, Divisional Court, [102].
27. *Miller*, UKSC [126–52].
28. Section 2 of the Scotland Act 2016 inserted subsection (8) into section 28 of the Scotland Act 1998.
29. More exactly: section 5 of the NI Act empowers the NI Assembly to make laws, but subsection 6 provides that "this section does not affect the power of the Parliament of the United Kingdom to make laws for Northern Ireland". Section 28(7) of the Scotland Act 1998 states that the section empowering the Scottish Parliament to make laws "does not affect the power of the Parliament to make laws for Scotland". An identical rule is made for Wales in section 107(5) of the Government of Wales Act 2006.
30. HL, Parliamentary Debates, 21 July 1998, vol. 592, col. 791.
31. Para. 14 of the Memorandum of Understanding and Supplementary Agreements between the United Kingdom Government, Scottish Ministers and the Cabinet of the National Assembly for Wales. This document has been revised six times since it was introduced. The most recent text is available at: https://assets.publishing .service.gov.uk/government/uploads/system/uploads/attachmentdata/file/316157/ MoUbetweentheUKandtheDevolvedAdministrations.pdf.
32. DGN 10, Post-Devolution Primary Legislation affecting Scotland, para. 4. See also DGN 8 (Northern Ireland) and DGN 17 (Wales).
33. Section 2 of the Scotland Act 2016 and section 2 of the Wales Act 2017.
34. The Scottish and Welsh governments promptly signalled their refusal of legislative consent to the EU Withdrawal Bill as presented to Parliament. See: First Ministers of Scotland and Wales, Joint statement in reaction to the European Union (Withdrawal) Bill, 13 July 2017; Scottish Government, *Legislative Consent Memorandum* (12 September 2017), Welsh Government, *Legislative Consent Memorandum* (12 September 2017). For some comments of these contested contents, see Rawlings 2017 and Bowers 2017.
35. See section 31 of the Scotland Act 1998.
36. Now it is section 12 of the UK Withdrawal Act.
37. Scottish Continuity Bill [2018] UKSC 64.
38. It was approved on 20 June and received Royal Assent on 26 June 2018, while the Supreme Court heard parties in July and issued its judgement in December 2018.
39. Section 29(2)(b) of the Scotland Act.
40. More precisely, Paragraph 7(1) of the Part 1 of Schedule 5 of the Scotland Act states: "International relations, including relations with territories outside the

United Kingdom, the European Union (and their institutions) and other international organisations, regulations of international trade, and international development assistance and co-operation are reserved matters."

Sub-paragraph (1) does not reserve: "(a) observing and implementing international obligations under the Human Rights Convention and obligations under EU law, (b) assisting Ministers of the Crown in relation to any matter to which that sub-paragraph applies".

41. More precisely, the UK Law Officers complained that section 17 of the Scottish Bill: (i) would have modified – illegitimately – sections 28(7) of the Scotland Act; (ii) related to the reserve matter of "the Parliament of the United Kingdom", set out in paragraph 1(c) of Part 1 of Schedule 5 to the Scotland Act.
42. Paragraph 1(2) of Schedule 4 of the Scotland Act lists a number of provisions which the Scottish Parliament cannot modify, amend or repeal. Now this list includes the European Union (Withdrawal) Act 2018.
43. *Francovich v Italian Republic*, C-6/90 and C-9/90, [1995] ICR 722; [1991] ECR I-5357.
44. Section 63/A of the Scotland Act.
45. The Supreme Court failed to analyse the legal effects of this new section of the Scotland Act also in the *Miller* case, where the new provision was considered only for the reconstruction of the legal framework created by the enactment of the Scotland Act 2016. In the Court's view, this framework merely supported the conclusion "that the purpose of the legislative recognition of the [Sewel] convention was to entrench it as a convention".
46. Section 28(8). See *supra* para. 4.
47. Reserved matters are set out in Schedule 5 of the Scotland Act 1998.

REFERENCES

Baldini, G., E. Bressanelli and E. Massetti, E. (2019), "No-one in control? Brexit and the challenge to the Westminster Model", paper prepared for the EUSA Biannual Conference, Denver, 9–11 May 2019.

Barczentewicz, M. (2017), "*Miller*, Statutory Interpretation, and the True Place of EU Law in UK Law", *Public Law*, Nov Supp (Brexit Special Extra Issue), pp. 10–24, at https://ssrn.com/abstract=2929738.

BBC News (2016), "Brexit: Sturgeon sets out key Scottish interests that must 'be protected'", 25 July, at https://www.bbc.com/news/uk-scotland-scotland-politics-36878081.

Boffey, E. (2019), "Case Comment: The UK Withdrawal from the European Union (Legal Continuity) (Scotland) Bill – A Reference by the Attorney General and the Advocate General for Scotland [2018] UKSC 64", *UKSC Blog*, 11 January, at: http://ukscblog.com/case-comment-the-uk-withdrawal-from-the-european-union-legal-continuity-scotland-bill-a-reference-by-the-attorney-general-and-the-advocate-general-for-scotland-2018-uksc-64/.

Bogdanor, V. (2016), "Brexit, the constitution and the alternatives", *King's Law Journal*, 27 (3), pp. 314–22.

Bowers, P. (2017), "The European Union (Withdrawal) Bill: Devolution", *House of Commons Briefing Paper 8154*, 24 November.

Burrows, N. (2000), *Devolution*, London: Sweet & Maxwell.

Craig, P. (2019a), "Constitutional principle, the rule of law and political reality: the European Union (Withdrawal) Act 2018", *Modern Law Review*, 82 (2), pp. 319–66.

Craig, P. (2019b), "Prorogation: constitutional principle and law, fact and causation", *U.K. Const. L. Blog*, 2 September, at https://ukconstitutionallaw.org/.

Dicey, A. V. (1885), *The Law of the Constitution*, 10th edn, ed. E. C. S. Wade.

Douglas-Scott, S. (2016), "Removing reference to EU law from the devolution legislation would require the consent of the devolved assemblies", *The Constitution Unit*, 13 June.

Elliott, M. (2017), "The Supreme Court's judgment in Miller: in search of constitutional principle", *The Cambridge Law Journal*, 76 (2), pp. 257–88.

Elliott, M. (2018), "The Supreme Court's judgment in the Scottish Continuity Bill case', *Public Law for Everyone*, 14 December.

Elliott, M., J. Williams and A. Young (2018), "The Miller tale: an introduction", in M. Elliott, J. Williams and A. Young (eds), *The UK Constitution after Miller: Brexit and Beyond*, Oxford: Hart Publishing, pp. 1–38.

Hart, H. L. A. (2012), *The Concept of Law*, 3rd edn, Oxford: Oxford University Press.

HC (2018), *Brexit: Devolution and Legislative Consent*, Briefing Paper, Number 08274, 29 March.

Henderson, A., C. Jeffery, D. Wincott, and R. Wyn Jones (2017), 'How Brexit was made in England', *The British Journal of Politics and International Relations*, 19 (4), pp. 631–46.

HL, Select Committee on the Constitution (2010), *12th Report of Session 2009–10, Referendums in the United Kingdom. Report with Evidence*, HL Paper 99.

Jowell, J. and D. Oliver (2000), *The Changing Constitution*, Oxford: Oxford University Press.

Leyland, P. (2016), "Brexit and the UK: charting the constitutional and legal obstacles", *Istituzioni del federalismo*, pp. 41–68.

McHarg, A. (2018), "Constitutional change and territorial consent: the *Miller* case and the Sewel convention", in M. Elliott, J. Williams and A. L. Young (eds), *The UK Constitution after Miller: Brexit and Beyond*, Oxford: Hart Publishing, pp. 155–201.

Moffat, H. and P. Hardy (2018), "What next as the UK Supreme Court rules on validity of Scottish EU Continuity Bill?", 18 December, at: https://www.dlapiper.com/it/italy/insights/publications/2018/12/scottish-eu-continuity-bill/.

Nicolaïdis, K. (2017), "The political mantra: Brexit and the transformation of the European order", in F. Fabbrini (ed.), *The Law and Politics of Brexit*, Oxford: Oxford University Press, pp. 25–48.

Parpworth, N. (2018), *Constitutional and Administrative Law*, 10th edn, Oxford: Oxford University Press.

Rawlings, R. (2017), "Brexit and the territorial constitution: devolution, regulation and inter-governmental relations", *The Constitution Society*, report.

Simson Caird, J. (2019), "Brexit and the constitution: seven lessons", *The Constitution Unit*, at https://constitution-unit.com/2019/06/04/brexit-and-the-constitution-seven-lessons/.

Smith, E. and A. Young (2017), "That's how it worked in 2014, and how it would have to work again", *U.K. Const. L. Blog*, 15 March.

Stewart, H. and R. Mason (2019), "Grave abuse of power if PM shuts parliament to force no-deal Brexit", *The Guardian*, 27 August, p. 1.

Tierney, S. (2017), "A second independence referendum in Scotland: the legal issues", *U.K. Const. L. Blog*, 13 March.

Twomey, A. (2018), "Miller and the prerogative", in M. Elliott, J. Williams and A. Young (eds), *The UK Constitution after Miller: Brexit and Beyond*, Oxford: Hart Publishing, pp. 69–90.

Williams, J. (2018), "Prerogative powers after Miller: an analysis in four E's", in M. Elliott, J. Williams and A. Young (eds), *The UK Constitution after Miller: Brexit and Beyond*, Oxford: Hart Publishing, pp. 39–68.

5. Globally alone: the UK's foreign policy after Brexit

Emidio Diodato and Serena Giusti

5.1 BRITISH FOREIGN POLICY'S DISCOMBOBULATION

The decision to trigger Article 50 of the EU Treaty (29 March 2017) is the outcome of a chain of promises made for electoral reasons that led to an unexpected result. The British leadership had to manage a situation that it was not prepared to face up to, opening up a period of incertitude and tension.

The absence of a plan for the post-European Union (EU) period is particularly striking in the field of foreign policy, a very traditional core pillar of the state. It is in foreign policy that national interests, so often invoked in the UK's process of retracting from the EU, are conceived and pursued. It is foreign policy that is meant to produce a country's role conception with a strategic vision, especially when terrifying decisions for the future of a country are taken. Therefore, the post-referendum confusion in terms of foreign policy trajectories is pretty bewildering, in particular for a country that has usually exhibited a certain pragmatism and clarity in the conduct of its foreign policy. On the one hand, initial disorientation signalled the discomfort of a government (at least under Prime Ministers David Cameron and Theresa May), reluctant but forced by a referendum to take the country back from Brussels. On the other hand, deficiencies in foreign policymaking have been unveiled, certainly heightened by Brexit.

Already in 2011, the Public Administration Select Committee (PASC), a committee of Members of Parliament appointed by the House of Commons that produces reports making recommendations to the government, warned that

> The Government has lost the capacity to think strategically [. . .] short termism and reaction to events predominate in recent Whitehall practice. The ability to articulate our enduring interests, values and identity has atrophied. Strategy is too often thought of as a plan for action or a document rather than a process which needs to be articulated constantly and updated regularly.

And a year later, in 2012, the same Committee said it had

> little confidence that Government policies are informed by a clear, coherent strategic approach, itself informed by a coherent assessment of the public's aspirations and their perceptions of the national interest . . . Policy decisions are made for short-term reasons, little reflecting the longer-term interests of the nation.

In addition, according to the Institute for Government, the Foreign Office had lost 24 per cent of its staff since 2010 and 12 per cent of its budget.[1] Both reports point out government difficulties in discerning what were good (and bad) interests for the country.

So, while the United Kingdom (UK) should have undertaken a process of revision of its foreign policy in terms of conception and methodology, Brexit suddenly broke into the British political landscape inaugurating a period of obfuscation and chaos. The antecedent lack of strategic thinking, along with the urgency of prospecting reliable and attractive trajectories of foreign policy, brought a revival of classical ready narratives that resonated easily with a large public. Such a revival appeared the quickest and easiest answer to an unexpected situation that needed to be resolved convincingly both internally and externally in order to not squander the country's status and authority.

Since Cameron became prime minister in 2010, a certain dissatisfaction with the EU has emerged, along with a desire to play a more relevant role in global politics and not to be limited by EU membership. However, this aspiration of widening the external political horizon had been expressed only vaguely, and no alternative to the process of European integration was a realistic prospect. In his infamous speech on Europe (23 January 2013), Cameron, for instance, hinted at a goal, securing prosperity, which the UK maintained the EU should have treated as a top priority. He stressed that

> The challenges come not from within this continent but outside it. From the surging economies in the east and south. Of course a growing world economy benefits us all, but we should be in no doubt that a new global race of nations is under way today.

While calling his European partners' attention to the global dimension of contemporary challenges, he implicitly invited them to overcome traditional eurocentrism, a vocation that the UK, a traditional eccentric power '. . . that reaches out and turns its face to the world' (Cameron 2013), had already cultivated. However, at that time, Cameron was not considering the exit of his country as a viable option but rather the contrary, provided that the EU was able to drastically reform itself according to five principles: competiveness, flexibility, reversibility of power from the centre to member states, democratic accountability and fairness. Cameron's position was not so different from that of Prime Minister Margaret Thatcher who, in her celebrated 1998 Bruges speech, made it clear that 'Britain does not dream of some cosy, isolated existence on the fringes of the European Community. Our destiny is in Europe, as part of the community.' She remarked, however, that the Community is a cooperative space made up of sovereign countries with their identities and that the UK would have opposed its transformation into a political and economic union. She was dismissing a specific aspect of the European Community (EC), but not the whole European project in itself. The later British opting-outs from the European Monetary Union, the Charter of Fundamental Rights of the EU and some aspects of the areas of freedom, security and justice are fully in line with the Bruges spirit. A consistently minimalist approach to integration has characterised the UK's membership of the EU, allowing the country to balance its participation with an endemic scepticism regarding the evolution of the European project (Geddes 2013).

Given the many exemptions the UK has been conceded, it seems that Cameron's U-turn regarding the EU had an electoral rather than an 'ideological' justification. The 2014 European Parliament elections that marked the successful affirmation of the UK Independence Party (UKIP), led by Nigel Farage,[2] alarmed both the Labour and the Conservative parties which, by placing the question of the country's EU membership at the top of their political agendas, contributed to prioritising an issue that was not detected as being of chief importance for the country – issues such as stagnating wages, the housing crisis and problems with the National Health Service were far more crucial. In other words, in a very short space of time the UK's permanence in the EU turned into a vital issue, one connected to the very essentials of the state – a defence of national interest and sovereignty.

On 29 November 2014, Cameron, before the upcoming general election, devoted another speech to the EU, focusing on the question of migration and EU's citizens' access to British welfare, depicted as one of the main problems for the country's future. The prime minister also affirmed that he would "rule nothing out" (including leaving the EU) if his attempts to "get a better deal for Britain" from the other member states did not work. To the surprise of many, Cameron came out of the 2015 general election much stronger than expected, and with a promise to take power back from Brussels through a "new deal". The concessions that Cameron finally obtained in the new deal with the EU (European Council, 18–19 February 2016) neither calmed down the Eurosceptic fringes of his own party, nor the opinions of many British citizens who tended to identify the EU as responsible for their poor conditions in life. The renegotiation was a crucial mistake, not only because it did not coagulate the members of his own cabinet, but also because it unveiled the EU's inflexibility on the 'free movement of people' principle (this being one of the four freedoms on which the very European project construction is based), fuelling anti-Europe sentiment in the country.

Concomitantly, the migration crisis just after the Eurozone crisis further devaluates membership in the EU. Cameron believed that he could marginalise and contain his EU adversaries – some members of his own party were willing to defenestrate him – by sticking to his electoral promise of calling a referendum, one that he thought he could win. After a fierce campaign for, and mainly against Europe, the 'leavers' won the 23 June referendum and Cameron resigned as prime minister, leaving the country in a vacuum and with no clear design for the UK's future role in international politics without the EU's anchor. The leavers had 'endogenized' the referendum campaign by emphasising the presumed negative aspects of European integration for domestic politics (e.g. demonising migrants and scapegoating them for social problems while blaming the EU for its policies on open borders and lack of control). Foreign policy was relegated to the sidelines during the campaign. Even later, under the leadership of prime ministers Theresa May and Boris Johnson, much of the emphasis on leaving the EU related to 'taking back control' of migration (not asylum seekers and refugees, but rather EU migrants) and escaping the jurisdiction of the European Court of Justice (CJEU), and to be able to 'write and judge on our own laws', as May (2017b) put it in her speech at Lancaster House.

Emphasis on the aforementioned issues made the EU's status as a powerful global actor (Hill 1993) an irrelevant matter. Although the ontological limits of the European polity that requires foreign policy to be an intergovernmental policy, the EU has gradually strengthened its external leverage and presence. This is even more the case, considering that major recent progress in the EU deals with foreign policy, although many grave divisions persist on other fronts.[3] Once out of the Union, the UK's foreign policy will be influenced yet again by the EU, while important assets will have been lost – negotiation and bargaining powers, leverage and conditionality (positive and negative) – assets that the organization has developed especially since the end of the Cold War. The UK will also renounce political advantages – diplomatic practices, the system of delegations constituting the European External Service, international trade agreements already in place or about to be negotiated – offered by a collective and consolidated polity such as the EU. The UK will lose its grip on those areas where access to EU markets is still a powerful policy lever and where the EU is still considered a quite attractive power (such as the Balkans, Ukraine, North Africa and Turkey). Although the EU will probably shift from exercising a structural power (Keukeleire and MacNaughtan 2008) to a softer form of influence that the European Global Strategy (2016) has envisaged in support of resilience (Giusti 2019), it will still be an essential actor in the neighbourhood and further afield. Moreover, when rethinking the UK's foreign policy in a post-EU scenario, one should consider how the EU itself will be affected and what consequences it will face, both also relevant for the

UK. There are many hypotheses that can be advanced, such as an exacerbation of tension in Franco-German relations, a contestation of the free market principle or a return to protectionism. At extremes, the EU's disintegration could be contemplated, or its strengthening, as French President Manuel Macron wishes (*The Economist* 2019). Whatever form the EU will take, this will impact a UK that, in the meantime, will have no opportunity of framing the organisation's course.

The UK's choice reflects an old conception of sovereignty, ignoring that participation in supranational organisations or multilateral forums is a potent way of exercising influence and safeguarding national interests. States need to consider how their interests impact on other states, regional stability more widely, and global order generally, developing 'a constitutive interest in the preservation and expansion of the intersubjectivity of action-orienting mutual understanding' (Habermas 1971, p. 310). Neo-liberals and intergovernmentalists have been even more explicit, affirming that by belonging to regional/international organisations, states can pursue fully their national interests, albeit with a softer emphasis on sovereignty. States, as rational utility maximisers, frequently cooperate with one another through the construction of international institutions that lower transaction costs, increase information and reduce cheating. It is under this profile that the UK's choice must be considered. By leaving the EU, the UK may reconquer its full sovereignty at the price, however, of losing influence, especially if new foreign policy trajectories are ill defined.

So far, the UK's political leaders have mainly mentioned the concept of 'Global Britain' to substantiate the idea that a future outside the EU can offer greater opportunities for the British people. Relying on discourse analysis of official speeches on the UK's membership in the EU, and combining role theory and critical geopolitics, we will highlight the possible features of a Global Britain's role, showing the limits of this narrative.

5.2   SEEKING GLOBAL BRITAIN

As a matter of fact, the choice to leave the EU obliges the UK to redesign a new role for itself. We use role theory for discerning what the UK's ambitions are. A typology of national role conceptions that charts the number of roles expressed by decision makers, including contested roles, is a key topic in international relations (Walker 2017). Holsti (1970, p. 277) was the first scholar to stress "that policymakers of most states conceive of their state in terms of multiple sets of relationships and multiple roles and/or functions". He recalled, for example, Canada's roles as a mediator and a developer. More recently, Cantir and Kaarbo (2012) suggested that a profitable line of inquiry might be to ascertain empirically whether there is indeed broad consensus among foreign policy elites, and between elites and the broader domestic public. These approaches do not analyse a sufficiently long timeframe to be able to observe role change (Breuning 2017). Yet, rather than looking for explanations of single foreign policy decisions, scholars can explain long-term patterns of behaviour and historical junctures combining role theory and critical geopolitics. In particular, we will look at what scholars of critical geopolitics have defined as the "discursive practice" of "spatializing" international politics (Ó Tuathail and Agnew 1992, p. 192). According to this view, 'Global Britain' is not a concept that is immanently meaningful and fully realisable; instead it is a discursive 'event' that poses questions to us whenever it is evoked and rhetorically deployed (Ó Tuathail 1996, p. 14).

The concept of Global Britain has been nourished by popular and appealing narratives. As pointed out by Subotić (2016, p. 624),

> During the period of high anxiety, political actors do not create new narratives from scratch, nor do they significantly rewrite the existing ones. Instead, they use the wealth of multiple narrative tropes that exist in dominant state narratives to activate some elements of the narrative and deactivate others. This process manages to preserve the larger narrative template, thus maintaining a sense of order, stability, and ontological peace.

Narratives constitute a very sensitive material that can be either stimulated selectively or purposefully re-constructed. Any narrative will neglect some parts of the story while emphasizing others (Franzosi 1998). Narratives can, therefore, be easily manipulated, and yet still appear genuine, because they appeal to emotions, memories and to the identity of a people and of a nation. Narratives are revived especially when political leadership, lacking projectuality, is nevertheless able to instrumentally reframe them and adapt them to contemporary contexts.

In the wake of a post-Brexit plan for foreign policy, the leadership exactly recalled traditional narratives related to the global rather than continental dimension of the UK. If already Cameron was referring to the global rather than regional vocation of the UK, his successor, Prime Minister May and her Foreign Secretary of State Boris Johnson (2016–18) have repeatedly announced that the UK's future aim is to be a 'Global Britain', a vocation that has characterised the country for at least three centuries. However, re-running the past as a mythical experience holds a number of caveats, some examples being that the present cannot be the same as the past, different actors hold a different perception and assessment of what they have experienced, and the present cannot re-start exactly where it was fractured as things move on.

Even the Foreign Affairs Committee of the House of Commons (6 March 2018) has been critical on the government vision of a Global Britain (memorandum, 1 March 2018) as it is not clear how 'Global Britain' will differ from past UK foreign policy. The government identified "three centres of the global economy and political influence": in "North America, overwhelmingly the United States, in Europe and its neighbourhood; and in the Indo-Pacific region". The latter region is seen as "the centre of the world's growth" where the UK would have a huge advantage because of the Commonwealth. However, the Foreign Affairs Committee concluded that "For Global Britain to be more than a worthy aspiration, the slogan must be backed by substance" (Foreign Affairs Committee 2018b, p. 15). The idea of a 'Global Britain' regaining status seems to find the patronage of the monarchy, which has not taken any firm position regarding Brexit but rather contributed to reinvigorating the Commonwealth.[4]

So far, the most straightforward declination of the concept of 'Global Britain' is prevalently connected to the nostalgic project of the Commonwealth. This trajectory is quite controversial, since it has its roots in British colonialism. It is susceptible to contestation especially among the countries which were part of the British Empire.[5] The international trade secretary Liam Fox (2017a), while talking to a group of Commonwealth trade ministers, described his country in the colonial era as "A small island perched on the edge of the European continent [that] became a leader of world trade", neglecting the fact that the British Empire's power was established through violence in the name of alleged humanitarianism.

The idea of reconnecting to the Commonwealth recalls also the post-war period British foreign policy outlook, based upon the recognition that Britain belongs to three distinct spheres: Western Europe, the Atlantic community and the Commonwealth, as imagined by Winston Churchill.[6] The political choice which prevailed was to give priority to what was called the 'special relationship' with the United States, with the Commonwealth coming next, and Europe third. By the 1960s, all hope of organising the Commonwealth into something approaching a political region had completely failed; Britain became increasingly disillusioned about the possibilities of continuing and cultivating its 'special relationship' with the United States, and hence it turned to Europe. Since then, the country's destiny has been linked to the European project without, however, renouncing a strong dialogue with Washington and close relations with former colonies.

In the meantime, the Commonwealth countries have undertaken their own path: Canada, for example, is keen to protect the North American free trade agreement that US President Donald Trump would prefer to revise; Australia and New Zealand have long seen their future in the dynamic Asia-Pacific region; and India is aspiring to become one of the power poles of a multipolar international system and seeking to reach a trade agreement with the EU.[7] Some countries, such as Singapore, have surpassed Britain in per capita income and growth, and do not foresee any economic advantage in a closer relationship.

While recognising the UK's role as a coordinator within the group, the Commonwealth countries are unwilling to accept a sort of British post-imperial guide whose legitimacy would lie in the colonial legacy. Reception to the UK's possible role as a leading country in the Commonwealth, turning it into a new political and economic project, was in fact not enthusiastic. The Commonwealth countries would have preferred a strong Britain in the EU pleading for their own interests in that political arena (Oppermann et al. 2019). In terms of role theory, we can say that 'Global Britain' is purely the result of British elites' conception that does not meet the expectations of others, especially of those actors that would be primarily involved in the project. There is a dyscrasia between what the UK casts for its post-Brexit foreign policy and what the others expect from the country.

5.3   NARRATING POST-BREXIT BRITAIN

Prime Minister May first outlined her vision for post-Brexit Britain in her speech to the Conservative Party Conference on 2 October 2016:

> Brexit should not just prompt us to think about our new relationship with the European Union. It should make us think about our role in the wider world. It should make us think of Global Britain, a country with the self-confidence and the freedom to look beyond the continent of Europe [. . .] to forge an ambitious and optimistic new role in the world. (May 2016)

A year later, in her speech to the Lord Mayor's Banquet on 13 November 2017, the Prime Minister added:

> It is why we will use our relationships with the Commonwealth [. . .] to work with partners in Africa, Asia and beyond in building consensus and taking practical steps towards a global economy that works for everyone. (May 2017a)

On the one hand, the expression 'Global Britain' introduced by May sounds like an impressive and fashionable slogan. It appears as a rhetorical figure that tries to intercept the favour of those who see Britain regaining its independence and taking back control of the state through leaving the EU. According to Hill, for example, this idea refers "to the notion, trumpeted by the right-wing tabloids, that Britain is 'the greatest country in the world', and can regain its position as a great power" (Hill 2018, p. 187). On the other hand, May underlined that the UK should rethink its international role outside the EU. This point cannot be challenged. The outcome of the June 2016 referendum has obliged the UK to reconsider its role on the world stage. Of course, terms such as 'self-confidence' and 'ambition' are not straightforward concepts in foreign policymaking. Having said that, we need to understand whether there are *new elements* introduced by May when depicting 'Global Britain'.

In the aforementioned Churchill's three circles and, generally, in 'Churchill legacy' with respect to the UK's role in the world, we can envisage a claim for British leadership in Europe as the result of maintaining post-imperial control on the Commonwealth and the Anglosphere. After the Second World War, Churchill devoted himself to reshaping the popular understanding of British history as the history of the English-speaking peoples, and in support of the special relationship he wished to claim with Anglo-Saxon America and with the 'white' Commonwealth (Wallace 2005, p. 66). This legacy originates from the debates among liberal imperialists, who denied that British imperialism was colonial by intention. They instead persuaded themselves that, without benevolent attention from more developed peoples, less-developed peoples could never progress (Kearns 2009, pp. 29–30).

May's narrative partially draws from these aspects of Churchill's narrative. Yet, it completely omits that central to British debates on the British Empire was the idea that the population of Britain had produced not merely international power, but also a surplus of men who had been driven by economic pressure to found new 'Britains' across the ocean. At the beginning of the twentieth century, the eminent geographer Halford Mackinder wrote: 'There are now colonies in the old Greek meaning – independent nations tied to the mother country only by a sense of common ideas [. . .] Britain exercises little imperial control in these white men's lands' (Mackinder 1902, p. 345). This belief, which emerged from the debate on imperial preferences, inspired the idea of the white and racist Commonwealth. Of course, it was a sentiment generally associated with imperialism in the past.

May's narrative of Commonwealth relies on linguistic links rather than on the sense of racial superiority. As also Foreign Minister Boris Johnson wrote in *The Sunday Express*, introducing the London Commonwealth Summit of April 2018, the idea of 'Global Britain' refers to linguistic links and, at the same time, to new opportunities offered by the peoples of the Commonwealth. Indeed, "the Commonwealth's 53 members comprise a third of humanity. Of those 2.4 billion people spread across six continents, 60 per cent are under the age of 30. They are joined with us by ties of history and friendship and the English language" (Johnson 2018).

There is not benevolent attention from less-developed peoples. On the contrary, it is the UK which now needs its Commonwealth for shaping a post-EU role for the country. It seems a process of resuscitating old elements of that epoch, giving them a new collocation by fitting with contemporary political motherland necessities and thus forging a new relation of power imbalance (thought different from the past). As a matter of fact, there are no new elements to underline. Decolonisation produced a significant shift from a (post-)imperial Britain to a twentieth- and twenty-first-century international power. The UK's geopolitical destiny changed radically in late 1967 when the country was forced to withdraw from the military bases at Suez. This event, associated with the devaluation of sterling, generated a rethinking of the country's world role and of the same idea of Commonwealth as a way to preserve the empire (Hill 2018, p. 184). The UK joined the European Economic Community (EEC) in 1973 and this choice marked another turning point, although the country had already been participating informally in the system of foreign policy coordination in Europe. It is worth noticing that, after the Second World War, the UK had not taken advantage of the Marshall Plan. Rather, it had to repay the Lend Lease loans with which it had financed the war effort. To some extent, the European accession with the 1975 referendum took place as obligatory choices. They originated from the end of the British Empire and from the economic success of the European Community at the apex of the so-called *Trente Glorieuses*, i.e., the rapid economic growth in France and Europe between 1945 and 1975.

A second important turning point to consider is what occurred in the late 1990s, following the end of the Cold War. Upon winning the election with the New Labour Party, former Prime Minister Tony Blair reasserted the guiding principles of British foreign policy. He described the UK as a 'bridge' between the US and Europe. After two years in office, in his speech to the Lord Mayor's Banquet on 22 November 1999, Blair chose a similar image, labelling the special position of Britain as a 'pivotal power'. According to Wallace, it was "a restatement of Churchill's 'three circles' doctrine, without the lost British Commonwealth and Empire" (Wallace 2005, p. 55). However, the Blairite notion of the UK's international role as a 'bridge' and 'pivotal power' was the premise for global responsibilities after the Cold War, by virtue of British history, power, influence and values (Ritchie 2014, p. 97). In this perspective, "the images of bridge and pivot, like that of the three circles before them, have partly been about the avoidance of full commitment to European cooperation" (Wallace 2005, p. 57).

The interpretation of Blair's vision as a post-Cold War version of Churchill's conception of Britain is useful in order to understand continuity and change in national role conception after Brexit. There are affinities in avoiding full commitment to European cooperation, but in this case also differences. We can put May's 'Global Britain' along the same post-imperial road of the Churchill and Blairite visions of the UK as being the centre of three intersecting circles. Yet, there are dissimilarities related to the new historical context.

The first one "is that Europe is pushed to the margins" (Hill 2018, p. 188). In her Lancaster House Speech on 17 January 2017, May represented the Brexit referendum as a choice that would direct the country well beyond avoidance of commitments to European cooperation:

> A little over 6 months ago, the British people voted for change [. . .]. They voted to leave the European Union *and* embrace the world. (May 2017b, italics added).

The thesis "to leave *and* embrace" is that the referendum not only marked the exit from Europe but also the choice for something new, outside Europe. In her following Florence speech, indeed, May opened the doors to the EU through recalling the fluid and politically neutral concept of Europe:

> We may be leaving the European Union, but we are not leaving Europe. So we are proposing a bold new strategic agreement [. . .]: a treaty between the UK and the EU. (May 2017c)

However, the Florence speech did not clarify the UK's role in Europe and, above all, it focused on creativity rather than on concrete foreign policy proposals. Some days before this speech, the government had asked for "regular close consultations on foreign and security policy issues" (HM Government 2017b, p. 18). This proposal was a too fragile step forward from the previous white paper, in which, if the EU had any place in conceptions of Britain's role, it was only on the premise that the City of London would remain a European financial centre (HM Government 2017a, p. 43). It is worth remembering that the UK has long seen itself as a country that "punches above its weight" internationally (Bond 2018, p. 13). It has often underestimated how much the extra power it exerted after decolonisation came from its EU membership. May's awareness of the risks of EU isolation may explain her greater caution in Florence. Nonetheless, her idea of 'Global Britain' completely disregards the EU's role in building a global and liberal order.

The second and related difference is about globalisation. Britons voted to leave the EU having perceived the Euro crisis of 2010 and the immigration crisis of 2015 as sufficient reasons to "abandon the Titanic" (Clausi 2017, p. 108). The promise made by the British government to become a truly 'global' actor was a post-referendum one. During the referendum campaign, economic opportunities ranging from London's role as a global financial hub, as well as issues of migration and border control, prevailed over foreign policy discussions about the UK's soft (linguistic, diplomatic) or hard (nuclear, strategic) power (Hadfield 2018, p. 175). For many leavers, the referendum signified simply getting the country back from Brussels, and recovering sovereignty and border control (Browning 2018, p. 336). Most of the leave voters did not have liberal economic positions, or the propensity to intervene to protect global security. They were not in favour of promoting international trade, transnational supply chains of goods and services, or international law and human rights. If anything, they preferred to protect the British people from the risk of globalisation. It is the difference "between global Britain, which would be committed to free trade, low taxes, and deregulation and Britain First, a country in which immigration would be reduced to very low levels, and government would intervene to bring back manufacturing jobs and the close-knit communities of the past" (Gamble 2018, p. 4).

However, in the two years following the referendum a structured narrative about where the UK should go post-Brexit emerged inside the Conservative camp. Leavers in the cabinet, the PM, the Foreign Minister, but also the Secretary of State, David Davis, and the Minister for International Trade, Liam Fox, broadly supported a free market vision of the UK outside the EU. In economic circles, their narrative was often characterised as a "Singapore-on-Thames" strategy for the UK (Hix 2018, p. 7). Despite this, the Conservative elite view is held by a minority of the public; their speeches on 'Global Britain' provided what scholars of critical geopolitics have defined as the 'discursive practice' of 'spatializing' international politics. In addition to economic issues, they envisaged also the maintenance of world stability, and support for the rules-based international system:

> And we want to secure an agreement with the EU that provides the stability and confidence for EU and UK business and individuals to achieve our aims in maintaining and developing the UK's strong trading and economic links with the EU. (May 2018a).

In his December 2019 Queen's Speech, Prime Minister Johnson reiterated the point, saying that a future relationship with the EU would be based on a free trade agreement.

Two general aspects of globalisation deserve our attention in this regard. The first one is about the *politics* of foreign policy: namely, about the ideas and activities involved in getting and using power in foreign affairs. In the Prime Minister May's speech to the World Economic Forum in January 2017, for example, the focus was on the risk that extremist parties could gather support in Europe and worldwide by feeding off a keenly felt sense among some people against globalisation:

> I want to set out a manifesto for change that responds to these concerns and shows that the politics of the mainstream can deliver the change people need. (May 2017d).

Since the creation of the Department for International Trade after the referendum vote, Fox undertook many visits to all parts of the globe in order to find new allies. In a speech delivered in Malaysia, he stated:

> The UK government's ambition is to build a Global Britain – a nation that is outward-looking and internationalist, rejecting insularity and continuing to play a prominent role in global affairs. (Fox 2017b)

These narratives are certainly against the emerging populism and sovereignism in both Europe and world politics. The same can be said for Theresa May's speech at the Bloomberg Global Business Forum, during the United Nations General Assembly in September 2018:

> And internationally – as a Global Britain – we will champion our vision for the future of the global economy: a vision that is based on openness, innovation, competition, high quality and intelligent regulation. (May 2018b)

The second and related aspect of globalisation is about the *polity* of foreign policy: namely, about the structural elements that channel political processes and thus are essential prerequisites for political actions. Relevant in this regard is the expression 'Global nation' employed by Theresa May at the Munich Security Conference on 17 February 2018:

> We are a global nation – enriching global prosperity through centuries of trade, through the talents of our people and by exchanging learning and culture with partners across the world. (May 2018c)

The basic idea of 'Global Britain' is that Britain needs agility to react as global player, to be a flexible polity or container of power. This idea of agility and flexibility is applicable to both security and economic performance. For example, according to Fox:

> In an era of globalisation, it would not be in Britain's national interest to be tied too closely politically and economically to a model that was designed for the world of the second half of the 20th century. (Fox 2018a)

The most important thing to consider is that the model under critique is the continental/European one, considered as a too old transnational/regional model of deregulating markets. The EU is therefore seen as an obstacle to globalisation, a land of potential populism. In a speech at City Week 2018, Fox had already argued:

> Whatever one's view on the referendum result, it must be acknowledged that, outside the EU, this country will enjoy a new degree of economic agility. (Fox 2018b)

According to these arguments, in China, South East Asia and Africa there are new demands for British services with enormous potential growth for UK exports outside the EU. The European Union cannot provide the degree of economic agility that Britain needs. This is like saying that globalisation has dismantled the spatial structure of the world, once based on continent or regions, and Brexit is an effect of this rupture. This idea that the world has entered a new phase of globalisation is the main point of disruption compared to the past. According to the narratives on 'Global Britain', Brexit took place because continents are no longer a political reference in a truly globalised world. In the future, the United Kingdom will act globally *alone*, being the centre of the world's growth, thus giving relevance to North America and the European Union, but first of all to the Indo-Pacific region thanks to the huge advantage of being part of the Commonwealth.

5.4   CONCLUSIONS

This chapter has first highlighted how even before the Brexit decision UK foreign policy was missing a strong strategic thinking. The unexpected outcome of the referendum put British political leadership into disarray with no feasible pathway for foreign policy, as leaving the EU was not considered a realistic option. Furthermore, during the referendum campaign foreign policy issues took a backseat as domestic questions seemed of far more importance. The strategic vacuum has been filled by revitalising traditional narratives, rooted in the expansionist past of the country when it attained global status. The concept of 'Global Britain', however far-fetched, can easily gather a people's consensus and offer elites a ready-to-use project, though it does not realistically adhere to trends within the international system. We have discussed how the conception of the role of a 'Global Britain' conflicts with the expectations and inclinations of other actors in the international system. In particular, Commonwealth countries are reluctant to allow a possible strengthening of British leadership within the organisation, proving that 'Global Britain' is primarily a solipsistic conception rather than a relational one.

In the second part of the chapter, we have tried to evaluate the *politics* and the *polity* of the narrative of 'Global Britain', through which the Conservative elite has 'spatialized' international politics. Free trade and global security are the core elements of a Global Britain's narrative and this means that the *politics* of 'Global Britain' is presented as an anti-populist plan that sees in the UK a global *polity* more fitted to face globalisation than a continental polity such as the EU. However, this conclusion is not enough to disagree with the Foreign Affairs Committee's conclusions: the slogan 'Global Britain' must be backed by substance in order to become more than a worthy aspiration.

There are no doubts, as Hedley Bull once underlined, that the Commonwealth is a myth: "the central idea of the Commonwealth myth is that the Commonwealth combines the liberty of many states with the unity of one" (Bull 1959, p. 577). Of course, as Bull concluded, all political institutions contain myths and depend upon them for their working: "If the myth of the Commonwealth presents a distorted picture of reality, it also contains elements of truth" (p. 586). Only the future will tell us about this element of truth. However, the idea of 'Global Britain' and the related rhetoric of a post-EU globalisation is the fruit of a UK-centric perspective, disregarding the positions and the postures of Commonwealth countries and other areas considered as partners for UK foreign policy.

NOTES

1. See, at https://www.instituteforgovernment.org.uk/publication/whitehall-monitor-2018/workforce.
2. UKIP won 24 out of 73 seats, 26.77% of the votes, with an increase of 11 mandates.
3. See, for instance, the establishment on December 2017 of Permanent Structured Cooperation (PESCO) that has created an innovative institutional framework for the involvement of member states in common EU defence projects and, at the same time, making the EU a leading actor in the world security arena. In the same vein, the conclusions of the European Council in June 2018 have articulated the need for a stronger role for Europe regarding its own security by reinforcing defence investment, capability development and operational readiness.
4. During the April 2018 Summit, organisation leaders accepted that Prince Charles will become the next head of the Commonwealth, while Prince Harry, the Duke of Sussex, was appointed by Queen Elizabeth as a Commonwealth Youth Ambassador (April 2018). He has since stepped down from the role.
5. According to a 2014 YouGov poll, 59% of those interviewed felt the empire was something to be proud of; while only 19% thought it was something to be ashamed of. Almost half the respondents felt the colonies were better off for being colonised; only 15% felt they were worse off and 23% were not able to give an answer. Although many (36%) are uncertain, 49% of British people that think that, overall, former British colonies are now better off for having been part of the empire while a slim 15% oppose this view. A third of British people (34%) also say they would like it if Britain still had an empire. Under half (45%) say they would not like the empire to exist today. 20% don't know (https://yougov.co.uk/news/2014/07/26/britain-proud-its-empire/, accessed 17 October 2018).

6.   This is based on Churchill's idea of three circles shaping Britain's external projection in an attempt to keep together the country's interests and traditions including the European legacy (Churchill 1950). Churchill affirmed that while "The unity of the Empire is the foundation of our Party's political belief to which we shall remain eternally faithful", there is also "absolutely no need to choose between a United Empire and United Europe. Both are vitally and urgently necessary to our Commonwealth, to Europe, and to the free world as a whole." In Churchill's vision, "The first circle for us is naturally the British Commonwealth and Empire, with all that that comprises. Then there is also the English-speaking World in which we, Canada, and the other British Dominions and the United States play so important a part. And finally there is United Europe." The three circles are coexistent and inter-linked, and Britain would maintain great influence in every one of them. As Churchill underlined, "We stand, in fact, at the very point of junction, and here in this Island at the centre of the seaways and perhaps of the airways also have the opportunity of joining them all together."

7.   Prime Minister Theresa May raised the topic of a free-trade agreement with her Indian counterpart, Narendra Modi, who asked for more visas for Indian students and easier migration, in November 2016. May could not agree, as curbing immigration was one of the prime drivers for those who voted to leave the EU.

REFERENCES

Bond, I. (2018), "Plugging in the British EU foreign policy", March, Centre for European Reform, London.

Breuning, M. (2017), "Role theory in foreign policy", *Oxford Research Encyclopedia of Politics*, New York: Oxford University Press.

Browning, C. S. (2018), "Brexit, existential anxiety and ontological (in)security", *European Security*, 27(3): 336–55.

Bull, H. (1959), "What is the Commonwealth?", *World Politics*, 11(4), pp. 577–87.

Cameron, D., "Prime Minister David Cameron's speech on the future of the EU and the UK's relationship with it", 23 January 2013, accessed 10 October at https://www.gov.uk/government/news/david-camerons-eu-speech--2.

Cantir, C. and J. Kaarbo (2012), "Contested roles and domestic politics: reflections on role theory in foreign policy analysis and IR theory", *Foreign Policy Analysis*, 8, pp. 5–24.

Churchill, W. S. (1950), "Conservative mass meeting: a speech at Llandudno, 9 October 1948", *Europe Unite: Speeches 1947 & 1948*, London: Cassell, pp. 416–18.

Clausi, L. (2017), *Uscita di sicurezza. Brexit e l'ideologia inglese*, Rome, Manifestolibri.

Foreign Affairs Committee (2018a), *The Future of UK Diplomacy in Europe*, Second Report of Session 2017–19, London: House of Commons.

Foreign Affairs Committee (2018b), *Global Britain*, Sixth Report of Session 2017–19, London: House of Commons.

Fox, L. (2017a), *Speech at the first Commonwealth trade ministers meeting*, 9 March, accessed 10 October 2018 at https://www.gov.uk/government/speeches/commonwealth-trade-ministers-meeting-towards-a-free-trading-future.

Fox, L. (2017b), *Malaysia and Britain: partners in a post-Brexit world*, 5 April, accessed 10 October 2018 at https://www.gov.uk/government/speeches/malaysia-and-britain-partners-in-a-post-brexit-world.

Fox, L. (2018a), *Brexit and beyond: Britain's place in the world in the 2020s*, 1 May, accessed 10 October 2018 at https://www.gov.uk/government/speeches/brexit-and-beyond-britains-place-in-the-world-in-the-2020s.

Fox, L. (2018b), *Global Britain: the future of international trade*, 23 April, accessed 10 October 2018 at https://www.gov.uk/government/speeches/global-britain-the-future-of-international-trade.

Franzosi, R. (1998), "Narrative analysis, or why (and how) sociologists should be interested in narrative", *Annual Review of Sociology*, 24, pp. 517–54.

Gamble, A. (2018), "Taking back control: the political implications of Brexit", *Journal of European Public Policy*, 25(8), pp. 1215–32.

Geddes, A. (2013), *Britain and the European Union*, Basingstoke: Palgrave Macmillan.

Giusti, S. (2019), "From a regional hegemony to a global power in potency: the EU's Global Strategy", in S. Giusti and I. Mirkina (eds), *The EU in a Trans-European Space: External Relations across Europe, Asia and the Middle East*, London: Palgrave, pp. 21–42.

Hadfield, A. (2018), "Britain against the world?: Foreign and security policy in the 'age of Brexit'", in Benjamin Martill and Uta Staiger (eds), *Brexit and Beyond: Rethinking the Futures of Europe*, London: UCL Press, pp. 175–82.

Habermas, J. (1971), *Knowledge and Human Interests*, trans. J. J. Shapiro, Boston, MA: Beacon.

Hill, C. (1993), "The capability-expectations gap, or conceptualizing Europe's international role", *Journal of Common Market Studies*, 31(3), pp. 305–28.

Hill, C. (2018), "Turning back the clock: the illusion of a global political role for Britain", in M. Benjamin and U. Staiger (eds), *Brexit and Beyond: Rethinking the Futures of Europe*, London: UCL Press, pp. 183–92.

Hix, S. (2018), "Brexit: where is the EU–UK relationship heading?", *Journal of Common Market Studies*, 56(51), pp. 11–27.

Holsti, K. J. (1970), "National role conceptions in the study of foreign policy", *International Studies Quarterly*, 14(3), pp. 233–309.

HM Government (2017a), "Future partnership paper on foreign policy, defence and development", 16 September, accessed 12 October 2018 at https://assets.publishing.service.gov.uk/government/uploads/system/uploads/attachment_data/file/643924/Foreign_policy__defence_and_development_paper.pdf.

HM Government (2017b), "The United Kingdom's exit from and new partnership with the European Union", February, Cm9417, Crown Copyright, Her Majesty's Stationery Office, London.

House of Commons, Public Administration Select Committee (2011), *Who does UK National Strategy? Further Report with the Government Response to the Committee's First Report of Session 2010–11*, 28 January, HC713, accessed 10 October 2018 at https://publications. .parliament.uk/pa/cm201011/cmselect/cmpubadm/713/713.pdf.

House of Commons, Public Administration Select Committee (2012), "Strategic thinking in government: without national strategy can viable government strategy emerge?", 17 April, HC1625, accessed 10 October 2018 at https://publications.parliament.uk/pa/cm201012/cmselect/cmpubadm/1625/1625.pdf.

Johnson, B. (2018), "Commonwealth has key role to play in the bright future for Britain: article by Boris Johnson", 13 March, accessed 10 October 2018 at https://www.gov.uk/government/speeches/commonwealth-has-key-role-to-play-in-the-bright-future-for-britain-article-by-boris-johnson.

Kearns, G. (2009), *Geopolitics and Empire: The Legacy of Halford Mackinder*, Oxford: Oxford University Press.

Keukeleire, S. and J. MacNaughtan (2008), *The Foreign Policy of the European Union*, Basingstoke: Palgrave Macmillan.

Mackinder, H. J. (1902), *Britain and the British Seas*, London: William Heinemann.

May, T. (2016), "Speech: Britain after Brexit: a vision of a global Britain", Conservative Party Conference, 2 October, accessed 10 October 2018 at https://www.politicshome.com/news/uk/political-parties/conservative-party/news/79517/read-full-theresa-mays-conservative.

May, T. (2017a), "PM speech to the Lord Mayor's Banquet 2017", 13 November, accessed 10 October 2018 at https://www.gov.uk/government/speeches/pm-speech-to-the-lord-mayors-banquet-2017.

May, T. (2017b), "Speech: The government's negotiating objectives for exiting the EU", Lancaster House Speech, 17 January, accessed 12 October 2018 at https://www.gov.uk/government/speeches/the-governments-negotiating-objectives-for-exiting-the-eu-pm-speech.

May, T. (2017c), "PM's Florence speech: a new era of cooperation and partnership between the UK and the EU", 22 September, accessed 12 October 2018 at https://www.gov.uk/government/speeches/pms-florence-speech-a-new-era-of-cooperation-and-partnership-between-the-uk-and-the-eu.

May, T. (2017d), "Davos 2017: Prime Minister's speech to the World Economic Forum", 19 January, accessed 12 October 2018 at https://www.weforum.org/agenda/2017/01/theresa-may-at-davos-2017-her-speech-in-full/.

May, T. (2018a), "PM speech on our future economic partnership with the European Union", 2 March, accessed 12 October 2018 at https://www.gov.uk/government/speeches/pm-speech-on-our-future-economic-partnership-with-the-european-union.

May, T. (2018b), "PM speech at the Bloomberg Global Business Forum", 26 September, accessed 12 October 2018 at https://www.google.com/search?q=PM+speech+at+the+Bloomberg+Global+Business+Forum%3A+26+September+2018&ie=utf-8&oe=utf-8&client=firefox-b.

May, T. (2018c), "PM speech at Munich Security Conference", 17 February, accessed 12 October 2018 at https://www.gov.uk/government/speeches/pm-speech-at-munich-security-conference-17-february-2018.

Ó Tuathail, G. (1996), *Critical Geopolitics: The Politics of Writing Global Space*, London: Routledge.

Ó Tuathail, G. and J. Agnew (1992), "Geopolitics and discourse: practical geopolitical reasoning in American foreign policy", *Political Geography*, 11, pp. 190–204.

Oppermann, K., R. Beasley and J. Kaarbo (2019), "British foreign policy after Brexit: losing Europe and finding a role", *International Relations*, at https://doi.org/10.1177/0047117819864421.

Ritchie, N. (2014), "A citizen's view of 'national interest'", in Timothy Edmunds, Jamie Gaskarth and Robin Porter (eds), *British Foreign Policy and the National Interest: Identity, Strategy and Security*, Basingstoke: Palgrave Macmillan, pp. 85–101.

Subotić, J. (2016), "Narrative, ontological security, and foreign policy change", *Foreign Policy Analysis*, 12(4), pp. 610–27.

Thatcher, M. (1988), "Speech to the College of Europe, Bruges, September 20", Margaret Thatcher Foundation, accessed 22 October 2018 at https://www.margaretthatcher.org/document/107332.

The Economist (2019), "Macron's view of the world", 9 November.

Walker, S. G. (2017), "Role theory as an empirical theory of international relations: from metaphor to formal model", *Oxford Research Encyclopedia of Politics*, New York: Oxford University Press.

Wallace, W. (2005), "The collapse of British foreign policy", *International Affairs*, 1, pp. 53–68.

PART II

THE ECONOMICS OF BREXIT

6. The role of social capital explaining Brexit

Pompeo Della Posta and Scheherazade S. Rehman

6.1 INTRODUCTION

The European Union (EU) structure necessitates its member states to coordinate across policy and legal arenas on a broad range of economic, political and social issues. Of the now 27 member states, 19 countries have moved from a single market (in which goods, services, people and capital move freely) towards a currency area, commonly referred to as the Eurozone. Over the last decade, the EU and the Eurozone have faced innumerable challenges and crises that have overlapped, amongst others, the Greek debt crisis, the immigration and refugee crisis, the annexation of Crimea by Russia, the rise of populist parties, high unemployment and anemic economic growth, the growing terrorist threats, and the June 2016 UK referendum on EU membership (Brexit). Several observers argue that the latest serious challenge to the EU of a UK exit from the EU's single market, i.e., Brexit, may be a blessing in disguise and a hard but necessary lesson to skeptical EU members about why the EU is a desirable and necessary supranational structure for Europe: if that is true, then, Brexit may have finally laid bare the pros and cons of leaving the EU community.

The first part of this chapter analyzes the possible reasons behind Brexit. It tracks the performance of the UK economy and examines the social capital issues of increasing economic inequality and ethnic diversity up until 2016, when the Brexit vote was taken, arguing that both factors served as drivers that created a fertile socioeconomic ground for populism towards Brexit. It is our conclusion that Brexit occurred mostly because of a shrinking social capital, i.e., softer social factors rather than deteriorating hard economic factors, including actual immigration.

The second part of the chapter examines the protracted UK exit process from 2016 to 2020 in an attempt to demonstrate that it was also the result of continuing issues related to social capital, i.e., growing fear of losing the benefits of being an EU member that pressed Brexit into a shambolic process. We show the slow shift of the British electorate mood from celebrating the vote to leave the EU in 2016, to second guessing their decision and having misgivings about leaving the EU once the negotiated settlement became a reality in 2018 and 2019, and then shifting back to a pro-Brexit stance exemplified by the results of the late 2019 surprise general election. We contend that both the vote for Brexit and the later resistance against giving up EU member benefits by the British electorate are related to an actual reduction in, and in some cases a perception of, decreased social capital, rather than only just hard economic factors. In doing so we examine the political carnage in the UK, from 2016 to 2019, over the decision of how to leave and the negotiation of the future relationship with the EU-27, including the thorny issue of what to do with the Northern Ireland border, which remains open. The chapter also examines possible outcomes of the Brexit process, including the likelihood of a messy "no-deal" exit of the UK from the EU.

6.2   THE ROLE OF SOCIAL CAPITAL LEADING TO BREXIT

6.2.1   The Pre-Brexit UK Economy

One of the many puzzles that have characterized Brexit has been that it occurred in an atmosphere of low unemployment rate in the UK, especially if compared to most Eurozone member countries. The unemployment rate in the UK was 5.3% in 2015 and 4.81% in 2016, recovering after the higher rates characterizing the global financial crisis, when it peaked to about 8%. As shown in Figure 6.1, these results compare extremely well with those of the European Union, where the unemployment rate, for example, peaked to 10.81% in 2013 (after the euro area crisis) and did not manage to go below 9.38% in 2015 and 8.53% in 2016, and much better with the euro area (with unemployment rates respectively of 11.92% in 2013, 10.83% in 2015 and 10.01% in 2016).[1]

Moreover, in the UK the recovery from the 2008 global financial and economic crisis has been much faster than in its Eurozone counterparts, hit severely also by the negative effects of the public debt deleveraging that occurred during the 2011–12 Eurozone crisis: in 2014 the UK's GDP growth was above 3%, much higher than the 1.33% and 1.74% respectively of the euro area and EU, that were still resentful of the austerity policies imposed on them as a way to solve the euro area crisis. The slowdown of 2015 and 2016 did not prevent the UK from growing still more than both the EU and the euro area.

Finally, GDP per capita in PPP international $ reached a level of $42,656 in 2016, increasing constantly from the about $35,289 in 2007. A similar

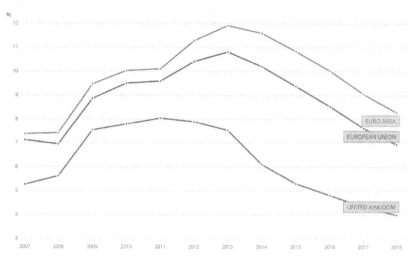

Source: https://data.worldbank.org, from International Labor Organization, ILOSTAT database.
Data retrieved September 2018.

Figure 6.1   *EU unemployment, % of labor force (modeled ILO est),*
              2007–17

trend has been followed also by EU and euro area countries (International
Comparison Program database of the World Bank, https://data.worldbank.org,
retrieved April 20, 2019).

The data reported above (especially if one focuses mainly on the figures
relative to the unemployment rate) may suggest that the choices made by the
British people were not grounded on a solid economic rationale, but they must
have been driven also by sociological motivations that may have been influenced by the role of social capital, as we are going to argue below.[2]

6.2.2   The Role of Social Capital

6.2.2.1   What is social capital?
Rather than focusing on "hard economic factors," social capital refers to
"softer social factors" (Putnam, 2017), namely to social networks and the
associated norms of trustworthiness and reciprocity or the "features of social
organization, such as trust, norms and networks that can improve the efficiency
of society by facilitating coordinated actions" (Putnam, 1993, 2000). Social
capital reflects the quality of both institutions and relationships of a community and it is, therefore, a variable that may be identified with both objective

(i.e., structural) and subjective (i.e., cognitive) elements, at both the macro and micro level (Figure 6.2).

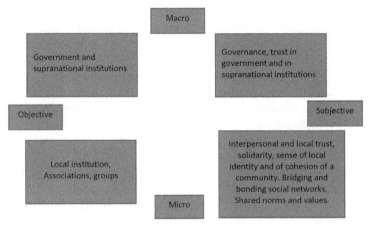

Source: Based on Grootaert and van Bastelaer (2001).

Figure 6.2   *Dimensions of social capital*

Among the subjective micro indicators we find, for example, the quality of personal relationships, including *bridging* – namely connecting – social networks and safety nets and trust, which is relevant at both the micro and macro level (Coleman, 1988).[3] Two of the main elements that have been singled out in the literature as needing special attention, however, are economic inequality and ethnic diversity.

6.2.2.2   Two relevant factors affecting social capital

6.2.2.2.1 *Economic inequality*
Inequality within both developed and developing countries has been increasing over time worldwide (Das, 2003; Della Posta, 2018a).[4] Wilkinson and Pickett (2009) show a negative correlation between economic inequality and trust. As a matter of fact, *within countries* inequality can undermine the cohesion of a community and induce a free riding behavior that would reduce the provision of public goods and the quality of democracy, and would increase the sense of frustration and favor populism.[5] Several authors, however, suggest that there may be a "tolerance" for inequality. Hirschman (1981), for example, explains it with the fact that people hope to have the same chance to enjoy, in the future,

the same higher incomes of rich people. *Equity* (namely equality of the starting points), then, might be more relevant for explaining social conflicts than *equality* (namely equality of the final outcomes) (de Soysa and Vadlamannati, 2018). In other words, economic inequality might be a necessary, but certainly not a sufficient determinant of popular protests and political conflicts.

It should also be distinguished between wealth inequality and income inequality (Alacevich and Soci, 2017). The bursting of the housing bubble accompanying the global financial crisis, then, might have played a role in depriving older people of the safety net they thought they could have relied upon, thereby explaining their voting behavior. This might have been particularly the case in the UK (and in the USA).

6.2.2.2.2 Ethnic diversity

An additional erosion of trust – and therefore of social capital – could be derived from migrations, induced by *cross-countries* inequality (Della Posta, 2018a) and quite often strongly opposed by people living in the countries of destination. As a matter of fact, according to Putnam, the inflow of migrants within a country induces *ethnic diversity* (defined in the literature also as *heterogeneous ethnicity* or *ethnic fractionalization*), which would risk destroying the social cohesion of a community, leading people to "hunker down," and to be less social, less trusting, and less altruistic (Putnam, 2007; Rhys, 2008; Belton et al., 2014).[6] Moreover, migrations might strengthen the network of incumbent domestic residents, who might feel not just entitled but even morally committed to defend the territory where they were born against the "invasion" of strangers – especially if they are also foreigners – what can be dubbed as *nativism*. This may occur, however, in spite of the economic effects of migrations, that might actually be positive, for example because migrants integrate in the host countries exhibiting a complementary rather than substitutive nature (it is sufficient to think that migrants work mostly as elderly care takers or as manual workers in physically demanding jobs that native residents do not want to take any more).

Moreover, Abascal and Baldassarri (2015) use the same database as Putnam (2007) and reach the opposite conclusion as to the effects of ethnic diversity on social capital and potential conflicts. To simplify their argument, they show that it is not ethnic diversity per se that matters, but rather the income of migrants: if white *poor* people were to move to a mostly white and wealthy neighborhood they would be equally undesired and regarded with suspicion, while if non-white but high-income newcomers were to settle down, little or no issue of ethnic diversity would be raised against them by their neighbors.

Similar conclusions had been reached by Letki (2008), who analyzes the effects of the racial context on various dimensions of social capital in British neighborhoods and by Gesthuizen et al. (2009) for whom cross-national differences in social capital in Europe would depend more on economic inequality and historical background than on ethnic diversity.

A final point to be made is relative to the possibility that the perception of ethnic diversity may well be endogenous, namely that the causation order may actually be reversed, since it might be the initial endowment of social capital to determine how ethnic diversity is perceived. In strong communities, where the sense of solidarity and trust is well developed and where social capital is rather strong, ethnic diversity might not produce any of the negative effects mentioned above and it might well be perceived as an opportunity rather than as a threat.

6.2.3   Social Capital in the UK

We are now in a position to discuss the possible explanations for Brexit and the role that social capital may have played.[7] As argued by Dustmann et al. (2017), the reasons for Brexit can be found in the many elements that also provide a fertile socioeconomic ground for populism. As a matter of fact, the UK is not alone, as populism has affected other EU countries as well. Therefore, studying the reasons for Brexit may assist us in understanding the current populist wave in the EU.

McAndrew et al. (2017) list as reasons for Brexit, together with immigration and inequality, also an anti-establishment sentiment (that may well be the result of both of the preceding issues), as well as concerns associated with the need to reaffirm national identity (as well exemplified by the slogan of the UK "leave" supporters: "we want our country back").

It is possible to argue that de-industrialization and technological progress, together with the effects of de-localizations, caused a loss of unskilled jobs and resulted in rapid social changes and internal income redistribution, thereby "leaving behind" large sectors of the population (a phenomenon that has also played a role in the USA).

In particular, the focus is on four main divides in the British population based on age, education, ethnicity and geography. Older people voted in favor of leaving the EU more than young people did (75% of people aged 18–24 voted to "remain," while only 37% of people aged more than 75 voted the same way).[8] Matti and Zhou (2017) analyze the results of the June 2016 referendum in the UK at the local government level and tested the factors that influenced the electoral outcome. Their conclusions confirm that the referendum results are also explained by demographic, rather than economic, variables.

The old/young people divide over Brexit is still puzzling, though, considering that older people should be more aware than younger people of the historic reasons for the inception of European integration – first of all the desire to avoid other world wars on European soil. But it might well be that this argument in favor of the EU is considered as "passé" and is therefore no longer sufficient, as the specter of a world war has dimmed so much that it does not justify giving up sovereignty to the European Union.[9]

Not only age, but also education impacted Brexit votes. Seventy percent of people with no higher education voted in favor of leaving with 68% of those with a degree or higher being in favor of remaining. Moreover, being white rather than black or belonging to ethnic minorities (BEM) also made a difference: 54% of white people voted in favor of the "leave" option, while 69% of BEM voted in favor of the "remain" one. Finally, a further relevant variable was the regional distribution of votes, with the "leave" votes mostly concentrated in rural areas.

One could argue, then, that

> the population seems to be split into two groups. In one group are young, well-educated individuals living in the big cities who embrace globalization, free trade, and free migration and are supportive of the EU; while in the other group are people living in rural areas who tend to be older and have less education, and fear globalization and distrust the EU. Their distrust is translated into votes for populist parties . . . . Moreover, the share of votes going to anti-EU parties has been increasing in recent years.[10]

It should be observed, however, that there are no clear economic reasons for these conclusions as old people have been affected relatively less by negative economic shocks and globalization, given their initial capital endowment and their guaranteed pensions, while less-educated people have been impacted quite substantially by those very same issues and would have clear reasons to complain (as they are the "losers" of the crisis and of globalization, for whom international trade has actually been a zero-sum game). It is difficult to find similar economic reasons in older people.[11]

Similarly, the data show that the unemployment rate amongst white British citizens was only 4% but the majority (54%) voted in favor of the "leave" option. This was paradoxical because the majority of non-white British citizens had much higher unemployment rates – ranging from 7% amongst Asians, 10% blacks, to 11% of mixed ethnicity – and they voted to "remain."[12]

Such observations strengthen the hypothesis that social capital must have played a role in Brexit, although there is one key exception with regard to "trust in others," given that this indicator has remained relatively stable over the last couple of decades in the UK (as shown by data provided by the Centre for Social Investigation, Nuffield College, Oxford, and the World Value Survey data).

The UK and the rest of Europe, however, are characterized by the deterioration of "trust" in the European Parliament and in the European Union,[13] thereby also contributing to the explanation of the recent wave of success of populist parties in some regions of continental Europe.

Other measures of social capital have also decreased in the UK (still as shown by the Centre for Social Investigation, Nuffield College, Oxford, and data from the World Value Survey). Associations with voluntary organizations, for example, have declined significantly over time: the percentage of the UK population that is active with one or more organization fell from 52% in 1993 to 43% in 2012.

The data above are consistent with the observation made by Sarracino (2010) that overall the UK indicators of social capital have been decreasing systematically over the last few decades, also in line with the increase of economic inequality with which it is negatively correlated. Loungani (2003), for example, reports that the Gini coefficient in the UK at the beginning of the 2000s had reached a value of 0.37, starting from a value of 0.27 in the 1980s.[14] Although in more recent years such a value had stabilized (for those data see the Figure "Disposable Income Inequality in the UK," in the Standardized World Income Database v8.0, 2019), the decreasing value of most indicators of trust could be due, then, also to the persistence of high income inequality. So, even if unemployment remained low and income did not perform badly, a large part of the British population may have been unhappy because of the persistently high degree of inequality that, moreover, in 2014 had started increasing again.

An important role, in the end, may have been played by the "lack of connection." Old or poorly educated people, and those living in rural areas, for example, might have "felt alienated from cosmopolitanism," as argued by McAndrew et al. (2017) who also state that "connectedness" to others and to localities is positively correlated to favorable attitudes towards the EU.

This might well explain the enigma of the similar behavior followed by old people, poorly educated people and people living in rural areas: they all have in common the feature of "disconnectedness," reducing the sense of belonging and of participation. This is also consistent with the role that economic inequality might have played in Brexit, which may increase the sense of "disconnectedness" (especially if perceived as economic "inequity," as discussed above). And in turn, this is coherent with the role played by social capital because in the end "connectedness," together with its corollaries of participation and inclusion, is a crucial and critical component of the subjective and micro-level social capital. It goes without saying that such a sense of "disconnectedness" is amplified if, as is the case in the UK, relatively old and poorly educated people are concentrated in rural areas, where the "leave" vote prevailed.

It has to be acknowledged, though, that the broader category of "disconnectedness" (no matter whether real or perceived) cannot encompass the white/BEM divide, since, if anything, BEM are surely less connected than white people. This is, then, precisely where the fear of heterogeneous ethnicity starts playing a role in Brexit. Still, analyzing things from a rational point of view, it should be difficult to reconcile the Brexit outcome with such an aspect, for the simple reason that a large number of immigrants into the UK have come from outside the European Union. Moreover, the UK would have had in the past the option to limit the inflow of immigrants from new EU accession countries, in particular from Bulgaria and Romania and had decided not to do it. This last point has probably been the most misinterpreted or, at least, misrepresented by politicians in order to collect the popular vote ahead of the Brexit referendum. It should be underlined also that, still quite paradoxically and surprisingly, the way heterogeneous ethnicity is usually approached ignores the fact that the successful outcome of a multi-ethnic society like, for example, the USA can be brought as evidence that ethnic diversity may actually be a source of economic strength rather than weakness.

Charron and Rothstein (2014) argue that not only economic inequality and ethnic heterogeneity may affect "trust" at the macro level, but also civic participation and institutional quality. They enlarge their analysis to subnational variations of trust and find strong and robust evidence that institutional quality – measured as a public sector that allocates services impartially and without corruption – is the strongest determinant of regional variations in trust within countries, while the others are not significant. It is not difficult to understand the role that the quality of institutions may play in providing the necessary support for trust at the macro level. However, this might well be a two-way relationship, since the quality of institutions itself may be the result of some of the components of social capital, including civic participation, through which it would be possible to monitor and favor the correct behavior of institutions.

Economics, however, also still plays a role in affecting social capital. As a matter of fact, it is difficult to separate the two. Economic globalization, for example, certainly bears some responsibility for both the higher degree of inequality within the UK (due to the unskilled jobs displacement from North to South and from West to East), and for the economic effects produced by the large migratory movements also induced, among other factors, by the increase in *cross-countries* inequality (at least between developed and least developed countries). An additional example is provided by Zoega (2017), who argues that the global financial and economic crisis might have had long-lasting effects reflecting in a deterioration of trust towards institutions and in polarization in politics, "often ending with the rule of populist right-wing parties, as also shown by Funke (2016)." Moreover, financial crises are often followed by rage and anger, as described by Galbraith (1954) and Aliber and Kindleberger (2014).[15] This may create, then, the ideal conditions for populist movements to emerge, even in countries characterized by flexible labor markets that have been able to recover from the financial crisis as quickly as the UK has done.

Within countries inequality and insecurity, no matter whether real or only perceived by some sectors of the population (determined also by ethnic fractionalization and the financial crisis), have created a situation whereby relying simply on an economic recovery would not necessarily take care of their dissatisfaction. Thus Zoega (2017) proposes that the EU should focus on common interests (following the principle of subsidiarity), increase positive externalities,[16] and reduce negative externalities.[17]

In other words, as argued by Dustmann et al. (2017), populist electoral choices – including then, we add, the threats to the process of European unification – can be avoided by taking care of the "losers" from both technology and globalization advancements.

This is particularly true today – still in our view – when two of the three main reasons behind the process of European integration, namely the threat of communism and the fear of new wars, are not there anymore. The third one was the protection of Europe against the challenge coming from global economic and political superpowers.

British citizens, legitimately of course, believe that they are better able to protect themselves and their future economic and social well-being by remaining on their own and leaving the EU, rather than adhering to a united Europe.

Time will tell whether they are right.

6.3   THE ROLE OF SOCIAL CAPITAL AND THE UNFOLDING OF BREXIT

The preceding sections have discussed the role the reduction of social capital (perceived and actual) played in leading the UK down an arduous decision to exit the EU single market. The two key elements of disconnectedness, a persistently high economic inequality and the fear of ethnic diversity (i.e., larger ethnic heterogeneity), served as drivers to create a fertile socioeconomic ground for populism ahead of the 2016 Brexit vote. This section of the chapter examines the process of Brexit after the vote. It follows the populace's exit vote in 2016, calling for a "hard" exit, to a chaotic scramble by the population and politicians to orchestrate a "softer" Brexit and even second guess the Brexit decision, and then with some degree of Brexit fatigue vote a decisively pro-Brexit government into power in late 2019. Unlike the factors leading up to Brexit, the post-vote Brexit process, on the surface, seems to be driven more by hard economic factors, i.e., loss of terms of trade rather than social capital. We attempt to show that the protracted UK exit process from 2016 to 2019 was demonstrative of the growing fear of losing economic benefits associated with being an EU member and influence over Northern Ireland, and resulted in political chaos and a muddled Brexit process which may have spillovers into loss of social capital, but it is too early to tell. We trace the slow shift of the

British electorate mood from celebrating the vote to leave the EU in 2016 to second-guessing their decision and having misgivings about leaving the EU once the negotiated settlement become a reality in 2018 and 2019, and then reverting once more to a pro-Brexit mood after prolonged uncertainty and Brexit fatigue. In doing so we examine the UK political chaos over the decisions on not only how to leave but also how to try and navigate a future relationship with the EU-27. This includes the key issue of the Northern Ireland border in a post-Brexit world. The following section serves to show that we also associate the growing resistance to a "hard" Brexit by the British electorate to issues related not only to fears of economic fallout from Brexit but also those that spill over to reduce social capital. A lack of a clear social block supporting the Brexit process and the ensuing social and political fragmentation could reflect a deeper lack of social capital. Sound social capital would be a linchpin to enact a speedy and coherent Brexit process, but the British experienced difficulty in finding a clear, coherent and linear approach to implement Brexit. This could be a further sign of the weakness of social capital in the UK. However, for the time being, this can only be just a conjecture. The following section not only examines this journey but also the possible outcomes of the Brexit process, including the likelihood of a messy "no-deal" exit of the UK from the EU.

6.3.1   Brexit Process

On June 23, 2016, the UK held a national referendum on whether it should leave or remain in the EU. The voter turnout was 71.8% (~30 million people) with 51.9% of the people voting to leave the EU versus 48.1% voting to remain in the EU. The breakdown across the UK for the yes vote to leave the EU was 53.4% for and 46.6% against. It is worth noting that internally, while England (53.4% vs 46.6%) and Wales (52.5% vs 47.5%) voted for Brexit, Scotland (62% vs 38%) and Northern Ireland (55.8% vs 44.2%) voted against Brexit.

In its aftermath, the upheaval Brexit caused in UK politics and to its economy was palatable. PM David Cameron resigned. Theresa May emerged as the "unity" candidate and became PM in wake of the Brexit referendum vote. She then invoked Article 50 of the Treaty of Lisbon on March 29, 2017, triggering the two-year process to negotiate a "hard" UK exit. May, sensing trouble with her promised "hard" Brexit plan, shocked the markets and the public by calling snap elections on June 8, 2017 (even though elections were not due until 2020) in what is now seen as a failed attempt to strengthen her political hand domestically with respect to Brexit. However, this backfired and the snap election resulted in her losing a majority in Parliament.[18]

Following this, May continued to engage in an uphill battle with her own Tory party and Parliament to come to an agreed upon UK withdrawal plan for the EU exit. Subsequent high profile resignations in mid and late 2018 of May's cabinet members (for example, Foreign Secretary Boris Johnson, a front-man for Brexit and David Davis, "Brexit minister" in charge of negotiating the country's split from the EU) left the UK government in disarray. The problems for Brexit were further exacerbated when not only the UK Parliament but the EU also rebuffed what was known as May's main negotiated exit plan for Brexit, the "Chequers plan." May resorted to threats to call for a second snap election in late 2018 to push her own party and Parliament to come to a Brexit agreement so that she could make an UK-EU agreement in good faith. This, however, fell on deaf domestic ears, and the UK Parliament rejected three versions of May's Brexit withdrawal plan. This left May's government in a state of disarray ahead of the March 29, 2019 exit deadline. In the week leading to the exit deadline, the UK saw one of the largest marches in its history of over a million citizens in London demanding a second Brexit referendum. The March 29 deadline passed with May having no draft UK plan to present to the EU for negotiation and the UK was forced to ask the EU for an extension. The EU granted the UK its first extension[19] on March 28 for a period of 54 days (until May 22) in the midst of increased domestic pressure on PM May to step down. In reality, however, the EU's decision forced a much shorter deadline of April 12 due to the May 23 European parliamentary elections. The EU had insisted that if they were to consider the option of a long extension for the UK, it could not simultaneously maintain "legal order" in the EU if the UK did not take part in the European Parliamentary elections in May. This effectively forced a new deadline of April 12 on PM May's government or the country would suffer a no-[withdrawal]deal Brexit as it was the last date by which the UK had to decide whether or not to hold European Parliament elections. On April 11, in an emergency session, the EU granted May her second extension of Article 50 until October 31, 2019 which de facto mandated that the UK cooperated with the EU with "sincerity." This second extension mandated that PM May move ahead and hold European parliamentary elections, which further undermined her government's credibility.

Until June 2019, there were three critical Brexit dilemmas within the UK. First, PM May was unable to govern a majority in the UK Parliament in support of a negotiated settlement (binding Withdrawal Agreement and non-binding Political Declaration). By the March 29, 2019 exit deadline, it was clear that PM May could not get parliamentary backing for any version of the withdrawal plan within her own party and its partnership with the Northern Ireland Democratic Unionist Party (DUP) (and nor from opposition MPs). The parliamentary stance was that it would not consent to the EU's "rule-making authority" as it would result in "Brexit in Name Only" (Norway is an example of this type of EU free trade agreement (FTA)). Second, a key negotiation sticking point for all parties (not only the Conservatives led by May, but various parties in the UK Parliament and the EU-27 itself) were the special trade concessions regarding the Northern Ireland border during the transitional Brexit period and in the event of a no-deal Brexit, otherwise known as the Irish "back-stop." A free trade area was proposed across all sectors with a customs union for Northern Ireland where the UK had to implement the EU's common external tariff in full. This meant that the UK would not be able to operate an independent trade policy, despite statements to the contrary. The third dilemma concerned the UK's ability to forge ahead with FTAs with non-EU countries in a timely fashion.

Brexit is multifaceted and it was clear by May 2019 that PM May could not survive politically as she could not bring about an internal consensus (within her own party and the UK Parliament) and achieve a tentative October 2019 UK–EU agreement. May ultimately resigned on June 7, 2019 and Boris Johnson became the new UK PM on July 22, 2019. Johnson had a deadline of October 31, 2019 and while he managed, against all odds, to strike a slightly altered deal with the EU for Brexit, he failed to reach the deadline due to his own Parliament's resistance to the new plan. In part, his deal resolved most of the issues of the Irish back-stop and the UK ability to sign FTAs with non-EU countries, but parliamentary backing was still an issue and ultimately forced, yet again, another UK general election. This is discussed in more detail in Section 6.3.5.

Johnson's withdrawal agreement was finally approved by the UK Parliament in December 2019 and gained Royal Assent in January 2020, having been put through several politically complex steps of EU legal process. It was then presented to the European Council (27 heads of government) and required approval from at least 20 countries which must represent 65% of the population; following this, the draft agreement was ratified by the European Parliament. A transition period until the end of 2020 has been enacted to smooth the pathway to post-Brexit relations. This will allow UK and EU businesses and others to prepare for new post-Brexit rules. The commonly referred to "worst-case" scenario of a no-deal Brexit has been avoided. If, at some stage in the future, the UK has a change of heart and wants to re-join the EU with a second referendum, it will have to apply like any other non-member country.

6.3.2   A Negotiated Brexit Settlement

De facto, Brexit means the UK will leave the EU single market, customs union, common agricultural policy and the common fisheries policy and the UK will cease to contribute towards the EU budget and involvement in crafting common EU policies.[20] PM May's government initiated the process to put forward the plan for its formal post-Brexit relationship with the EU in December 2017, which subsequently led to the fall 2018 UK government's white paper on *The Future Relationship between the United Kingdom and the European Union*, otherwise known as the "Chequers plan."[21] The plan was an all-encompassing attempt to put the binding Withdrawal Arrangements and non-binding issues known as "Political Declarations" under one umbrella. The formal Withdrawal Agreement is a binding protocol that determines the nature of the UK–EU-27 FTA specifically related to the issue of the Northern Ireland border (Irish back-stop), the UK's financial settlement obligation of £39 billion for leaving, and EU-27 and UK citizen's rights in the aftermath of Brexit. The Political Declaration, on the other hand, is a non-binding attempt to navigate the future relationship of the UK–EU-27 post-Brexit on a wide range of issues ranging from economic cooperation and security protocols to aviation and nuclear power, to legal governance. It attempts to layout the frameworks needed to enforce the withdrawal agreement (Mobility Framework and the Joint Institutional Framework).

PM May's overall negotiated settlement plan was an attempt, through a binding withdrawal agreement and non-binding political declarations towards ". . . ensuring trade cooperation, with no hard border for Northern Ireland, and global trade deals for the UK." Thus, it is important to note that ". . . while the official binding withdrawal agreement and the non-binding political declarations are two separate documents and are different in nature, they are part of the same negotiated Brexit settlement package."[22] Moreover, the binding withdrawal agreement only covers the period from the UK's exit date until the end of 2020. While new UK–EU-27 agreements can be struck, they will have to follow the basic tenets laid out in the political declaration. As such, both are equally important for a successful Brexit.

PM May's attempted comprehensive negotiated settlement went seriously awry. She severely miscalculated the shifting mood of the British public and her own party MPs as her Chequers plan never reached the EU for a vote. The plan and its numerous forced subsequent revisions were repeatedly voted down by her own Parliament and she suffered resounding defeats at the hands of her own MPs. May was given two extensions by the EU at the eleventh hour of April 12 and October 31. It appeared at that point that the UK government had only three choices left; a no-deal Brexit, a long delay involving holding European parliamentary elections on May 23, 2019, or hold a second referendum to revoke Brexit altogether. May had no choice but to opt for the second choice and hold European parliamentary elections in the aftermath of the second extension. Any new plan by the British government would invariably be a "softer Brexit" than the envisioned "hard" Brexit that former PM May or current PM Johnson originally promised.

In early summer 2019, May's various versions of the withdrawal plan, which was a compromise proposal that would keep British industry and agriculture in the EU single market and customs union while restricting the free movement of citizens and services between the UK and the EU, had all but been rejected by the EU as well. The UK plan was seen by the EU as undermining the multifaceted EU single market conciliations and hard-fought compromises for the past six decades. The EU was generally opposed to any long-term arrangement that would afford the UK special trade status with Northern Ireland and is very reticent to allow the UK to bypass EU single market harmonized good and services regulations and standards while having access to its single market. Moreover, the UK mostly only wants a "goods" agreement with the EU single market and this is unacceptable to the EU who sees the UK cherry-picking parts of their EU single market. The EU rightly believes this will undermine competitiveness and skew the level playing field for its remaining 27 member countries. Johnson's October 2019 negotiations, while outlining broad ideas and, in part, resolving most of the issues of the Irish back-stop and the UK ability to sign FTAs with non-EU countries, delayed the details of the FTA for Brexit (see Section 6.3.5). In the end the withdrawal agreement was ratified by the UK on 23 January 2020 and by the EU on 30 January 2020; it came into force on 31 January 2020.

6.3.2.1   The "binding" withdrawal arrangement
There were three critical components to the binding withdrawal agreement. First, is the monetary cost of exit which the UK bears (approximately £39 billion); second, the question of what happens to the Northern Ireland border given a new formal Free Trade Agreement (FTA) relationship with the UK and EU-27 since Ireland will remain in the EU; and third, what happens to UK citizens living elsewhere in the EU and EU citizens living in the UK. It should be noted that the main road block for former PM May's withdrawal agreement with both her own Parliament and the EU, had been the issue of the Northern Ireland border in the event of a "no-deal" Brexit. Johnson managed to renegotiate a softer version of the Northern Irish border deal which is discussed in Section 6.3.5.

6.3.2.1.1   Formal UK–EU FTA/FCA relationship post-Brexit
The UK envisioned its formal post-Brexit relationship as a proposed "customs system" – the Facilitated Customs Arrangement (FCA). The plan met with serious skepticism from the EU as it was seen to include proposals for the UK to preserve EU rules as they pertain to "goods" and to treat the UK/EU as a "combined customs territory." With respect to agriculture and trade, the various draft plans the UK had released envisioned a UK–EU "common rulebook for all goods including agri-foods" while the UK additionally would commit (in all other sectors) towards ongoing harmonization with EU rules (where pertinent) to afford seamless trade with Ireland. Essentially, this would mean that UK goods intended for the UK market would be subject to domestic

tariffs and trade policies but UK goods intended for EU markets would be charged EU tariffs and would also entail that the UK collected tariffs on behalf of the EU. While the UK Parliament would still have the prerogative to not adhere to any future EU rules there would, however, be "consequences" for UK–EU trade if that were the case. One of the key elements of the UK draft plans (for a formal Brexit relationship with the EU) was and is the politically charged issue of having a "visible border" with the Republic of Ireland. Disagreement over how to handle the Northern Ireland border emerged as the single most divisive issue that derailed May's plans for an FCA with the EU prior to the April 12 deadline. Additionally, beginning January 1, 2021, the UK envisioned that it would be able to make trade deals without EU approval.

EU members are party to 40 trade agreements with more than 70 countries which vary in scope but tend to include easier trade rules and market access, and reduced import and export tariffs/taxes. In a "no deal" Brexit, the UK would immediately no longer be a signatory to those trade deals. May attempted to "replicate" the EU trade agreements in the event of a no-deal scenario to attain "continuity and stability" as these deals were valued at approximately 11% of total UK trade. By spring of 2019, the UK had only completed eight out of the 40 "continuity" deals and had yet to secure key partners like Japan and Turkey.[23] The UK had signed "mutual recognition agreements" (not FTAs) with the USA, Australia and New Zealand. While the Australia and New Zealand deals reproduce all aspects of the current EU agreements with regard to recognizing product standards, the US agreement benefits certain sectors more than others (e.g., the pharmaceutical sector). See Figure 6.3 for the UK's top ten trading partners.

It should be noted that these "continuity" trade deals are complicated as the UK cannot replicate all the EU agreements as they pertain to specific EU law. Many countries are waiting for Brexit to be fully resolved before entering into any trade deals with the UK. The UK would have to default to the World Trade Organization (WTO) trade rules for all countries with which it has no formal trade agreement, thus allowing the flow of trade to be uninterrupted, albeit increased tariffs and barriers for certain industries would be incurred.

6.3.2.2 Northern Ireland "Back-Stop"

At the heart of Brexit, the most contentious issue has been the 499km land border between the UK territory of Northern Ireland and the Republic of Ireland (an EU member). The 1998 Good Friday Agreement brought about a long sought-after peace (demilitarization) after 40 years of violence between Northern Ireland (UK) and the Republic. This also removed barriers to free movement of goods and people. In a post-Brexit world, no one wants to see the return of a "hard" border within Ireland which would include passport and customs checkpoints. There is genuine concern for all parties involved that

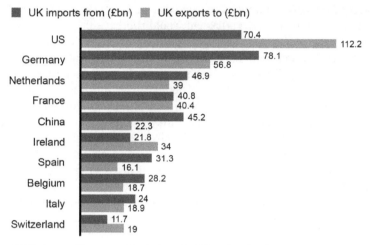

Source: UK Balance of Payments, *The Pink Book*, Office of National Statistics, UK, 2018.

Figure 6.3   UK's top ten trading partners (2017)

peace would be difficult to maintain within Ireland if this were to happen. However, this is where the agreement ends. While both the EU and UK agreed there could be no return to a hard border, they disagreed over how this Irish back-stop, in case of a no-deal Brexit, was to operate.

In an attempt to ensure that there is no return of a "hard border" between Northern Ireland and the Irish Republic once the UK left the EU, the EU insisted on an Irish back-stop arrangement. This would only come into play in January 2021 if there was no concrete UK–EU agreement. This was akin to an insurance policy in the event of a delayed or failed EU–UK formal (trade) agreement on the nature of their relationship post-Brexit. Under this EU Irish stop-gap plan, Northern Ireland would effectively remain part of the EU's customs union, in most parts of the single market, and the EU VAT system would thereby adhere to most EU regulations and standardization until such time that the UK–EU free trade agreement could be finalized. However, this would mean that there would be a customs border on goods moving between Northern Ireland and the rest of the UK. The EU insisted on a customs control border with the UK as it exited the EU single market and its customs union so that UK business could not evade EU tariffs and customs controls. This EU plan would have effectively kept the whole UK in the EU customs union for a limited period of time. It is important to note that throughout the transition period until December 31, 2020, the UK–EU trade relationship would more or less stay as it was and nothing would change until January 1, 2021 when a new permanent UK–EU free trade arrangement was to be put into place. The Irish back-stop was there just in case there was a delay between the transition period ending on December 31, 2020 and the new UK–EU free trade agreement beginning, safeguarding a "no hard border." This, however, meant that while there would be no checkpoints for goods within Ireland, trade with Northern Ireland and mainland UK would have a customs barrier thereby effectively creating a "soft" Irish Sea border between Northern Ireland and the rest of the UK (as is currently the case).

May and her Parliament had struggled to find common ground with regard to any agreement (albeit temporary or just in case) that created a new "soft" border in the Irish Sea between Northern Ireland and the rest of the UK – it was "unacceptable" to the British Parliament. Her goal was to keep the whole of the UK aligned with the EU while she negotiated a UK–EU free trade deal. While there was some internal UK political wriggle room for a possible temporary Irish back-stop deal, May at the time insisted that it would need to be "time-limited" or else the UK could potentially be tied to the EU open-endedly as currently there was no assurance of a UK–EU withdrawal deal. May's own cabinet, party, and Parliament were in perpetual disarray in attempts to find common ground on the issue of being a signatory to any agreement that could potentially keep the UK in a perpetual customs union with the EU (in the event of a no-deal). Moreover, May had a very difficult time convincing the DUP, which would not agree to any arrangement that treated Northern Ireland differently from the rest of the UK, even temporarily. The EU was skeptical about any time-limit on the Irish back-stop plan as they were understandably worried about the resurrection of a hard border if there was no UK–EU trade deal. They argued that the back-stop would only be removed once the UK–EU formal withdrawal (trade) deal had found a way around a hard border.

As a compromise, May had argued that it should be a UK back-stop and not just an Irish back-stop if a UK–EU FTA could not be enacted by January 1, 2021. Essentially, this would mean that while the UK would leave the EU sometime in 2019, it would remain in the EU single market until December 31, 2020 and then remain in a customs union indefinitely until such time as a FTA was enacted. This, however, did not sit well with May's Tory Brexiteers and other Conservative MPs because it bound the UK to EU rules and regulations for a long period of time which, they believed, undermined the Brexit vote. The EU was also against this expanded version of a back-stop stating that it allowed the UK to remain in the single market indefinitely without any EU membership obligations.

The subsequent EU–UK Brexit plan agreed by Boris Johnson in October 2019 substituted May's controversial back-stop plan with a legal customs border to be installed between Northern Ireland and the Republic of Ireland (which remains part of the EU). It should be noted that this new deal, in practice, would make the real customs border between Great Britain and the "island of Ireland," with goods being checked at the points of entry in Northern Ireland. This is discussed further in Section 6.3.5.

6.3.2.3 Financial settlement

The discussion of the Brexit financial settlement or the so-called "divorce bill" over post-Brexit payments the UK needs to make to the EU can be summed up largely in two categories. First, there was a discussion about whether the UK was required to pay an "exit bill" to cover unsettled obligations once it left the EU. The EU claimed that the UK was obliged to continue to pay into the EU budget according to the seven-year cycle (multiannual financial framework, MFF) from 2014 to 2020 (the UK was a signatory). This bill was estimated to be about £50 billion (approximately US$62 billion). On the flip side, the UK had entitlement to EU assets, for example, a 16% share of the European Investment Bank (EIB) worth approximately £8.8 billion. Initially, this was a hotly contested topic on both sides and the estimates of the bill ranged from £36 billion to £50 billion. However, by late 2018, a financial settlement of $39 billion was seen as the most likely by all parties involved. The issue of continuing disbursements the UK would need to make to the EU for special access to EU markets (goods, services and financial), however, were yet to be resolved fully. Agreements of the formal trade deal within the withdrawal framework were well on their way even amidst no sign of May's Parliament approving any unified British proposal to send to the EU.

It is important to remember that the central issue in the financial settlement is that Article 50 does not spell out financial liabilities, so we were in unchartered waters of trade negotiations. May's position was a particularly difficult one as the UK was internally split on whether it had the MFF obligation which was originally estimated at £39 billion. The EU position that trade negotiations should not be linked to the UK's Brexit financial obligations was not gaining traction in the UK. Either way, the final amount paid by the UK for its past commitments would most certainly impact the outcome of future continuing payments to the EU through a UK–EU trade deal. However, due to the Brexit delay, the new estimate of the divorce bill was now £33 billion under PM Johnson's plan. This is discussed further in Section 6.3.5.

6.3.2.4 Citizen's rights

The withdrawal agreement would effectively end the "free movement of people" burden for the UK. A proposed "mobility framework" would be set up to allow UK and EU citizens to travel with relative ease between the territories for work and study. Currently, 4.5 million UK and EU citizens will be impacted, of which 3.2 million are EU citizens living in the UK (this includes citizens of Iceland, Liechtenstein, Norway and Switzerland, who all have various agreements with the EU). Of the estimated 1.3 million UK citizens living in the EU, the majority reside in Spain, Ireland, France, Germany and Italy, in rank order.[24] In the event of a no-deal withdrawal, the EU emphatically stated that there would be no side-deal on citizen's rights and the mobility framework had to be part of the larger withdrawal agreement. This created a lot of labor uncertainty for UK citizens in the event of a no-deal withdrawal, in particular, as while May had indicated her willingness to allow EU-27 citizens to remain in the UK, the same could not be said for the EU-27 governments treatment of UK citizens within their borders.

6.3.3   Non-Binding Political Declarations

The UK hoped to manage other future critical issues, such as economic and security cooperation, governance and institutional legal frameworks with the EU through "non-binding" political declarations. The political declarations would serve to provide a basis for taking into account both the UK and EU red lines and principles post-Brexit. The wide areas of the topics under the non-binding UK–EU-27 political declarations were designed to maintain the spirit of Article 50 of the Treaty on European Union within Brexit. The political declaration committed the UK to "an ambitious, broad, deep and flexible partnership across trade and economic cooperation, law enforcement and criminal justice, foreign policy, security and defense and wider areas of cooperation."[25] The EU hard red lines are mainly concerned with maintaining EU principles and rules, and primarily that EU law will supersede UK law in the post-Brexit relationship. The EU core values and rights, especially with respect to human rights law, were an EU precondition to any UK–EU-27 trade agreement.

Other issues under the political declarations include future protocols on cooperation on data protection; cooperation in services and investment; transport, energy, fishing, competition and agriculture policy; security partnership and foreign, intelligence and defense policy and the legal institutional framework; a commitment by the UK to fund a portion of the Northern Ireland PEACE PLUS program; the UK open to rejoining the European Investment Bank, and UK participation in EU programs (science, culture, overseas development, defense, foreign policy and space) which would be subject to EU law and require a financial contribution from the UK, all of which are still to be determined.

6.3.3.1   Governance and institutional issues
The negotiated settlement anticipated a transition period ending on December 31, 2020 to smooth the pathway to post-Brexit relations and allow UK and

EU businesses and others to prepare for new post-Brexit rules. Additionally, a "Joint Institutional Framework" was proposed to be established to interpret UK–EU agreements. While each territory would utilize its own courts, UK courts would be obliged to refer to EU case law on UK–EU agreements (utilize a common rulebook). It should be noted that under this arrangement, cases could still be referred to the European Court of Justice (ECJ), the interpreter of EU rules, although the ECJ would not have the authority to resolve disputes between the UK and EU.

6.3.4   Future Brexit FTA/FCA Relationship

The outcome of the UK–EU trade deal can take a variety of shapes and shades. In its simplest form the UK could simply remain in the EU customs union but rest assured the EU would want some form of reparation for the privilege of access to the customs union without membership obligations. Alternatively, the UK and EU can use existing agreements, such as the European Economic Area (EEA) or the EU–Canada-style free trade agreement (FTA). A last possibility is the so-called nuclear option of the UK exiting without a deal – the "No-deal" scenario. After briefly reviewing below the first three options, this section focuses on the last and most undesirable scenario as the other options are discussed elsewhere in this book.

6.3.4.1   UK–EU customs union
In the short to medium term it would seem that a quick way to solve this impasse would be to simply create a UK–EU customs union until such time a technically workable Northern Ireland border agreement is carved out. This would effectively remove any UK–EU customs checks but the UK would have to agree to the EU's single (internal) market regulatory rules between Northern Ireland and the UK mainland. This solution, however, would have been difficult to sell within the UK as a UK–EU customs union would have meant that PM May's "Facilitated Customs Arrangement" proposal and any UK strategies to create FTAs with non-EU countries would have had to be shelved. The UK Conservative Party's "Hard Brexit" supporters would not have supported any agreement that would restrict the UK's ability to sign new trade deals with non-EU countries. PM May could not even get the parliamentary backing of her own party and the DUP to create a UK–EU customs union. Moreover, the DUP would not vote for any agreement that instituted any "new" EU trade regulations between Northern Ireland and the rest of the United Kingdom. PM Johnson's plan was also short on details with regard to the trade agreement.

6.3.4.2 UK–EU Free Trade Agreement (FTA)

An EU free trade agreement (FTA), such as the EU–Canada deal was a non-starter for PM May, and also subsequently for PM Johnson, as an FTA would have effectively put Northern Ireland within the EU's regulatory and customs control which was unacceptable to the UK (Johnson himself and all parties in the UK Parliament).

6.3.4.3 UK joins the European Economic Area (EEA)

A seemingly reasonable solution would have been to take Norway's path and for the UK to have joined the existing European Economic Area (EEA), allowing for free movement of goods, services, capital, and people. This was also seen as the last resort if there were a no-deal Brexit.

6.3.4.4 No-deal Brexit

The reality of a protracted withdrawal settlement and a no-deal exit was still likely. The UK had missed many Brexit deadlines in 2019 (March 29, April 12, and October 31). The reality of a no-deal Brexit was still probable under PM Johnson. First, Johnson's Brexit plan with a new agreement on the Irish "soft" border was rejected by Parliament on October 22, 2019 for "fast track" debate and approval. This legally forced Johnson to ask the EU for a three-month extension. EU leaders were in turn forced to reconsider another extension for the UK, extending the deadline to January 31, 2020. In the wake of the EU extension, Johnson called a general election on December 12, 2019 in the hopes of getting a clear mandate to meet the new January deadline. Johnson won a landslide victory and, of course, the Brexit deal was approved by a large majority later that month.

It is highly probable that if the UK–EU Brexit agreements had faltered or if future deadlines were missed, the UK would have been taken to court by the EU. Moreover, lack of a deal would have been extremely disruptive to manufacturing supply chains for both the UK and EU, and the political fallout would have been multifold; a no-deal would have branded the UK symbolically as the reason for new political divisions within the EU, it would have complicated matters on the United Nations Security Council, and weakened security and antiterrorism efforts – not to mention the unresolved thorny issue of a hard physical border between the UK and Ireland.

While there were numerous deals and no-deal outcomes possible for the UK–EU breakup, it should be noted that a no-deal was the official default option under Article 50 of the Treaty of Lisbon with respect to the actual withdrawal treaty. If this were to occur, the UK would default into a WTO relationship with the EU and, in all likelihood, over time become a "multi-deal" Brexit as many bilateral agreements would in all probability ensue.

It should be noted that in the absence of a government negotiated settlement, the UK Parliament had always had the right to pass a withdrawal treaty (needing a majority vote) without the involvement of the PM's office. In fact, it voted and claimed that right in spring 2019 just ahead of the March 29 deadline. However, it failed to pass any of its own numerous versions of a Brexit deal thus far discussed. Alternatively, Parliament had the option to overturn Brexit. If the latter more radical (but less likely) option had been taken, the House of Commons would in all probability have had to introduce a new referendum process. This would have required coordination with the European Council and an EU extension beyond January 31, 2020 for the settlement agreement. It should be noted that although the door for a second referendum was reopened in late October 2019 when PM Johnson's fast-track Brexit failed in Parliament, it was slammed shut with the Conservative Party's landslide victory in the December 12, 2019 general election. Regardless, a no-Brexit deal was still a possibility as the January 31, 2020 deadline loomed and if it were to occur the EU and the UK would be in uncharted waters.

PM May's office had struggled with the reality that the House of Commons would not approve any Brexit deal she put forward and, as feared, she had to step down. The delayed Brexit deal had already forced the UK to participate in the May 2019 EU parliamentary elections to ensure a seamless changeover. Subsequently, PM Johnson's leadership style, although creating more confusion, ironically brought the UK closer to a Brexit deal. However, both the EU and UK were still ill-prepared to deal with the aftermath which would have required renewed and intense negotiations with regard to the most pressing problem of the UK–EU FTA and that of Northern Ireland. This would have been a Herculean technical challenge which, in all probability, would have needed more time and included the UK paying a new financial settlement bill. In all likelihood all entities would have had to quickly put into place some provisional arrangements to resolve the many technical problems so as to ease the UK goods, services and capital access to and from what would be effectively the EU border (Ireland). The movement of people issue was expected to be a more of a medium-term matter as neither side was in any rush to revoke work and study visas. Nonetheless, a no-deal Brexit would have been difficult for both sides, impacting manufacturing and jobs negatively in the short to medium term. The downsides of a no-deal were not lost on either side, bolstering pro-EU MPs' calls for a second Brexit referendum. Although, at that time, the negotiations had been acrimonious, it seemed more likely than not that some form of UK–EU withdrawal deal would probably happen, probably with several extensions as no one wanted to see a no-deal Brexit. There were, however, many who argued that a bad deal would be worse than no deal for both parties.

The so-called nuclear option of the UK simply leaving the EU with no settlement agreement in place was plausible. This would almost assuredly (in the short to medium term) have destabilized markets, exchange rates and the economic outlook. The EU leadership was keenly aware that the nuclear option of the UK simply leaving the EU with no deal in place would only force all parties to revert back towards the EEA. This was not an undesirable outcome for the EU.

A no-deal UK–EU-27 stalemate would have invariably led to fresh general elections in the UK and de facto increased uncertainty and instability for both the UK and the EU. It was thus increasingly likely that both the UK and EU would push for an interim arrangement due to the dire specter of a no-deal scenario sometime prior to the end of the transition period of December 31, 2020 as the hard Brexit was due to be enforced on January 1, 2021.

The political landscape in the UK was shifting given that the initial British electorate unease of leaving the EU permanently was being replaced by Brexit uncertainty and fatigue, and eventually the landslide electoral mandate for the Conservatives under Johnson to "get Brexit done." While pressures on the issues of the Irish back-stop and the UK's future ability to sign FTAs with non-EU countries had eased with the new Johnson plan, his chances of bringing about Brexit by January 31, 2020 were still suspect at the time. However, the withdrawal agreement was ratified by the UK on 23 January 2020 and by the EU on 30 January 2020; and it came into force on 31 January 2020.

6.3.5   Final Brexit Deal?

As many predicted in early 2019, any Brexit negotiated settlement would have involved a new UK prime minister – May resigned on June 7, 2019 and ushered in a controversial Boris Johnson on July 22, 2019, who then subsequently had to call for general elections on December 12, 2019 because he could not push Brexit through by its October 31, 2019 deadline. Much to everyone's surprise Johnson fast-tracked a new agreement with the EU but unfortunately not his own Parliament and missed the October deadline. The new EU–UK Brexit deal replaced PM May's controversial Irish back-stop plan, but much of her trade deal remained intact. Essentially, the plan calls for the UK to exit the EU customs union in its entirety which would allow the UK to negotiate trade deals with other countries in the future without EU permission (a key issue for the UK). A legal customs border will be installed between Northern Ireland and the Republic of Ireland (which remains part of the EU); however, in practice, the real customs border will be between Great Britain and the island of Ireland, with goods being checked at the points of entry in Northern Ireland. Practically speaking, there will be no duty tax on goods being exported from Great Britain to Northern Ireland but "goods at risk" of being moved into the

Republic of Ireland will incur duty tax. A joint EU–UK committee will decide the list of goods at risk at a future date. The discussion on UK tax refunds of goods at risk that incurred duty tax but did not end up in the EU is also to be discussed at a later date. Citizens and private transactions are not impacted by this duty tax. It is important to note that with respect to the regulation of goods, Northern Ireland will keep to EU single market rules rather than UK rules. This is practical since it removes the need for product standard and safety checks between the Ireland and Northern Ireland border, and falls under the auspices of the so-called "all-island regulatory zone." This, however, necessitates border product standard and safety checks between Northern Ireland and Great Britain which, under Johnson's October 2019 plan, have opted out of EU single market rules. These checks will be facilitated by a joint agreement (Joint Committee) between EU and UK officials. On the issue of value added tax (VAT), Northern Ireland will incur EU law on VAT but only on goods (not services) and its VAT rate will be different from UK VAT. An additional key consideration of Great Britain's agriculture aid to Northern Ireland will also be negotiated by the Joint Committee but will be in line with the amount Northern Ireland currently receives from the EU Common Agriculture Policy (CAP). The plan calls for EU and UK Citizen's Rights to remain unchanged after Brexit, in both the UK and the EU. The so-called "divorce bill" has slightly lowered from approximately £39 billion to £33 billion due to the delay in Brexit between March 29, 2019 and October 31, 2019 (as the UK continued to contribute to the 2019 EU budget and will continue to do so for the 2020 budget). Due to the subsequent new Brexit deadline of January 31, 2020, this "divorce bill" will be lower slightly again. The withdrawal agreement was ratified by the UK on 23 January 2020 and by the EU on 30 January 2020; it came into force on 31 January 2020. Most importantly, there was no change to the transition period which ends on December 31, 2020. The future of UK–EU relationships is not legally binding as it continues to fall under the "political declaration." Both sides have agreed to work towards an FTA and have agreed to reconvene in June 2020 while both "uphold[ing] the common high standards [. . .] in the areas of state aid, competition, social and employment standards, environment, climate change, and relevant tax matters." The reality of a finalized Brexit is still some time off, and a potentially bumpy road lies ahead.

6.4   CONCLUDING REMARKS

It is difficult to understand the source of Brexit by simply looking at economic causes. The UK, for example, has experienced lower rates of unemployment and higher growth rates than most of its EU neighbors in the post-Eurozone crisis era. We conclude that the populist uprising in the UK leading to the vote for Brexit was, at least in part, a result of growing mistrust and a reduction of trust and of social capital. This mistrust manifested itself due to two distinct issues: first, increasing economic inequality, which was part of a more general, actual or perceived, feeling of "disconnectedness" characterizing older and unskilled British citizens and those living in rural areas, and second, a larger ethnic diversity. Both of these factors served as a driver to create a fertile socioeconomic ground for populism towards Brexit and may have undermined the cohesion and the sense of belonging and trust of the British community, namely its social capital.

We conclude that the perception of decreased social capital (i.e., economic well-being and growing fear of losing the benefits of being an EU member) has, at least in part, resulted in what is best described as a shambolic Brexit process. This was demonstrated in the shifting mood of the British electorate and its political establishment during the post-Brexit referendum era. The UK has been left second-guessing their "hard" Brexit decision and having misgivings about leaving the EU once the negotiated settlement became a reality in 2018; and Brexit has now rolled into 2020 with its third prime minister since the referendum. While the withdrawal agreement came into force on 31 January 2020, the British still struggle to find a clear and coherent path to implement Brexit serves possibly as a further sign of the weakness of social capital in the UK. However, for the time being, this is only conjecture. In all likelihood there will be some semblance of a compromised "soft" Brexit and the UK will most likely join a "special" FTA-semi customs union agreement with the EU by paying into it in some format. Regardless, on January 1, 2021 the new UK–EU political and economic relationship is set to begin in earnest.

NOTES

1. All data above are taken from https://data.worldbank.org, accessed October 15, 2018.
2. A different conclusion, though, can be reached in the case of the yellow-green coalition – comprising the 5 Star movement and the Lega – in Italy, of Syriza in Greece, or of the right-wing governments in some Eastern European countries. Also, those experiences contain some populist and nationalist elements. In those cases, however, it is possible to see more clearly than in the case of the UK (given the low unemployment rate of the latter), that the bad economic situation might have played a role in the spreading of populism and nationalism.
3. Social capital, however, may also have *bonding* – rather than *bridging* – features. In such a case the connections are limited to a close circle of friends and families, excluding other people. *Bonding* social capital further strengthens economic inequality and is close to the idea of "cronyism," a word that became popular during the South East Asian economic and financial crisis in the second half of the 1990s.
4. This might be the result of sudden changes in the pattern of trade, changing the distribution of income (see e.g., Colantone and Stanig 2016; Dippel et al. 2015, as reported by Dustmann et al., 2017) and also because of technological develop-

ments or more favorable fiscal regimes towards high income citizens (Della Posta, 2018b).

5. See Fadda and Tridico (2017) and Center for Economic Reform (2016) for the connections between economic inequality and populism. According to Zoega (2017) populism presents the following features: anti-establishment; nativist or nationalistic; and charismatic leaders who articulate the nativist, anti-establishment policy messages, usually offering simplistic and incoherent policy proposals that sound appealing to disgruntled voters and who propose economic policies that are not good for innovation and future prosperity.

6. Similar negative effects of rising immigration on native populations are also highlighted by Dustmann et al. (2005).

7. As for the endowment of social capital (considered as based on five main criteria, relative to health, equality, crime, freedom and satisfaction), the relatively high crime rates and low availability of health services in the USA make it rank 129 (which is, quite surprisingly, worse than China, India and Brazil, ranking respectively 37, 84 and 115). As for European countries, Germany ranks 5, France 16, Italy 26 and the UK 28 (http://solability.com/the-global-sustainable-competitiveness-index/the-index/social-capital, accessed April 20, 2019).

8. This is what has been dubbed the "Ryanair effect," referring to the fact that young people see themselves more as European citizens, given the frequency with which they can fly to and from the continent.

9. This argument, however, might not hold if one thinks of the historical cultural distance between Britain and continental Europe. Even the famous 1946 Churchill speech suggesting the creation of the United States of Europe did not imply that the UK should have been part of it.

10. Ipsos MORI, "How Britain voted in the 2016 EU referendum", September 5, 2016; YouGov UK, "How Britain Voted," June 27, 2016.

11. A different conclusion can be drawn, however, when considering the negative wealth effect on older people, presented as a result of the dramatic fall of house prices resulting from the crisis.

12. See https://www.ethnicity-facts-figures.service.gov.uk/work-pay-and-benefits/unemployment-and-economic-inactivity/unemployment/latestdiversity.

13. In continental Europe a deterioration of trust in national parliaments has also been observed (Dustmann et al. 2017).

14. The same is true for the United States, where it has increased over time so as to reach the value of approximately 0.4. In other developed countries (Japan, Canada and many European countries), however, the redistributive policies that had been adopted allowed the Gini coefficient to remain rather stable over the last decade (OECD, Standardized World Income Inequality Database).

15. In the euro area, the euro has been blamed for not being able to shield its members against the 2008 financial crisis, and, in fact, blamed for having worsened it. The euro is also blamed for creating the crisis of 2011–12 (especially if compared to other non-euro EU members). It is difficult to argue that the euro played a specific role in Brexit, although it did create a heightened sense of mistrust in anything associated with the EU and its European institutions, given the severity of the euro area crisis.

16. As in the fight against terrorism, reducing tax evasion, agreeing on a common migratory policy, protecting the environment and – we should add – showing that it can actually operate in favor of European citizens by reducing some costs, for example, roaming for phone calls across Europe.

17. He mentions, in particular, the need to regulate capital inflows in order to avoid their destabilizing consequences, although doing so would have created new problems between the EU and the international community.
18. PM May was politically weakened in the June 2017 snap election and has had to rely on support of 10 MPs from Northern Ireland's Democratic Unionist Party in the subsequent votes.
19. The extension had to be approved by all 28 EU members – the UK plus EU-27 remaining members.
20. The UK officially withdraws from the European Union ("Union") and the European Atomic Energy Community (Euratom) in accordance with Article 50 of the Treaty on European Union (TEU). TEU applies to Euratom by virtue of Article 106a of the Treaty which established the Euratom Treaty.
21. The white paper received its nickname, the "Chequers Plan", because it was agreed by the UK cabinet at Chequers, the PM's country residence.
22. Letter written to PM May by European Commission President Jean-Claude Juncker and European Council President Donald Tusk, January 15, 2019.
23. The eight deals are with Caribbean countries (Cariforum), Pacific Islands, Israel, Palestinian Authority, Switzerland, the Faroe Islands, Eastern and Southern Africa, and Chile.
24. Trends in International Migration Stocks: The 2017 Revision, Economic and Social Affairs, United Nations publication, POP/DB/MIG/Stock/Rev.2017, December 2017.
25. Available at https://assets.publishing.service.gov.uk/government/uploads/system/ uploads/attachment_data/file/759021/25_November_Political_Declaration _setting_out_the_framework_for_the_future_relationship_between_the _European_Union_and_the_United_Kingdom__.pdf.

REFERENCES

Abascal, M. and D. Baldassarri (2015), "Love thy neighbor? Ethnoracial diversity and trust reexamined," *American Journal of Sociology*, 121(3) (November), pp. 722–82.

Alacevich, M. and A. Soci (2017), *Inequality: A Short History*, Washington, D.C.: Brookings Institution Press.

Aliber, R. Z. and C. P. Kindleberger (2014), *Manias, Panics and Crashes*, 7th Edition, Hoboken, NJ: John Wiley & Sons, Inc.

Belton, W., Y. Huq and R. U. Oyelere (2014), "Diversity and social capital in the U.S.: a tale of conflict, contact or total mistrust?," *IZA DP* No. 8384, August.

Center for Economic Reform (2016), "Conference report: Brexit and the economics of populism," Ditchley Park, Oxfordshire, November 4–5, 2016.

Charron, N. and B. Rothstein (2014), "Social trust, quality of government and ethnic diversity: an empirical analysis of 206 regions in Europe," *Working Paper Series* 2014:20.

Colantone, I. and P. Stanig (2016), "Global competition and Brexit", *BAFFI CAREFIN Centre Research Paper* No. 2016-44, Bocconi University.

Coleman, J. S. (1988), "Social capital in the creation of human capital," *American Journal of Sociology* 94, pp. S95–S120.

Das, D. K. (2003), *The Economic Dimensions of Globalization*, Basingstoke: Palgrave Macmillan.

de Soysa, I. and Krishna Chaitanya Vadlamannati (2018), "Income Inequality, equity and state terror 1976–2016," *Scienza e Pace/Science and Peace*, available at https://ntnuopen.ntnu.no/ntnu-xmlui/handle/11250/2593168.

Della Posta, P. (2018a), "Economic inequality and conflicts: an introduction," *Scienza e Pace/Science and Peace* 8(2), pp. 7–36.

Della Posta, P. (2018b), *The Economics of Globalization: An Introduction*, Pisa: ETS.

Dippel, C., R. Gold and S. Heblich (2015), "Globalization and its (dis-)content: trade shocks and voting behavior," *NBER Working Paper* No. 21812.

Dustmann, C., B. Eichengreen, S. Otten, A. Sapir, G. Tabellini and G. Zoega (2017), *Europe's Trust Deficit: Causes and Remedies*, London: CEPR Press.

Dustmann, C., F. Fabbri and I. Preston (2005), "The impact of immigration on the British labour market," *The Economic Journal* 115(507), pp. F324–F341.

Fadda, S. and P. Tridico (eds.) (2017), *Inequality and Uneven Development in the Post-Crisis World*, Abingdon: Routledge.

Funke, F. and P. T. Dunwoody (2016), "The aggression-submission-conventionalism scale: testing a new three factor measure of authoritarianism," *Journal of Social and Political Psychology* 4(2), 571–600.

Galbraith, J. K. (1954), *The Great Crash*, Boston, MA and New York: Mariner Books.

Gesthuizen, M., T. V. D. Meer and P. Scheepers (2009), "Ethnic diversity and social capital in Europe: tests of Putnam's thesis in European countries," *Scandinavian Political Studies*, 32(2), p. 121.

Grootaert, C. and T. van Bastelaer (2001), "Understanding and measuring social capital: a synthesis of findings and recommendations from the social capital initiative," *Social Capital Initiative Working Paper* No. 24 , The World Bank, available at https://web.worldbank.org/archive/website01360/WEB/IMAGES/SCI_W-24.PDF.

Hirschman, A. O. (1981), "The changing tolerance for income inequality in the course of economic development," in A. O. Hirschman, *Essays in Trespassing: Economics to Politics and Beyond*, Cambridge: Cambridge University Press.

Letki, N. (2008), "Does diversity erode social cohesion? Social capital and race in British neighbourhoods," *Political Studies* 56(1), pp. 99–126.

Loungani, P. (2003), "Inequality: now you see it, now you don't," *Finance & Development* (September), pp. 22–3.

Matti, J. and Y. Zhou (2017), "The political economy of Brexit: explaining the vote," *Applied Economics Letters*, 24(16), pp. 1131–4.

McAndrew, S., P. Surridge and N. Begum (2017), "Social identity, personality and connectedness: probing the identity and community divides behind Brexit," November 12, University of Bristol, available at https://osf.io/preprints/socarxiv/w95xa/.

Putnam, R. (1993), *Making Democracy Work: Civic Traditions in Modern Italy*. Princeton, N.J.: Princeton University Press.

Putnam, R. (2000), *Bowling Alone: The Collapse and Revival of American Community*. New York: Simon & Schuster.

Putnam, R. (2007), "E pluribus unum: diversity and community in the twenty-first century: the 2006 Johan Skytte Prize Lecture," *Scandinavian Political Studies* 30(2), pp. 137–74.

Putnam, R. (2017), Hearing before the joint economic committee congress of the United States. One hundred fifteenth Congress, First Session, May 17, 2017: "What do we do together?: the state of social capital in America today."

Rhys, A. W. A. (2008), "Civic engagement, ethnic heterogeneity, and social capital in urban areas: evidence from England," *Urban Affairs Review* 44(3), pp. 428–40.

Sarracino, F. (2010), "Social capital and subjective well-being trends: comparing 11 Western European countries," *The Journal of Socio-Economics* 39(4), pp. 482–517.

Trends in International Migration Stocks: The 2017 Revision, Economic and Social Affairs, United Nations publication, POP/DB/MIG/Stock/Rev.2017, December 2017.

UK Balance of Payments (2018), *The Pink Book*, Office of National Statistics, UK.

Wilkinson, R. and K. Pickett (2009), *The Spirit Level: Why More Equal Societies Almost Always Do Better*, London: Allen Lane.

Zoega, G. (2017), "Increase trust to stem the rise of populist movements," *Vox CEPR Policy Portal*, November 3, available at https://voxeu.org/article/increase-trust-stem -rise-populist-movements 2017.

7. UK dithering over Brexit: on the European single market and its regulatory model

Annette Bongardt

7.1 INTRODUCTION: UK DITHERING OVER LEAVING THE EU

In June 2016 the United Kingdom (UK) decided by an in–out referendum on its European Union (EU) membership to leave the Union. Having dithered over its departure from the Union for two and a half years, the 12 December 2019 UK parliamentary elections set the country on course to leave the Union on 31 January 2020, almost ten months after the original Brexit date, and to do so in an orderly way through the ratified EU–UK withdrawal agreement. The December 2019 elections resulted in a large parliamentary majority for the Conservative Party in government, committed to 'get Brexit done' at the next occasion (31 January 2020), and put the government in a position to at last ensure ratification of the (renegotiated) withdrawal treaty with the EU. The withdrawal treaty enshrines a transition period that keeps the UK effectively in the single market of the EU until the end of 2020, meant to facilitate the transition to the final bilateral EU–UK trade (and wider) relationship. The UK is entitled to ask once (in June 2020) for a time-limited prolongation of the transition period.

Since its Brexit vote the UK dithered over leaving the EU (taking about nine months to trigger the exit provisions of the EU after the referendum, not finding majorities in parliament for approving the withdrawal treaty and its renegotiated version), rather asking for repeated extensions of the exit period that maintain the status quo and postponing any hard choices. This chapter considers the possible role the single market of the European Union therein. It discusses the properties of the European single market and its wider (growth) framework to shed light on what exactly the UK stands to give up when exiting the internal market. To do so, Section 7.2 examines the state of the internal market and the possibility of a truly single market in terms of market opening, regulation, and the institutional environment (including structural reform), respectively. Section 7.3 focuses on the single market as the EU's vehicle for (quality) growth and its governance set-up. Section 7.4 addresses what the UK gave up when opting for Brexit, from the point of view of the internal market's status quo and also the possibility of creating a truly single market (after all, the single market is a work in progress), and considering what the UK could or might have wanted to do in response. Section 7.5 discusses the UK's ambivalent stance towards the single market cum regulatory model and highlights the nature of the Brexit-induced difficult choices facing the UK. Section 7.6 concludes on the UK's single market Brexit dilemma, which will become acute only after Brexit, at the end of the transition period.

7.2 THE SINGLE MARKET OF THE EU: ON THE STATUS QUO AND THE POSSIBILITY OF A TRULY SINGLE MARKET

7.2.1 Market Liberalization and its Limits in Light of European Varieties of Capitalism

A well-functioning internal market promotes competition, innovation, better services and lower prices for consumers. At its inception in the mid-1980s, the '1992' single market project was motivated by the need to regain competitiveness and promote growth through a truly common market. At the time the emphasis was on liberalization. The '1992' project required market opening in hitherto closed sectors (services and production factors) whereas goods markets, which had become re-segmented along national lines by member state protectionist measures in the 1970s in the aftermath of the two oil crises, were to be subject to what was presented as an essentially technical deregulation exercise. Implementation turned out to be more complicated, not least since the state is also a player in the economy in European varieties of capitalism.

The logic of the single market is based on straightforward economics, namely on the realization of the efficiency properties associated with the free movement of goods, services, persons and capital (the 'four freedoms'), plus the right to establishment, in an enlarged domestic market.[1] By and large, the single market's evolution has been driven by an efficiency and competitiveness rationale.[2] Market scale has also increased over time. Today the single market of the EU, with its more than 500 million consumers, is the world's largest market in terms of purchasing power.

The single market's performance hinges on the interplay between market liberalization, competition and regulation. If functioning well the internal market provides a formidable platform for promoting EU competitiveness and growth. Globalization has further increased its importance, notably diminishing EU external trade barriers in line with successive multilateral agreements under the World Trade Organization (WTO) umbrella and an ever-increasing number of EU trade agreements with third countries.[3] The prospect of unrestricted access to the internal market stands out as the most important factor in making EU membership attractive. Internal market participants comprise not only the member states of the Union (from initially six founding members up to 28, post-Brexit 27) but in addition three (out of four) members of the European Free Trade Association (EFTA) that integrate the European Economic Area (EEA). As EEA members they have gained unrestricted access to and fully participate in the single market of the EU.[4] Switzerland, while not an EEA member, shadows its membership.

To a certain extent, the single market is still a work in progress. Efforts to complete the single market have continued beyond the official single market programme deadline at the end of 1992 and also much beyond the initially envisaged legislative measures.[5] Today the single market framework is largely in place, but still below potential. There are several reasons for this. Single market liberalization is not yet complete, notably as far as the single market in services and labour mobility is concerned.[6] There is also a compliance and transposition deficit with respect to single market directives.[7] Moreover, there are still gaps in the single market.

To start with, any late or incorrect transposition of directives by even one member state leaves the single market incomplete in that given area and thus impairs market performance. Also thanks to strong commitment by the Commission, the process of tackling the transposition and compliance deficit is on course. The European Commission's (2018) single market scoreboard evidences that the EU's average transposition deficit has decreased steadily since 1997 and, since 2012, has stood below the 1 per cent target set by the European Council (except in 2016) and often close to the 0.5 per cent target of the 2011 Single Market Act. The Commission notes that the total number of pending infringement cases is down to their lowest level ever. New infringement cases mostly concern the environment (44 per cent) and transport (11 per cent) sectors (leaving the single market incomplete in areas that are important for EU growth), free movement of goods and market surveillance (11 per cent) and taxation (8 per cent).[8] Services replaced environmental impact among the top three areas with the cases of longest average infringement duration (the new ranking is headed by air transport, followed by the free movement of persons and Union citizenship, services, environmental impact, and indirect taxation).

Gaps in the single market are of particular importance. They condition future growth performance as they regard new areas with a high growth potential.[9] New – digital and green – growth areas are of course key objectives of the Europe 2020 strategy for putting the EU on a higher-growth path. The

2011 and 2012 Single Market Acts had reinforced the aim to redirect the single market towards high-growth areas. The problem remains that in those sectors market opening does not suffice. It also requires conducive market rules. The success of measures under the Single Market Acts then depends on the implementation of measures that fall in the single market and in the Europe 2020 strategy domains and their two different methods, the Community method and soft coordination, respectively. The first facilitates market opening (market making), whereas delivery of market rules (market correcting measures) by the second strategy is more complicated, based as it is on coordination with open outcomes (open method of coordination).[10]

A digital single market and an energy union feature among the Commission's priorities for deepening the single market.[11] Tearing down regulatory walls is a challenge common to both and it needs to be tackled. A digital single market needs to be created from what have been national, segmented markets. As for energy union, the Energy Union Framework Strategy launched in 2015 has faced persistent challenges: from regulation to European network infrastructure and links to more active consumer roles.[12] According to the European Commission's own assessment, it had been delivered by 2019.[13]

Trade in services trails trade in goods, despite the importance of services in the EU economy (about 75 per cent of GDP). Strengthening services trade is hence key for potentiating the single market's growth potential, but it equally needs to go beyond liberalization, requiring more common standards and EU-wide rules for competition (Mion and Ponattu, 2019).[14] With services being by nature less suitable for cross-border trading, the European Commission points out that service trade integration calls on the one hand for facilitating the cross-border provision of services, the recognition of qualifications and establishment outside the home country but that it also highlights the need for structural reforms at the EU and national level in order to do away with a range of obstacles of regulatory, structural and behavioural nature. Those obstacles (to business opportunities, innovation and investment, including those arising through new technologies and new business models and more integration in EU and global value chains) are addressed through various strategies, namely in the Single Market strategy, the Digital Single Market strategy and the renewed EU Industrial Policy Strategy, while the European Semester promotes related reforms at national and euro area levels.

To the extent that market liberalization in European mixed economies calls for adequate regulation, the challenge for the EU is to define the rules of the game in the single market in way that is compatible with reaping the benefits of single market scale. This is notably true for directing the single market towards potential high-growth areas, where market liberalization has to be complemented by European market rules. Nor does market liberalization by itself do away with frictional (cost-increasing) market barriers and distortions created by member state interventions in the economy. That does not mean, of course, that market rules were not needed or desirable in light of the European model (for instance for environmental or consumer protection or as a forward-looking EU industrial policy). Also note that EU regulation is mostly risk regulation (as is the case of financial regulation), which leaves significant room for different member state preferences in the EU (OECD 2015).[15]

Competence distribution in the EU and the efficacy of associated policy instruments are likely to condition the prospects for single market completion and hence growth in the foreseeable future. Policy effectiveness will hinge importantly on the success of action programmes and soft coordination.

At present, and although the '1992' project might be near completion, there is no truly single market. It is therefore hardly surprising that the single market should not have exhausted the expected economic benefits and have been underperforming compared to its growth potential. That said, the limits of the planet (natural resources, pollution) impose limits on economic growth. There may also be limits to promoting growth in the EU due to the inherent preferences of ageing societies in European mature economies.[16]

In European varieties of capitalism the completion of the single market and realization of a 'genuine single market' (akin to 'genuine EMU') hence needs to go beyond market liberalization and better coordinate market rules and institutions. As Pelkmans (2016) puts it, this calls for rethinking the single market from the economics side and implementing the necessary policies and actions under that rationale: EU member states would need first and foremost to recognize the single market as a club good. They would then need to take the necessary actions to assure intra-EU mobility to realize its full benefits, considering that markets are often and to different degrees regulated, and that other interventions take place at the sub-national level. A truly single market would then require: first, unrestricted free movement plus the right of establishment; second, EU regulation where appropriate and justified by market failures, or mutual recognition when it is accepted; and third, that other, member state interventions in their home markets are either non-distortive or negligible for the EU economy, or combined in some effective way at EU level. That would require the implementation of a coherent set of actions at the EU level and at the interface between member states and the EU.

The completion of the single market hinges both on increased sovereignty sharing and political willingness and commitment by member states. As further discussed in the ensuing section, it also requires sufficient (openness to) preference convergence to sustain the EU's regulatory model.

7.2.2   Regulation: The Economic Case and the Issue of Preference Convergence

In European varieties of capitalism, regulation and issue of the role of the state are intertwined. Frictions between the EU trade-led integration model and member state intervention in the economy already began to be felt from the 1970s onwards. At the time of the single market programme, they came to be addressed more effectively through a new approach to regulation, in response to the need to overcome the segmentation of the common market in goods – resulting from things like different technical specifications or consumer protection and environmental standards – to boost its performance.

Despite the considerable weight of services in the EU economy (about 75 per cent of EU GDP) and in member state economies, services have been lagging behind goods in EU market integration, and cross-border trade in services still trails intra-EU goods trade. Their large weight in the economy, the slow liberalization of the sector and the overall lack of competition imply that in the EU there is a great potential for efficiency and productivity gains, and consequently untapped growth potential, in services (especially in protected sectors and professions). The fate of the services directive has showcased that regulation is critical for the successful liberalization of services, and indeed for the sustainability of the European project.[17]

The services directive envisaged liberalizing consumer and business services except in areas with specific legislation, as is the case for financial services.[18] Still, the directive that is in place falls short of the original comprehensive proposal for services liberalization. Notably, the home country principle was abandoned, the scope of the directive limited (for instance regarding health services) and member states were allowed to impose general obligations for service providers on their territory. As a result of abandoning the home country principle, which implies mutual recognition through the acceptance of national standards, competition between national regulatory systems in the internal market was avoided. The implementation of the directive not only suffered substantial delays at the member state level but its economic impact was held back through barriers at the national level, with particular incidence in the construction and business services sectors.[19] The European Commission advocates the use of European standardization to remedy these problems and promote market integration also in services and not only in goods and future high-growth areas like the digital single market.[20]

What the case of services liberalization also illustrates is that it is the convergence of preferences that conditions (the possibility of) European standards. In services liberalization, the real issue was never whether liberalization would take place, once national regulations that constitute invisible (frictional) barriers to trade are incompatible with the common market and market integration, and that the objectives of services liberalization and the freedom of establishment were already enshrined in the Treaty of Rome. Rather, the issue was how market integration would take place in the EU – in a market-making or market-correcting way.[21] The possible options range from mutual recognition of national regulations (market-making, the default option) to European, harmonized (market-correcting) regulation. Regulation in the EU has come to make use of all options relating to the degree of preference convergence between member states, from the home country principle to European standards, or some combination of the two, with common standards for essential requirements and home country control for the remainder.

Whereas European regulation requires preference convergence, diverse national preferences can be accommodated through the principle of mutual recognition of national standards. However, in line with the theory of fiscal federalism, the subsidiarity principle only covers diversity of preferences and not heterogeneity rooted in technical or administrative differences. The Commission introduced market monitoring as a new approach to gain in-depth insights into market functioning to help sort out to what extent desirable pro-competitive reforms are held back by member states in the name of heterogeneity (of technical or administrative differences), which cannot be justified by diverse preferences.

Regulation is meant to remedy market failures, but bad regulation could also give rise to regulatory failure. Currently, most EU rules refer to risk regulation, which pursues safety, health, environmental and consumer protection objectives. This risk regulation concerns mostly goods and services markets – among which are financial market regulation and supervision, and network industry aspects – and only occasionally labour and capital markets.[22] On a more horizontal level, it includes environmental regulation and consumer protection and rights. In Pelkmans' (2012) view, there is general acceptance of an economic-evidence-based regulatory logic at the EU level, which has been embraced by the Commission but has not yet trickled down to the EU legislator (the Council of the EU, the European Parliament) to the same extent. EU regulatory thinking has come to enshrine the 'better regulation' logic, together with cost–benefit analysis and other quantification of impacts. The European Commission has a deregulation (and better regulation) agenda, which already dates back to the 2007 action programme on reducing administrative burdens; yet, a lot of regulation is national and beyond its reach. The EU has also developed a standard cost model to quantify the red-tape costs of EU legislation.

In European integration terms, the completion of the single market meant a qualitative shift from trade- to regulation-based European integration, which in turn called on member states to jointly define the economic order to avoid the segmentation of the single market. It put the issue of regulation – after all, market rules involve values and beliefs – not only on the economic but also on the political agenda.[23] The fact that single market integration to date has come to occur more through market-making (mutual recognition, which is the default option) than market-correction (dependent on preference convergence on European standards), which a priori would be more adequate for mixed economies, testifies to the difficulties in preference convergence across European varieties of capitalism. Arguably, the significant leeway enjoyed by member states tests the limits of the European model and of integration.

On an international level, the EU has become a global standard setter in some areas (most recently in data protection matters). More generally, however, EU trade policy (i.e. the recent proliferation of EU comprehensive (deep) free trade agreements), has magnified single market issues and societal concerns with respect to market rules and regulation in an international trade context. For the EU those open up the possibility of higher economic benefits (competitiveness, growth) associated with unrestricted trade and investment over a larger area, as well as the potential to enhance the EU's influence on the world order. However, given that WTO trade barriers (tariffs) were already low, most benefits would be expected to accrue from doing away with non-tariff, regulatory barriers.[24] European comprehensive free trade agreements, in particular the EU–US Transatlantic Trade and Investment Partnership (TTIP), which did not go ahead, and the EU–Canada Comprehensive Economic and Trade Agreement (CETA), which did, which stirred up fears in the public sphere as to a possible pre-emption of European standards through regulatory cooperation and/or a race to the bottom in standards.[25] To be sustainable, the EU needs to address public concerns as to the impact on the European model in order to ensure domestic support.[26]

7.2.3 Modernization of the Framework in which Markets and Economic Actors Operate

In European varieties of capitalism, member state intervention goes beyond market rules, shaping the business environment and thereby also growth prospects. The need for a modernization of European varieties of capitalism gained urgency with the slowdown in European productivity improvements, which stood in marked contrast with US performance in the 1990s. The fact that it occurred despite wide-ranging liberalization under the single market programme led to a consensus across member states to embark on an EU-wide economic reform strategy to put the EU on a higher growth path. It was as a continuation of the single market's supply-side liberalization and efficiency rationale with different means, which added EU-level coordination to coordination through the market where market liberalization alone would have been insufficient. The importance of improving productivity stands out at a time of global productivity slowdown.[27]

The Europe 2020 strategy represents a shared understanding that an insufficient modernization of European varieties of capitalism, which fails to adapt to changed competitiveness factors (innovation capacity and speed of adaptation to changing circumstances), impairs single market performance (notably growth and productivity).[28] Member states committed to agreed common benchmarks. They notably include headline indicators for the modernization of their economies such as employment levels, research and development, climate and energy performance indicators, schooling and higher education levels, and reduction of social exclusion and poverty. The strategy accommodates the various national realities, traditions and preferences by allowing each member state to find its own path towards the common EU targets within a decade-long time frame. It was thought that mutual learning in a long-term framework would allow for preference convergence over time, to the benefit of individual member states and the EU as a whole.[29]

However, the loose approach to economic coordination – featuring EU-wide performance targets while instruments for implementation remained at the member state level – failed to deliver on welfare state and market-structural reform. Member state compliance with commitments has in general been mixed at best, although some member states were willing and able to put soft-coordination instruments to good use and modernize their economies. The asymmetry across member states, however, means that growth spillovers went unrealized.

Leaving aside the fact that a coordinated EU response to common challenges – notably globalization, the new economy, demographic ageing, or climate change – would promote EU growth (and promote the EU's global standing), the modernization of national institutional frameworks and redirection to new quality growth areas (digital, green) should have been in the interests of each individual member state, too. As it turned out, political economy constraints were often strong; positive spillovers from trade proved not a strong enough argument for triggering domestic reform; countries did not take ownership of reforms; and public and peer pressure did not work. Overall, soft coordination failed to produce the desired growth effects. The European Semester process meant to tighten coordination and make it more effective has not brought about any fundamental change. The fundamental issue remains, namely that competences and instruments have remained at the member state level and that member state commitments are non-enforceable. It is likely to restrain possible trade spillovers into growth in the foreseeable future.[30]

As for modernization in the industrial policy domain, EU industrial policy specifically aims at promoting growth and competitiveness in the manufacturing sector in order to foster reindustrialization.[31] Instruments range from creating appropriate framework conditions (e.g. smart legislation) to EU support programmes (Cosme, Horizon 2020, Galileo and Copernicus) for sectors with geostrategic implications and a high degree of public intervention and for high-potential areas.[32] European industrial policy has been strengthened, for instance in the context of the European energy union.[33] Nevertheless, the EU's role is merely complementary and supportive with regard to member state industrial policy. Member state actions are only loosely coordinated towards smart and sustainable growth goals under the Europe 2020 strategy. They are, of course, subject to EU competition policy that aims to guarantee a level playing field for competition in the single market.[34] The EU's state aid regime, which is focused on addressing market failures, assumes special importance in the industrial policy context. It allows subsidies that promote the competitiveness of sectors and companies, provided that they do not distort competition in the single market. To that extent, competition and industrial policy can be thought of as complementary.[35]

Still, growth needs to be sustainable in the long run and should not only be a short-term concern to exit the crisis. Sustainable growth requires (a shift to) consumption and production patterns that are environmentally (and socially) sustainable. For that to happen environmental constraints have to be internalized.

Yet, what has happened so far falls short of an integrated forward-looking strategy for sustainable growth. The EU has gained competences in the field and has bits and pieces in place.[36] It addresses sustainability concerns under the heading of different policies and with different governance methods. This is not a problem in itself, provided that those were to amount to a comprehensive approach towards the common good, correcting market failures and creating the right incentives for economic agents for growth that are sustainable in the long run. It still falls short today, however. The von der Leyen European Commission's New Green Deal is a welcome development that promises a comprehensive approach and which put sustainable growth on top of the EU's (growth) agenda.

It is probably fair to say that sustainable growth became secondary in the refocused Lisbon agenda on growth and jobs, even more so in the face of crisis impacts. The green growth dimension has tended not to be integrated with the digital and inclusive growth dimensions (more interconnected), despite the large potential associated with linking the digital and energy agendas (notably smart grids).[37] The Europe 2020 strategy's headline targets are moreover focused on climate and energy, which de facto reduce the environmental dimension to energy and resource efficiency (obviously very important) but fall short of sustainable development. The EU committed to the Paris Climate Agreement, under which global warming is to be contained, but has found it difficult to agree on a binding path that would limit emissions in line with the 1.5° goal and de-carbonize the union by 2050.

7.3   ON THE SINGLE MARKET AS THE EU'S VEHICLE FOR (QUALITY) GROWTH

Economic growth is an objective of the Union. The question remains what kind of growth the EU aims at and whether the EU framework is conducive to growth. The Treaty of the European Union (TEU) goes beyond economic growth for growth's sake ('whatever kind of growth') by establishing the objective of quality growth. It thereby acknowledges that growth can only be economically and politically sustainable in the long run if environmental constraints are taken care of (are internalized) and if economic growth serves a model of society that is aligned with European (social, environmental) values.[38] After all, the single market of the EU is at the core of what the EU does, so that the delivery of socioeconomic results assumes importance beyond the narrower growth and competitiveness concerns also for the sustainability of the political European integration project.[39]

The internal market is to provide a level playing field on which economic agents compete. It is the EU's vehicle for delivering growth. But the EU largely relies on the European economic (growth) agendas, the Lisbon strategy (2000–2010) and its successor, the Europe 2020 strategy (2011–20) for delivering on those broad growth objectives of the single market (Bongardt 2015). Economic growth is to be achieved in a way that makes social and environmental concerns compatible with, and indeed the motor of, quality economic growth. To that end, the Europe 2020 strategy aims at growth that is inclusive (social), smart (digital) and also green (sustainable).

The idea is to create a growth-enhancing environment for markets and firms to operate in. It reflects a consensus across member states that in the reality of European varieties of capitalism market opening alone would not produce the desired economic results. Rather, institutional frameworks required modernization, above all at the member state level, so as to transform common challenges like globalization, the new economy, demographic ageing, or climate change into economic opportunities and growth. The European growth agendas feature a notion of competitiveness that captures a wide range of conductive and long-term competitiveness determinants rather than focusing on more narrow and immediate factors (such as unit labour costs).

However, the EU's growth objectives face an EU governance set-up that is uneven, which has had a bearing on implementation: while it facilitates decision making and implementation in the single market domain (where the EU has either exclusive or shared competences) the same does not hold true for other growth-enhancing policies. The European growth agendas, which pursue single market aims by other means, are a case in point, and so is EU industrial policy. Although member states recognized that institutional modernization was in their national interest, and that they would thereby contribute to a European common good (i.e. increased EU growth through trade (spillovers) across member states of the Union), they were reluctant to transfer competences to the EU level. As a result, economic coordination came to rely on soft coordination of member states' commitments.[40] In the industrial policy domain the EU has only been granted a complementary competence. It means that the EU can take actions but only in support of those taken by member states (which accounts for the thrust of actions taken).

The need for economic growth features prominently on the contemporary international policy agenda. At the level of the EU and its members, the call for growth has tended to be framed in the context of an exit from the twin effects of the global financial and sovereign debt crises and the need to deal with crisis legacy costs at the member state level, in more recent times reinforced by looming trade conflicts and uncertainty surrounding the international trade system. The urgency in the crisis context gave rise to an almost unanimous call for growth. Economic growth is seen as a fundamental (albeit not necessarily sufficient on its own) step towards addressing a range of economic problems and challenges besetting the EU and its member states (such as macroeconomic disequilibria, unemployment, budgetary imbalances, or the financing of European varieties of the welfare state). In this light, the adequacy and good functioning of the EU's framework for growth becomes ever more important for delivering economic results (competitiveness, growth, productivity), even more so at a time when the capacity of providing growth impulses through monetary policy and fiscal policy is facing constraints, both within and beyond the Eurozone. However, the (very belated) increasing salience of climate change means that economic growth can no longer be discussed while disregarding environmental effects and goals, most notably those enshrined in the Paris Climate Agreement.

The EU's framework for growth has remained rather stable. While the EU – with the notable exception of the UK – has responded to the crisis by building up governance in its economic union part (within and beyond the Community framework and through a variety of mechanisms), with significant advances in some relevant areas (notably banking union), since 2012 least progress has been made with regard to economic coordination, especially so in the area of structural policies. The UK remained on the sidelines and on occasions even tried to block the process, as illustrated by the Fiscal Compact (Dorucci et al. 2015).[41]

7.4   WHAT THE UK GAVE UP: SINGLE MARKET OPTIONS AS AN EU MEMBER

The UK has traditionally taken a stance in favour of competitiveness, open markets and free trade, and it has been rather successful in moulding the EU along those lines. With Brexit, the UK loses its influence over the EU and its policies.

Repeated requests for extending the Article 50 TEU exit period to protract its EU exit date testify to the UK's reluctance to leave the Union and with it the main institution of which it was part as a member and whose shape it very much determined, the single market of the EU. The internal market may not yet be complete (notably in services or potential high-growth sectors) but as a club member the UK has benefited significantly from unfettered access to the world's largest internal market and its wider growth framework. There has also been progress in areas in which the UK takes a particular interest, like the energy or digital sectors. There is even a lot of space for national preferences in regulation in the single market. Much of the governance of what constitutes the EU's wider growth framework is 'soft', meaning that the UK has always enjoyed significant leeway in acting and adopting its preferred policies, notably those covered by the Europe 2020 strategy and industrial policy.

In essence, in its quality as an EU member, the UK faced two basic options with regard to the single market's development and in light of the character-istics of the EU's growth framework. The first consisted in trying to improve the functioning of the single market within the limits of the present EU frame-work. As an alternative, the UK could have made itself the advocate of the implementation of a truly single market, rethought on the basis of economics and the common good (i.e. growth). After Brexit, both of these options become unavailable.

With regard to the first option, action plans and soft coordination loom large and need to deliver. The option includes deepening the single market to high-growth areas. The realization of a digital single market and of an energy union, which are two areas of interest to the UK, are in line with the Commission's and EU growth agendas. Their success, however, hinges on adequate European regulation. Given the EU governance set-up, in the EU market-making has proved easier than market-correction. National regulation might ignore impacts on the common good. European standards ultimately depend on sufficient preference convergence between member states. It remains to be seen whether the European Commission's market monitoring exercise will further European standards by distinguishing mere heterogeneity at the level of technical and administrative procedures from true diversity of preferences. The Commission is also committed to good regulation and has progressed on cutting red tape, which has been another area of interest of the UK.

Institutional modernization across EU member states in line with the Europe 2020 strategy would also benefit UK growth. As an EU member, the UK could have employed peer pressure to push for structural reforms in other member states. Also, preferences are of course not static but tend to evolve (if slowly). The UK could have tried to shape member state preferences. With respect to financial services regulations, the UK has often managed in the past to have its way by convincing other member states of the merits of its proposals, although with EMU its heterogeneous preferences became unsustainable. By the same token, the UK could have wielded a significant influence on the shape of trade agreements (like TTIP).[42] With the UK on its way out, what is under discussion is a stripped-down version on free trade in industrial goods.

Alternatively, the UK could have defended the much more ambitious strategy of creating a truly single market to unleash the single market's growth potential. This calls for rethinking the single market from the economics side and requires a host of actions at the EU and the member state level (notably that member states take ownership of the single market as a common good and act accordingly also at the national and supra-national level). The UK's chance of succeeding would always have depended on whether it was prepared to go along with any functional governance needs and sovereignty-sharing that this might imply.

Note that within the present setting member states including the UK have enjoyed significant leeway with regard to actions promoting growth and employment. This is true for regulation but also for industrial policy. The EU's industrial policy aimed at reindustrialization supports UK actions. Also, to the extent that member states modernized their economies under the European economic reform strategies (e.g. by bringing up skill proficiency to targets) they are better prepared to cope with structural change. Like other EU economies, the UK has had to come to grips with offshoring from developed to developing countries in the context of globalization, a phenomenon first observed in manufacturing and then also in services trade. In the UK, too, significant offshoring of manufacturing was followed by services, while the impact in the country was uneven in terms of spatial implications, especially affecting those regions with a higher share of routine occupations (Gagliardi et al. 2015). In the end, much depends on the right national policies. The EU framework on industrial policy does not supplant member state actions on reindustrialization. Member state policy is only constrained to the extent that state aid must not distort the level playing field in the single market.

By way of conclusion, the European single market and the European growth strategies provide valid instruments for promoting growth. However, and crucially, the delivery of economic results – including the promotion of quality

growth, compatible with and building on social and environmental values –
hinges very much on member states' attitudes and actions.

7.5   THE UK: FROM AMBIVALENCE TOWARDS THE SINGLE MARKET CUM REGULATORY MODEL TO FACING BREXIT-INDUCED DIFFICULT CHOICES

For the UK, which had never warmed to the idea of a European political union,
the single market came to constitute the bedrock of its EU membership. Yet,
by invoking Britain's exit from the EU (Brexit) on 29 March 2017, the country
set itself on course to leave the Union within a two-year timeframe and with it
all of its institutions. Those institutions include the internal market of which,
incidentally, in the 1980s the UK (under Prime Minister Margaret Thatcher)
had been the chief promoter.

The realization of the European single market moved European integration
up to a higher level, from a free trade zone in goods and a customs union, to
a common market. The UK has shown unease with its implications. Not only
did coordination needs increase in consequence but there was a fundamental
change in the very nature of integration, from a trade-led to a regulatory model.
Far from taking issue with the associated economic benefits, what the UK
came to dislike were some of the single market's features or sovereignty costs,
above all its necessarily regulatory nature and the EU governance set-up to
make it function, particularly decision-making by qualified majority voting in
the Council of the European Union. The alleged sovereignty costs resulted in
some ambivalence in the UK's stance towards the internal market.

Nonetheless, the single market became even more central to the UK's
participation in the Union after the country opted out in the 1992 Maastricht
Treaty from accompanying the further deepening of European integration
from the internal market to European Economic and Monetary Union (EMU).
At the same time, however, with EMU the UK's preferences for an economic
union independent of monetary requirements had become incompatible with
European integration objectives and in the event not sustainable, once it is in
the interests of all present and future EMU members that interdependencies
between the internal market (economic union sphere) and the monetary union
sphere be internalized and spillovers accounted for, a fact to which the sovereign debt crisis added urgency (Bongardt and Torres, 2016). The latter notably
comprises financial regulation aimed at the common good of financial stability, and hence necessarily concerns the UK's large financial sector.[43] Yet, since
Maastricht the UK had kept at the margins of further European integration
initiatives, including crisis-driven economic governance advances, distancing
itself until it became the least integrated of all EU members.[44] It follows that

the vote for exiting the EU in the UK's June 2016 in–out referendum on its EU membership, translating into an affirmation of national control and preference for (repatriating hitherto shared) sovereignty, essentially meant leaving the single market and the customs union. After all, there was not much else to be left. In its letter to the EU triggering the EU's exit provisions (Article 50 of the Treaty on European Union, TEU), the UK government accordingly communicated its intention to leave the single market and the EU customs union.

Of course, EU (and by extension also European Economic Area, EEA) membership has conferred substantial economic benefits on its members, including the UK, through unfettered access to and (ever more) frictionless trade in the large European internal market.[45] Those, however, hinge on a country's willingness to go along with an enhanced degree of coordination and sovereignty sharing. Having opted to become an EU outsider, the UK is free to avoid those sovereignty costs but in turn faces the loss of club benefits. Among those are automatic (mutual) recognition of standards, participation in European standard setting (cum influence on global standard setting), or membership of European regulatory agencies; note that non-participation in all of those is liable to increase rather than reduce red tape and trade costs for outsiders.[46] The UK's referendum outcome in favour of Brexit faces the country with the inherent trade-offs between sovereignty repatriation and securing continued access to what is its principal market, the EU being not only its geographical neighbour but largest trading partner (as further discussed in Bongardt and Torres, Chapter 2 in this volume).

To complicate matters, by leaving the Union the UK leaves not merely one of the largest markets in the world but also turns its back on what is the EU's wider growth framework and socioeconomic model of development, at a time when world growth is slowing and when the UK became one of the EU member states with the lowest growth rate, following the Brexit referendum in 2016 and drawn-out uncertainty as to when and whether Brexit would take place and whether it would be orderly or disorderly.[47] At the same time, the UK's global Britain strategy, meant to roll over or substitute the EU's international trade deals with third countries, failed to deliver on creating any valid alternative to the internal market.[48] What we have witnessed is that, having triggered Brexit, the UK has been trying to find ways to preserve (as much as possible of) the benefits it enjoyed as an EU member but without the associated sovereignty costs, thus far without much success.

The EU, on its part, has consistently stated that it will not compromise on the single market, its constituent four freedoms being indivisible, and its integrity (including its institutional ecosystem to function) and the decision-making autonomy of the remaining EU-27. Respecting those red lines, it made it also very clear that there exists a range of options available for a bilateral privileged relationship post-Brexit, but that all come with conditions attached. In essence, on an economic benefit/sovereignty continuum, the UK always faces, albeit to different extents, a trade-off between available economic benefits and national control, where more benefits are granted at the expense of more sovereignty sharing. That said, only a combination of membership of the EEA and the customs union could give the UK economic benefits akin to those that it enjoys as an EU member. Still, as an EU outsider it becomes a rule taker (customs union and single market alignment) rather than as in the past a rule maker in conjunction with the other EU members (Bongardt and Torres, Chapter 2 in this volume). On the other hand, the extent to which the UK aligns to single market rules conditions the comprehensiveness of any future bilateral free trade agreement.

7.6   CONCLUSION: THE SINGLE MARKET BREXIT DILEMMA, ACUTE AFTER BREXIT

Before exiting at last on 31 January 2020, the UK had been dithering over Brexit. It had displayed ambiguity towards the single market, for which understanding the issue of regulation and governance (sovereignty) is key. Despite having been the chief promoter of the single market, the UK came to dislike its regulatory nature and its governance (notably qualified majority voting in the Council), both of which are critical to ensure its good functioning. Still, it is the issue of financial regulation, which is in the economic union sphere, where the UK's interests (City of London's) have ultimately come to collide, and arguably became incompatible, with the interest of the Eurozone in safeguarding the public good of financial stability), once the UK opted out from EMU membership. The vote for Brexit in the UK's in–out referendum in June 2016 transformed a latent conflict into a dilemma: the UK needs to make hard choices in terms of economic benefit/sovereignty trade-offs as those determine whether and under what conditions the EU grants it continued access post-Brexit to what is its largest market.[49]

The cost of Brexit (i.e. the foregone benefits associated with the single market and its growth framework) go a long way towards explaining why the UK only triggered Brexit after a delay of nine months following the referendum, insisted on a transition period in the withdrawal treaty and, in the face of its inability to ratify the withdrawal treaty in parliament, did not leave on the scheduled Brexit day of 29 March 2019 but pleaded with the EU for repeated extensions of the Article 50 period (thereby keeping it in the EU and all of its institutions).

To be sure, the UK would be able to preserve beneficial privileged access and trading conditions also as a third country to the EU if it became a member of both the EEA and the EU customs union post-Brexit. However, this comes at a sovereignty cost (higher than EU membership), as it implies having to abide by EU rules and regulations without having a say. Put differently, rather than a rule maker in conjunction with the other EU member states, the UK would become a rule taker. On the other hand, as a member of the EU customs union, it would not be free to set its own tariffs, nor have its own trade policy. Still, even as a third country to the EU, the UK's degree of access to the single market and hence the benefits that can be preserved will be conditioned by the concessions that it is prepared to make in terms of sovereignty.

Remarkably, in the years since the UK voted for Brexit in the June 2016 referendum, the country developed no Brexit strategy and even less a consensus on what are its aims with regard to the bilateral relationship with the EU or model of society post-Brexit. Until the 12 December 2019 parliamentary elections it had even remained unclear whether the UK would in the end leave the EU and by implication the single market in a disorderly fashion (cliff-edge scenario), through a ratified (re-)negotiated withdrawal treaty with the EU, or even revoke its exit. UK ratification of the withdrawal treaty ensured a time-limited status quo transition period and came with a political declaration setting out the future bilateral relationship. On the basis of the UK's red lines, the future trade relationship can only be a free trade agreement. Still, from the EU's point of view its comprehensiveness hinges not least on UK level playing field commitments on workers' rights, taxes, state aid and environmental and consumer protection to the EU.

The UK December 2019 elections ensured that the UK was able to leave the EU at the end of January 2020 in an orderly fashion. Still, withdrawal was always thought to be the easy part in comparison with the subsequent, likely drawn-out and complex, negotiation of the future bilateral trade (and wider) EU–UK relationship. It is only after the transition period that the issue of single market access will bite. In any post-Brexit trade agreement, alignment with single market rules will come up. After Brexit, the hard choices are still before the UK.

NOTES

1. It was the European Commission which first set out the economics of common market completion (European Commission, 1988) at the time when the 1992 project was launched. Baldwin (1989) drew attention to the fact that the study underestimated benefits by not accounting for dynamic growth effects. For a textbook treatment on the economics of the single market, which accounts for market scale and competition effects, see Baldwin and Wyplosz (2015).
2. For a discussion see Bongardt and Torres (2012, 2013).
3. For a discussion see Bongardt and Torres (2019).
4. The EEA includes EFTA members that wish to fully participate in the internal market without having to become full members of the EU and to participate in common policies (at present these are EFTA members Iceland, Norway and Liechtenstein, but not Switzerland). As a prerequisite, they must comply with the

EU's legal and regulatory framework (the internal market relevant *acquis*, which may cover some flanking policies such as social policy, consumer protection and environment policy), without having a vote in decision-making. They also have to pay a financial contribution (which is used to reduce economic and social disparities in the EEA). Even Switzerland, although not an EEA member, shadows it through more than 120 bilateral agreements with the EU.

5. At the time the minimum required legislative measures were set at close to 300. In 2015, a total of 1,115 directives, together with 2,953 regulations, were in force to ensure the functioning of the single market. Note that there has been a noticeable reduction in the number of internal market directives in a quest to reduce red tape (http://ec.europa.eu/internal_market/ /performance_by_governance_tool/ transposition/index_en.htm). As of 30 November 2017, 1,038 directives and 4,100 regulations were in force to ensure the functioning of the single market (European Commission 2019), which are in turn embedded in an ecosystem of institutions.

6. The issue of services is taken up in the next section. As for labour mobility, suffice it here to say that labour mobility is one of the four fundamental freedoms of the internal market, but that frictions have arisen in particular with regard to national welfare systems, which have been built on stable populations, and are a national competence.

7. The underlying issue is that directives have to be transposed into national law at the member state level. This is not the case of regulations, which are applicable with immediate effect across the EU.

8. The UK now evidences a below-average transposition performance.

9. They were identified in the Monti report (2010) and taken up by the Single Market Act (2011) and the Single Market Act II (2012). The Single Market Acts aimed at redirecting the internal market towards new areas with a high growth potential to enhance internal market results. The Single Market Act II (2012) launched a second set of priority actions to support four drivers for new growth: fully integrated networks in the Single Market, mobility of citizens and businesses across borders, the digital economy and social entrepreneurship, cohesion and consumer confidence (see, at http://ec.europa.eu/internal_market/smact/docs/single-market -act2-keyactions_en.pdf).

10. Or, to put it differently, the transmission mechanism between the single market domain and adequate market rules (largely in the Europe 2020 domain) did not deliver.

11. The Juncker commission's priorities also comprised a Single Market Strategy, a Capital Markets Union, an Action Plan for fairer corporate taxation (notably with a minimum floor), and labour mobility, in order to create a deeper and also fairer single market (http://ec.europa.eu/priorities/internal-market_en).

12. See https://ec.europa.eu/energy/en/topics/markets-and-consumers/single-market -progress-report.

13. See https://ec.europa.eu/commission/news/energy-union-vision-reality-2019-apr -09-0_en. The Commission's proposal to shift to qualified majority voting in the Council on taxation met with resistance by member states. On the other hand, Brexit facilitated the capital markets union part of the financial package.

14. The authors furthermore suggest targeting investments in digital infrastructure and innovation capacity in regions that are lagging behind in order to enhance growth.

15. For instance, the Netherlands and the UK have the lowest product regulation in the OECD (and are both EU members), while the UK's low labour protection levels are similar to countries such as the USA, Canada or Australia.

16. The issue of growth in mature societies begs the question whether the very pref-
    erences of society might not result in lower growth (lower consumption, more
    old-age savings). Immigration might of course change that to a certain degree.
17. See, at http://ec.europa.eu/growth/single-market/services/index_en.htm. As for
    the European project, opposition to the original Services Directive is widely
    regarded to have contributed to negative referendum outcomes in France and the
    Netherlands on the 2004 European Constitution.
18. The 2006 Services Directive was to be implemented by 2009. It was the result of
    a compromise, for the sake of which the degree of ambition and sectoral reach of
    the original 'Bolkestein' proposal (named after the responsible Commissioner) for
    services liberalization had become watered down.
19. See European Commission (2015), figure 1.
20. The Commission holds that while "The current system is mainly focused on prod-
    ucts (. . .), there is significant potential for further integration both in products and
    in service markets through the use of standards (for instance in the digital single
    market)" (European Commission 2015: 55).
21. Negative or positive integration, in the terminology of Tinbergen (1954).
22. See Pelkmans (2012).
23. Regulation thereby became more political – see Tsoukalis (1989).
24. As Egan and Pelkmans (2015) put it, that would mean not to primarily focus on
    removing or reducing non-tariff barriers to trade but to focus on the established
    objectives of regulation. They argue that regulatory cooperation would then need
    to get down to the key business of regulation, that is, helping regulators to become
    more efficient and effective in achieving their goals in line with those established
    objectives.
25. See Egan and Pelkmans (2015). Reservations have also been voiced with respect
    to regulatory cooperation as far as consumer preferences are concerned (the other
    main issue is the investor–state dispute settlement). With respect to regulatory
    competition, it is the prospect of an obligatory regulatory cooperation council in
    particular that has raised concerns that stricter EU regulation in line with consumer
    preferences (on issues such as environmental regulation, workers' rights, con-
    sumer standards) might come to be pre-empted. It allegedly happened in the case
    of the (voluntary) transatlantic economic dialogue on regulation, which is part of
    the transatlantic dialogue (Haar et al. 2016).
26. As discussed in Bongardt and Torres (2017).
27. Possibly related to the exhaustion of the underlying technological paradigm.
28. Note that unreformed European market institutions were not apt to transform
    challenges (globalization, new technologies, demographic ageing, climate change)
    into economic opportunities as they were largely created in a very different
    market and technical environment (in what the French refer to as the 'les trente
    glorieuses'. It denotes the period after the Second World War that offered rather
    stable and predictable conditions for growth). When conditions in the business
    environment changed (markets becoming volatile and often rather small, techno-
    logical change accelerated, new technologies made an appearance, competences
    became obsolete faster, etc.), firms' competitiveness factors changed. The ade-
    quacy of the conditions in which markets and the state operated in European mixed
    economies were adequate for boosting productivity, and growth became a critical
    issue for competitiveness and growth.
29. On the issue of preference convergence in the EU, see Bongardt and Torres
    (2013).

30. Economic coordination problems had an additional effect in the Eurozone, where interdependencies between member states are larger. The lack of reforms at the member state level gave rise to negative spillovers from the uncoordinated economic union side to the monetary sphere of the Economic and Monetary Union (EMU), and even put at risk the survival of the euro. The appearance of external pressure (in the form of market pressure or conditionality under adjustment programmes) somewhat increased reform efforts.

31. The target is to raise the share of industry in EU GDP from currently 15.1% to 20% by 2020 (http://ec.europa.eu/growth/industry/policy/eu/index_en.htm).

32. Regardless of Brexit, the UK manifested its wishes to continue participating in European programmes like Horizon 2020, Galileo, and even defence.

33. The European battery industry is a case in point. It was identified as a strategic value chain for the EU, with a strategic action plan. It is subject to a separate report that accompanies the Energy Union report (European Commission 2019).

34. EU competition policy was created and competences given to the EU already at the time of the Treaty of Rome when the common market cum customs union objective was established, a fact that testifies to the importance attributed to competition policy for internal market performance. Competition in the single market is key for providing economic agents with incentives for innovation and productivity improvements. EU competition policy aims at single market integration and is guided by maintaining a level playing field. To that end the European Commission can undo or prevent distortions of competition in the internal market by means of antitrust, and merger control, and state aid control.

35. According to the Commission, industrial policy and competition policy are to be complementary, at the core of a new competitiveness policy framework, in which the EU's state aid regime is critical in overcoming possible frictions (http://ec.europa.eu/growth/industry/policy/competition/index_en.htm).

36. The general EU framework for growth also conditions green growth. Apart from that, the EU has gained competences with respect to sustainability-relevant policies over time. Since the Lisbon Treaty climate change and energy policy have become shared competencies next to environment policy (although unanimity voting requirements hold back decision-making in areas as important as environmental and energy taxation and energy sources).

37. This fact looks particularly worrying if one considers that the digital and energy areas are heralded as the basis of a possible third industrial revolution.

38. Article 3(3) TEU establishes that "The Union shall establish an internal Market. It shall work for the sustainable development of Europe based on balanced economic growth and price stability, a highly competitive social economy, aiming at full employment and social progress, and a high level of protection and improvement of the quality of the environment. It shall promote scientific and technological advance."

39. See Begg et al. (2015) for a conceptualization of sustainable European integration.

40. That is, the open method of coordination (OMC), with no sanctions for non-compliance.

41. See Bongardt and Torres (2016) for a discussion of the implications of Brexit for EMU.

42. See Messerlin (2015) for a discussion of the services dimension in TTIP. The UK (next to Germany) is one of the USA's biggest trade partners in Europe and as such has taken a great interest in the successful completion of TTIP with regard to low-

ering trade and non-trade barriers, even more so since the economic significance of TTIP critically depended on services.

43. The UK takes a special interest in the City of London, given the weight and importance of the financial sector to its economy, which has put it on collision course on shared EU rule making.

44. For a graphical illustration, see Wolfstädter and Kreilinger (2017).

45. See https://www.bertelsmann-stiftung.de/fileadmin/files/BSt/Presse/Press-Relea se_EU-Single-Market-boosts-per-capita-incomes-by-almost-1000-euros-a-year _20190508.pdf. The UK benefited significantly from the single market, albeit with regional differences (the South benefiting more than the North) that are the largest in the EU (Mion and Panattu (2019)).

46. With the UK out of the EU, the EU is set for an acceleration of financial regulation (https://www.reuters.com/article/us-eu-banks-exclusive/exclusive-europe -prepares-raft-of-post-brexit-banking-reforms-idUSKCN1SL195; consulted 28 June 2019). Post-Brexit, as a third country to the EU, the UK would depend on being granted equivalency of its rules to access the EU market. As opposed to mutual recognition in the single market, those can be easily revoked, as happened in the summer of 2019 to Switzerland (https://www.reuters.com/article/us-swiss -eu-explainer/explainer-why-switzerland-and-the-eu-face-a-battle-of-the-bourses -idUSKCN1TR141; consulted 28 June 2019). The EU's decision not to recognize the Swiss stock market regulations' equivalency has the effect of preventing EU-based banks and brokers from trading on Swiss exchanges.

47. See, at: https://ec.europa.eu/eurostat/tgm/table.do?tab=table&init=1&plugin=1& language=en&pcode=tec00115; and, at: https://ec.europa.eu/eurostat/tgm/graph .do?tab=graph&plugin=1&language=en&pcode=tec00115&toolbox=type.
The highest annual growth rates for real GDP in 2017 were recorded in Ireland (7.2%), Romania (6.9%), Malta (6.4%) and Slovenia (5.0%), while the lowest rates of change were registered in Belgium and the United Kingdom (both 1.7%), Italy (1.5%) and Greece (1.4%).

48. By the beginning of April 2019, the UK had signed no-deal continuity arrangements with Norway, Iceland, the Faroe Islands, Israel, Palestinian Authority, Switzerland, Pacific Islands, Caribbean countries, and East and South Africa. In June 2019, it agreed in principle to sign a free trade deal with South Korea.

49. In May 2019 the EU's market regulator, ESMA (European Securities and Markets Authority) had ruled that in the event of a no-deal Brexit at the end of October investment firms in the EU must trade about 6,000 EU-listed shares on exchanges in the bloc. The effect would be to force funds and other users to redirect trading from London to the EU (https://uk.reuters.com/article/uk-britain-eu -markets/french-market-watchdog-to-london-stop-trading-eu-shares-after-brexit -idUKKCN1TT1DQ, consulted 28 June 2019).

REFERENCES

Baldwin, Richard E. (1989), 'The growth effects of 1992', *Economic Policy*, 2: 247–82.
Baldwin, Richard E. and Charles Wyplosz (2015), *The Economics of European Integration*, 5th edn, New York and London: McGraw-Hill.
Begg, Iain, Annette Bongardt, Kalypso Nicolaïdis and Francisco Torres (2015), 'EMU and sustainable integration', *Journal of European Integration*, 37(3): 803–16.

Bongardt, Annette (2015), 'The transformation of the Single European Market: from the Lisbon strategy to Europe 2020', in José M. Magone (ed.), *Routledge Handbook of European Politics*, Abingdon and New York: Routledge, 746–62.

Bongardt, Annette and Francisco Torres (2012), 'Economic governance and sustainability', in Amy Verdun and Alfred Tovias (eds), *Mapping European Economic Integration*, Basingstoke: Palgrave Macmillan, 146–67.

Bongardt, Annette and Francisco Torres (2013), 'The issue of convergence of preferences and institutions', *Intereconomics – Review of European Economic Policy*, Forum, Springer, 48(2): 72–7.

Bongardt, Annette and Francisco Torres (2016), 'EMU reform and resilience in a re-dimensioned EU', *Journal of Economic Policy – Politica Economica*, XXXII(3): 575–96.

Bongardt, Annette and Francisco Torres (2017), 'Comprehensive trade agreements: conditioning globalisation or eroding the European model?', *Intereconomics*, 52(3): 165–70.

Bongardt, Annette and Francisco Torres (2019), 'Trade agreements and regional integration: the EU after Brexit', in Robert Looney (ed.), *Routledge Handbook of International Trade Agreements*, Abingdon and New York: Routledge, 296–306.

Dorucci, Ettore, Demosthenes Ioannou, Francesco Paolo Mongelli and Alessio Terzi (2015), 'Europe's challenging economic integration: insights from a new index', *VoxEU*, 15 April 2015 (http://www.voxeu.org/article/economic-integration-europe-insights-new-index).

Egan, Michelle and Jacques Pelkmans (2015), *TTIP's hard core: barriers to trade and standards*, CEPS special report no. 117, August, Brussels: Centre for European Policy Studies (CEPS) (https://ec.europa.eu/regional_policy/en/information/publications/working-papers/2018/the-geography-of-eu-discontent).

European Commission (1988), 'The economics of 1992', *European Economy*, No. 35, March.

European Commission (2015), 'A single market strategy for Europe – analysis and evidence', Commission Staff working document, Brussels, 28.10.2015 SWD(2015) 202 final.

European Commission (2018), 'The EU single market: single market scoreboard', edition 07/2018 (http://ec.europa.eu/internal_market/scoreboard/), consulted 26 April 2019.

European Commission (2019), 'The energy union: from vision to reality', 9 April (https://ec.europa.eu/commission/news/energy-union-vision-reality-2019-apr-09-0_en).

Gagliardi, Luisa, Simona Iammarino and Andrés Rodrígues-Pose (2015), 'Offshoring and the geography of British jobs', *VoxEU*, 5 November (http://www.voxeu.org/article/offshoring-and-geography-british-jobs).

Haar, Kenneth, Lora Verheecke and Max Bank (2016), 'Dangerous Regulatory Duet', London: Corporate Europe Observatory, Lobby Control, January.

Messerlin, Patrick (2015), 'The transatlantic trade and investment partnership: the services dimension', CEPS special report no.106/May 2015, Brussels: Centre for European Policy Studies (CEPS).

Mion, Giordano and Dominic Ponattu (2019), 'Estimating economic benefits of the single market for European countries and regions', Policy paper, Bertelsmann Stiftung (ed.) (https://www.bertelsmann-stiftung.de/en/publications/publication/did/estimatinerg-economic-benefits-of-the-single-market-for-european-countries-and-regions/).

OECD (2015), *Economic Policy Reforms 2015: Going for Growth*, Paris: OECD.

Pelkmans, Jacques (2012), 'The economics of single market regulation', in Amy Verdun and Alfred Tovias (eds), *Mapping European Economic Integration*, Basingstoke: Palgrave Macmillan, 79–104.

Pelkmans, Jacques (2016), *What Strategy for a Genuine Single Market?*, CEPS special report no. 126, January, Brussels: Centre for European Policy Studies (CEPS) (https://www.ceps.eu/publications/what-strategy-genuine-single-market).

Tinbergen, Jan (1954), *International Economic Integration*, Amsterdam: North Holland.

Tsoukalis, Loukas (1989), *The New European Economy Revisited*, 3rd edn, Oxford: Oxford University Press.

Wolfstädter, Laura and Valentin Kreilinger (2017), 'European integration via flexibility tools: the cases of EPPO and PESCO', Policy Paper 209, Berlin: Jacques Delors Institute.

8. Brexit and the future of the City of London: between deregulation and innovation

Leila Simona Talani

8.1 INTRODUCTION

This chapter draws a parallel between the monetarist practices adopted by the British government in the 1980s and the responses to Brexit that will allow the City of London to thrive. Just as Prime Minister Thatcher's monetarism responded to the needs and preferences of the British financial elite in light of the City's so-called "revolution" of 1986–87, deregulation practices ensuing from Brexit also meet the preferences of the British financial elite, especially at the dawn of a new innovation era. The chapter will conclude that Brexit represents the revenge of the ultra-liberals and will allow the City to emerge on the winning side of globalization.

The chapter is therefore structured as follows. In Section 8.2 the author analyses the evolution of deregulation and innovation in the City of London during Thatcher's era. In Section 8.3, the policies that will allow the City to thrive after Brexit are identified, noticing the similarities with the Thatcherite era. The Conclusion (Section 8.4) points at the continuity between deregulation and innovation practices in the 1980s and the policy needs of the City after Brexit.

8.2 DEREGULATION AND INNOVATION 80S-STYLE IN THE CITY OF LONDON

Despite the British financial sector's period of crisis during the Second World War, from 1945 onward, and particularly during the 1960s, a combination of regulatory changes and specific government policies led to a return to the City's economic prosperity and political power. These measures were primarily directed at allowing a set of wholesale, short-term parallel markets to be established and prosper in the City of London. They were the Euro-currencies parallel markets, especially euro-dollars, the euro-bonds market and secondary markets in sterling. Equally, the City's postwar revival was favored by the strengthening of some traditional activities, such as insurance, bullion dealing and the secondary market in foreign issued stock. Overall, the City's basic practices remained essentially commercial, and the changes have by no means eliminated the financial separation of the City and industry. Further, they have been actively pursued by the intervention of British authorities, primarily the Bank of England and the Treasury (Talani 2012).

By the 1970s, after a very short period of crisis connected to the change in the international role of sterling and to the development of new financial markets, the City, thanks to its institutional nexus with the Bank of England and the Treasury, had fully re-established its leading role in world financial markets and its dominant position in the domestic economic environment.

During the course of the 1980s, the City of London succeeded in securing and enhancing its national and international leadership, or hegemonic position, by relying on the new monetarist practices of the Thatcher government. From the end of the 1960s onward, orthodox Keynesianism, with all that it implied in terms of direct intervention of the government in the economy and policies supporting aggregate demand to achieve full employment, was increasingly considered an obsolete, or even dangerous, economic policy-making ideology and was progressively substituted by monetarism. Control of the money supply became the only objective of macroeconomic policy-making, and monetarism the only ideological credo. In turn, laissez-faire monetarism policies represented the City's preferred set of macroeconomic policies.

Laissez-faire was the policy of the City. Limiting state intervention and, most importantly, regulation, to the strictly necessary, was at the core of that "pragmatic adaptation" that had allowed the City of London to prosper uninterruptedly since its establishment (Talani 2018).

Restrictive fiscal policies were also profoundly embedded in the City's practices and ideological belief system. Finally, the laissez-faire perspective justifies why price control had to be realized necessarily by adopting the third element of Thatcher's monetarism; that is, control of the money supply.

As far as innovation is concerned, City market structures and institutions underwent major changes in the period between 1986 and 1988. This is known as the "City revolution", and it constituted a total changeover of the regulatory framework in which the City worked. By issuing a flexible normative framework privileging secondary norms (rule books) and self-regulating practices, the British legislature confirmed a tendency to grant the widest possible degree of autonomy and discretion to financial institutions; autonomy and discretion, which in turn are absolutely necessary for "pragmatic adaptation" to take place and hegemony to continue unhindered.

The City's revolution represents the last stage of a process which had already begun in the mid-1970s: the definitive submission of productive capital to financial capital. In other words, it revealed the almost complete absorption of the productive sector by the financial one, with all that it implied in terms of the prevalence of short-term considerations over long-term ones in the management of the British productive sector. From the mid-1980s revolution onward, short-termism had, indeed, become a structural characteristic of the British capitalist system. Both deregulation and innovation during the Thatcher era are now analyzed in more detail.

8.2.1   Deregulation: Thatcher's Monetarism

In order to understand how monetarist policies implemented in the course of the 1980s responded to the needs of the City, it is appropriate to identify the three basic elements of Thatcher's monetarism: (1) The promotion of laissez-faire, including the reduction of state intervention in the economy and of regulation of the private sector (especially the financial sector) to a bare minimum; (2) Restrictive fiscal policies relying explicitly on curtailing public expenditure; (3) Control of the money supply (Coakley and Harris 1983: 192).

As noted by Longstreth (1984), laissez-faire was the policy of the City. It was both the cause and the result of the way City markets operated after the developments they underwent during the 1960s. Its implementation allowed the City's financial markets, particularly the new parallel ones, to continue thriving in the global economy.

Restrictive fiscal policies were also profoundly embedded in the City's practices and ideological belief system. Cutting the deficit was interpreted as a means to achieve "laissez-faire" in the general sense that a reduction in state spending would have the visible effect of "rolling back the state" (Coakley and Harris 1983). In particular, reduction of the deficit was seen as essential for the retreat of the state from the City and its financial markets, as indeed deficit spending needs to be financed. Financing high deficits by means of bank lending was considered unacceptable because it would put under discussion the achievement of the goal of controlling the money supply. However, also borrowing through the sale of government bonds, and borrowing in other ways that did not increase the money supply, did not meet the preferences of the City. It was argued that the effect of government borrowing directly from the public would be to deprive the private sector of finance. This would lead to a "crowding out" effect which would eventually increase the interest rates paid by the government on gilt sales and drive private borrowers out of the financial markets (Coakley and Harris 1983: 198). In other words, financing high-deficit spending through direct government borrowing would bring borrowers away from financing private enterprises through financial markets lured by the high interest rates offered by the government, therefore reducing the turnover on the City's credit markets.

Finally, the laissez-faire perspective justifies why price control had to be realized by adopting the third element of Thatcher's monetarism: control of the money supply. Indeed, to allow free trade in financial markets, exchange rates could not be fixed, hence eliminating this tool to keep inflation rates under control. In a world of capital mobility there is a sort of trade-off between the stability of exchange rates and the ability to implement autonomous monetary policies, which means setting interest rates and the amount of the monetary aggregates. So, given the hegemony of the City of London and its laissez-faire/ free trade credo at the time, the only way to control the rise of prices was to adopt strict monetary policies and not target the exchange rate. Hence the British rejection of both the Exchange Rate Mechanism of the European Monetary System and, later on, Economic and Monetary Union.

8.2.2   Deregulation and the 1986–87 City Revolution

The first official piece of regulation relating to the organization of the City was produced only in 1976 and was urged by EC member states' pressure on the British government to harmonize the organization of its financial and banking system with the organic legislation of the other European countries.[1] Thus, the August 1976 White Paper attributed to the Bank of England the formal faculty of authorizing the activity of deposit-taking institutions and divided them into two major groups: *recognized banks* and *licensed deposit-taking institutions*. While for the second group some strict licensing and controlling requirements were provided, the first group of institutions, including the entire traditional banking system, clearing banks, merchant banks and discount houses, was still characterized by the privileging of informal prudential supervision criteria (Cianferotti 1993: 94).

The publication of the White Paper gave the City of London the legitimization to participate, and deeply influence, the content of the forthcoming first EEC directive on the coordination of laws, regulations and administrative provisions relating to banking activity. This required a prior authorization system for credit institutions to be set up by December 1979. Robin Hutton, a City merchant banker, succeeded in convincing the other member states in Brussels to abandon the project of adopting a communitarian banking law. He also succeeded in including in the EC banking directive the City's definition of "supervision": it had to be limited to prudential regulation and not influence banking management through the implementation of formal rules (Cianferotti 1993). Thus, despite British membership in the European Community, what had been recognized by Lord O'Brien, then Governor of the Bank of England, in 1973 as the major competitive advantage of the City of London over the other financial centers, notably, its "(. . .) freedom from vexations of banking legislation equalled in few countries in the world" (O'Brien 1973: 123), could, to a very large extent, be maintained.

In fact, the first Banking Act, receiving Royal Assent on April 4, 1979, although attributing to the Bank of England various powers, usually formal ones relating to the releasing of licenses and recognition, did not provide for the explicit imposition of any duties or responsibilities with regard to supervision, especially of the recognized banks (Ryder 1979: Introduction). Again, as in the 1976 White Paper, the document privileged the centrality of the system of informal supervision with significant discretionary powers on the part of the Bank of England to decide which institutions could obtain recognition as banks (Bank of England 1982: 34). It was a system which privileged once again the importance of the "personal factor" as the decisive variable in defining bank supervision and confirmed the traditional division between the *gentlemen* and the *others*. Thus, it is no surprise that in 1983, four years after the issue of the Banking Act, *The Economist* could claim: "London's Banks, theoretically governed by the 1979 Banking Act, in practice know no masters but the Bank of England and their own clubs" (*The Economist* 1983: 69).

The unrestrained deregulation of the financial markets undertaken during the first Thatcher government, however, increased not just individual salaries, but also the risks connected to the banking and financial practices of the City of London. The situation became worrying when one of the City's prominent bullion dealers,[2] Johnson Matthey, risked involvement in the financial collapse of one of its smaller parent companies, the recognized bank Johnson Matthey Bankers (JMB), on October 1, 1984 (Lawson 1992: 403). As the then Governor of the Bank of England stated, "We felt it was vital to prevent any contagious spread to other members of a central and traditional London market, any failure within which could have quickly sent serious shock waves through the UK banking system" (Leigh-Pemberton 1984: 473). Since this statement clearly reflected the concerns of the most important City representatives, it was decided that the problem be solved within the City itself: "The rescue operation was a characteristic of the City of London" (Leigh-Pemberton 1984: 473). Thus, the Bank of England, with the consensus of the City's major bankers, decided to buy JMB at the symbolic price of £1; a few months later, the Central Bank was able to establish, with the decisive (if reluctant) participation of the major City Banks, a Guarantee Fund of £150 million.

Even if it subsequently had no major consequences, the JMB crisis brought to the forefront how the lack of prudential supervision by the Bank of England could have worrying spillovers into City institutions' activities and returned the reform of the 1979 Banking Act to the government's agenda (Moran 1991: 79): "The Johnson Matthey affair doubtless has lessons for the Bank of England too, illustrating as it does the challenge for devising a supervisory regime which achieves regulation without strangulation. I can assure you that we shall be working on these lessons very seriously" (Leigh-Pemberton 1984: 473).

On December 17, 1984, Nigel Lawson, the Chancellor of the Exchequer, who in his memoirs claims to have been very critical toward the Bank of England's rescue of JMB (Lawson 1992: 404), made a statement to Parliament announcing the setting up of a committee to look into the UK system of bank supervision and make recommendations. This committee, however, was to be chaired by the Governor of the Bank of England, Leigh-Pemberton, and comprised various members, including leading representatives of the City such as distinguished commercial banker Deryk Vander Weyer, a former Deputy Chairman of Barclays Bank and one of the outstanding commercial bankers of his generation (Lawson 1992: 404). The report of the Leigh-Pemberton Committee, published in June 1985, proposed the unification of the supervision procedures of the licensed institutions and the recognized banks, as well as a more detailed filling up of the *returns* provided for by the authorized institutes. However, the report did consider the possibility of an explicit request by the Bank of England for information on the management of the single banks only in cases of need.[3] Overall, the report seemed to suffer from the impossibility of solving the inconsistency between two goals: On the one hand, the necessity to avoid worrisome situations of instability like the one experienced with the JMB crisis by providing a system of consolidated supervision; on the other, there was a need to maintain the momentum of the City's financial boom triggered by the unrestrained liberalization of financial and banking activities.

The City of London was indeed enjoying a moment of great prosperity by the mid-1980s, sustained by the government's implementation of high interest rate policies (Johnson 1989). Financial and business services, overlapping, if not identical to the overseas earnings of the City of London, increased from 1.9% of GDP in 1980 to 2.8% in 1986 and 1987 while the invisibles[4] balance rose from 0.7% of GDP in 1980 to 2.9% in 1986 when it peaked as in the mid-1970s (Johnson 1990).

However, as indicated by the *Financial Times*, "rising levels of profits have made it possible to escape the consequences of imprudent or fraudulent behavior. History shows that this is the kind of climate in which standards of business practices can easily deteriorate" (*Financial Times* 1985). Thus, the Leigh-Pemberton Committee report became in December 1985 a White Paper which allowed for the traditional involvement in the discussion of all parties concerned, before a specific draft law was presented to the House of Commons.

Bargaining between the City, the government and the opposition party about the reform of the 1979 Banking Act went on from the beginning of 1986 until the end of 1987. The major issues at stake were two: The first was the regulation of relationships between supervisors, auditors and management of banks. In the end, the solution to this problem was left to the discretionary judgment of the Bank of England. The second issue was the establishment of an external Board of Banking Supervision to assist the Governor in the exercise of his supervisory powers. Eventually, its configuration was that of an *advisory* and not of an *executive* body as demanded by the opposition.

It is true that the Banking Act 1987, in force from October 1, 1987, increased the supervisory powers of the government and of the Bank of England according to the necessities of the new deregulated financial markets. However, it ultimately confirmed the traditional flexibility of the British supervisory regulation privileging the discretionary powers of the Bank of England in its implementation. Indeed, the Banking Act 1987 maintained the fundamental provisions of the 1979 Act. It required the issue of an authorization to exercise banking activity which was subject to the acceptance of deposits in the United Kingdom and which could be withdrawn if one of the minimum criteria provided by the law was not fulfilled (Bank of England 1988: Sched. 3).

One major change was the elimination of the distinction between recognized and licensed institutions. This distinction had proven useless in coping with major financial crises, which usually tended to involve both categories of credit institutions. Generally, the bill did not aim at regulating every aspect of prudential supervision and the mechanics of continuing supervision were deliberately left to the implementation of the Bank of England without recourse to detailed statutory provisions (Lewis 1987: 51). Indeed, it was up to the Bank of England to decide if the owners and managers of an authorized institution were "fit and proper persons" (Bank of England 1988: Sched. 3, para. 1); if the management of the institution was carried out "with integrity and the professional skills appropriate to the nature and the scale of the activities of the institution concerned" (Sched. 3, para. 5); or if banking activity was exercised with a "general prudent conduct" (Ch. 3, para. 4(9)), with "adequate capital" (Sched. 3, paras. 4 (2) and 4 (3)), and "liquidity" (Sched. 3, paras. 4(4) and 4 (5)). The traditional British legislator tendency to regulate only the conditions of entry and exit from the banking activity, and leave to the discretionary and informal action of the Bank of England the implementation of prudential supervision, far from being reversed, was, instead, substantially confirmed by the new banking legislation (Cianferotti 1993: 138).

Paradoxically, the regulatory wave of 1986–87 seems to have been prompted by the deregulation undertaken in the first Thatcher administration (Gowland 1990). This, as shown by the elimination of the distinction between licensed and recognized banking institutions, and, even more, by the diversification of Building Societies activities allowed by the 1986 Building Societies Act, by increasing the competitive challenges to the financial operators produced as a major consequence the need of their de-specialization.

8.2.3   Innovation and the London Stock Exchange "Big Bang"

Another important area in which the process of deregulation produced a similar result was the relationship between the banking system and the stock exchange. Also, in this case the *re-regulation* (Gowland 1990) of 1986–87 concealed a phenomenon of liberalization of the markets and de-specialization of the operators.

The prelude to the 1986 London Stock Exchange reform, the so-called "Big Bang," was represented by the 1975 deregulation of the New York Stock Exchange, which brought about a reduction in transaction costs, and by the 1979 abolition of any control on foreign currency dealings in the UK. This decision, aimed at strengthening London's financial markets, was inevitably followed by a reform of the Stock Exchange which took the form of the 1986 Big Bang.

The London Stock Exchange (LSE) was increasingly being bypassed by big institutional investors. Not only were British investors using foreign securities firms for their purchases of overseas securities, but foreign securities firms operating in other markets were creating markets in British securities. This was associated with a decline in the competitive position of the London Stock Exchange, most evidently in relation with New York. As the costs for large institutional investors of dealing in New York were lower than in London, the London Stock Exchange was being increasingly bypassed. Moreover, technological innovation had the effect of making location as such increasingly less relevant for securities trading (Cianferotti 1993).

The 1986 Reform of the LSE included both the institutional-organizational aspect and the technological one, and was based on four main innovations: (1) Abolition of fixed minimum commissions; (2) Abolition of the distinction between *brokers*[5] and *jobbers* with the creation of the *market makers*; (3) Opening up of the Stock Exchange to external institutions; and (4) Introduction of new technologies aimed at offering a system of continuous bargaining through video-terminals.

The Big Bang represented a further step in the process of de-specialization and concentration of financial institutions, and was clearly prompted by technological innovation. With the creation of a single market operator, the *market maker*, able to exercise all the activities connected to the Stock Exchange practices,[6] the big groups, mainly linked to the clearing banks, were able, by acquiring Stock Exchange firms, to offer services grouped into banking (traditional finance and corporate advice), securities (equities and debt), capital markets and investment management (Skerrit 1986: 83). Even if the clearing banks had already entered the Stock Exchange by the mid-1970s through the acquisition of merchant banks, the consequences of the Stock Exchange reform were decisive for them. The merging of commercial and investment banking allowed them to strengthen their position as middlemen, a position historically defining the City's predominance in global financial markets. Consequently, the reform increased the economic and political power of the City's big institutions in the domestic context as well.

As a further guarantee of the autonomy of the financial sector in general, and of the City's big institutions in particular, the deregulation of the Stock Exchange was accompanied by the issuance of the Financial Services Act,[7] establishing a new regulatory framework for investment business activities. This piece of legislation regulating the activities of financial intermediaries broadly defined was, in fact, aimed at increasing the range of activities that the banks were able to exercise also by protecting them from the unfair competition of other institutions. Non-banking intermediaries would, indeed, be at an advantage given the mere fact that credit institutions were not allowed to issue securities (Cianferotti 1993). In addition, the transition from broking of new products to trading them in a mature market had greatly increased the risks of banking activities (Skerrit 1986: 83).

The system was based on the introduction of the authorization to perform any investment business activity[8] to be granted directly by the Securities and Investment Board (SIB), a self-regulating body, recognized by the government and thus performing public functions.[9] This authorization could also be obtained by membership in one of the five Self-Regulating Organizations (SROs)[10] authorized by the SIB, or in one of the Recognized Professional Bodies (RPBs) for which investment advice was only a secondary activity. There was also a category of financial intermediaries, which included the insurance companies, for whom authorization was automatic. Without authorization, investment business was considered a crime and the SIB was endowed with criminal prosecution powers as well as civil remedies. The SIB and SROs could exercise the traditional powers of the self-regulating bodies over the authorized societies: appropriate and effective sanctions as well as the suspension and even the withdrawal of authorization (Cianferotti 1993).

The deregulation and laissez-faire policies implemented in the Thatcher era, prompted by technological progress and allowing financial innovation to take place in the City, made the City of London more powerful and successful in the following decades. Can we hypothesize that Brexit, if proper Thatcher-style deregulation and laissez-fair policies are implemented, will represent the means through which the City will be able to gather the full benefits of technological innovation and of globalization, thus confirming once again its hegemonic position both domestically and internationally?

8.3 BREXIT AND THE FUTURE OF THE CITY OF LONDON

8.3.1 Brexit and the City 1: Fintech, between Innovation and Deregulation

The impact of Brexit on the City of London is a widely discussed issue. There is the possibility, that, if openness is reduced, as, for example, by closing the European single market to the UK as a consequence of a Brexit, all the advantages of globalization for the City of London could be off-set.

This might explain why, at the onset, the City of London was against Brexit. Indeed, the City of London Corporation has openly supported Britain remaining in the EU. A survey of 147 UK-based financial services firms found 40% chose the UK over other centres because of access to the EU. Of 98 fintech start-up business published by Innovate Finance, 81% voted to stay in the EU; this was comparable to the survey conducted by Tech London Advocates in 2015.[11] Not a single financial trade association had been favorable to Brexit in the debate leading to the 2016 referendum, and the representatives of major City institutions such as Lloyds of London, the London Stock Exchange, Aviva, Goldman Sachs, HSBC, Barclays, Prudential, RSA, Standard Life and Santander have all expressed their institutions' wish that Britain would decide to remain in the EU.

The reasons were initially very clear. If the UK stayed in the Single Market, the institutions based in the City would have a passport to operate everywhere else in the EU without the need to have separate businesses in other countries, with all that this means in terms of different authorization processes, regulation and staffing costs.[12] However, as an exit not only from the EU but also from the Single Market, has become a reality, it seems that the City's institutions have adapted themselves to the changing situation through their traditional "pragmatic adaptation." This takes the form of moving all EU services to another EU member state with the aim of keeping their passporting rights. As in the case of the announcement made by Deutsche Bank in March 2017, with Britain leaving the Single Market, thus losing passporting rights granted to EU members, banks would turn their London branches into subsidiaries that would require capital and move their EU booking hub to an EU financial center.[13] Frankfurt could emerge as a winner in a similar race, with Standard Chartered, Nomura, Sumitomo Mitsui and Daiwa Securities picking the city as their EU hub in the year after the Brexit vote, while Citigroup, Goldman Sachs and Morgan Stanley were considering the same location.

However, as Bill Blain, a strategist at Mint Partners in London, says, "They can move as many trading and investment assets to Frankfurt as they want, but the gravitational centre of the European financial universe will remain in London for some time – whatever Brexit we get."[14]

Also Irish authorities claim they achieved deals with more than a dozen London-based banks and finance houses to move some of their operations to Dublin in preparation for Brexit with US bank JP Morgan buying a landmark office building in Dublin and Bank of America Merrill Lynch, which already has a presence in Dublin, speaking of expanding in the city.[15]

Still, one year after the referendum, experts, such as Kieran Donoghue, head of international financial services at Ireland's Industrial Development Authority, were convinced that the mass exodus from London that was once feared was unlikely to materialize.[16] In his words: "This is a sensitive event for the financial services, they don't really want to leave decades of infrastructure in London, for them to leave is a disruption to business and a cost." "We do not think that London is going to disappear, but the industry will move to a more decentralised model."[17] Even more clearly: "Essentially there are going to be three or four centres in Europe that are going to grow in size, but not to the point that London becomes irrelevant."[18]

Moreover, the size of the EU market for the City of London should not be overestimated. Indeed, the Brexit impact papers published by the European Parliament make clear how, in 2015, only 23% of UK financial services revenues derived from activities relating to the EU.[19] That is to say that the remaining 77% was related to activities outside the EU.

Finally, so far London does not seem to have lost its capacity to attract especially technologically sensitive financial industry. Reuters reports that over half a billion dollars were poured into British financial technology companies in the first half of 2017, over a third more than the same period the year before according to trade body Innovate Finance in July 2017. This is a clear sign that the fast-growing fintech sector was betting on a post-Brexit favorable environment. UK-based fintech startups pulled in $564 million of venture capital investment in the first six months of the year 2017, more than half of which came from outside Britain. That was up 37% on the first half of 2016, and put Britain in third place globally for fintech investment, behind the United States and China.[20]

Fintech is a sector ranging from mobile payment apps to digital currencies like bitcoin, and one that the government considers as key for future economic growth. Therefore, the British government has identified fintech as a priority area, saying it provides 60,000 jobs and contributes around $9 billion to the economy. In the first six months of 2017, the global investment in fintech was $6.5 billion. Of this, just over half went into US startups and around $1 billion into China. A third of the investment into British fintech came from venture capital firms based in the United States.[21] In March 2019, London was already recognized as the global centre of fintech. At that time, the British capital already hosted 17 of the top 50 fintech companies in the world, and was globally recognized as the biggest existing cluster of successful fintech companies.[22]

The main reasons for this renewed confidence in the British economy post-Brexit are, according to Abdul Haseeb Basit, Head of Finance and Strategic Projects at Innovate Finance: "Britain's prowess in both conventional finance and technology, as well as light-touch regulation, its pro-business culture and even the fact that it is Anglophone make it difficult for other centres to compete, though many – such as Berlin and Paris – are trying."[23] He also claimed that: "while passporting rights – which give firms licenced in one EU country the right to trade freely in any other – had been a big concern for investors after Brexit, those worries had eased. Even if Britain loses passporting rights, that would affect only 20 percent of the almost 300 startups that are members of Innovate Finance."[24]

The real worry was that access to highly skilled workers would dry up with Britain leaving the EU, as an estimated 30% of the sector's workers were foreigners and most of them from the EU. In Basit's words: "Talent is the number one concern, and has been consistently since the referendum – we test (our members on) that every three to six months. So that's been fairly consistent – it's been a worry and until we have more certainty around that, it will remain a worry."[25] Moreover, "There is a lot of competition in the investment space – there's a lot of capital available and it's looking for good companies to invest in." "Were they to not invest in UK companies, they feel like they might miss an opportunity. The appetite is still strong."[26]

Thus, it seems that the competitive advantages secured so far by the City of London as a global financial center, such as its technological infrastructure and its high concentration of financial expertise, may well be able to survive.

8.3.2 Brexit and the City 2: The Revenge of the Ultra-Liberals

It might even be argued that Brexit could enhance the competitive position of the British financial center in the era of globalization, as it will actually require precisely those kind of policies which further enhance the City's hegemonic potential domestically and internationally: liberalization and deregulation.

It is indeed becoming increasingly clear that Brexit could actually work for the UK, providing that a specific set of policies are adopted, policies that go precisely in the direction of the kind of Thatcher-style measures strongly supported by the "ultra-liberals," the free-marketeers of the City. Two former Chancellors of the Exchequer, Philip Hammond and George Osborne, hinted at this when they underlined the structural changes that the British economic model would need post-Brexit. Even Jeremy Corbyn, the leader of the Labour Party, seemed very aware of the risk that Brexit poses in terms of moving towards an ultra-liberal, hyper-globalized capitalist system. Moreover, this is certainly in line with former prime minister Theresa May and her cabinet's claim that Brexit will make the UK more, not less, globalized.[27]

As almost verbatim claimed in the press, in order to stay competitive in the global economy post-Brexit, Britain will have to "adapt" and the UK's economic model will need to be reset.[28] Britain will have to become a sort of Hong Kong or Singapore of Europe. That would represent the completion of Margaret Thatcher City's revolution, and it may be no coincidence that almost all of the Brexiteers are hard-line nostalgic Thatcherites.[29]

So what are those measures and how are they likely to shape the future of the City outside the EU? Or, put another way, how will "pragmatic adaptation" unfold in the case of "Brexit"? First of all, the British government will have to declare the adoption of unilateral free trade. By reducing tariffs on all imports to the UK of both goods and services, the country can easily benefit from lower global prices, in exchange for no tariffs and no control on imported goods. According to HMRC, routine customs declarations could be made electronically and goods cleared at ports in seconds.[30] This, of course, will undermine the productive base of the country, thus exacerbating further the divide between finance and industry already at the core of the British capitalist system. As during the Thatcher era, the losers will be workers, who will have to endure much higher unemployment and a reduction of the welfare system as the economy adjusted.

Contrary to expectations, migration will not necessarily decrease post-Brexit, as the competitiveness and productivity of the City of London, and of the British economy as a whole, will have to be maintained by allowing migrants in. However, migration quotas and skills will now be controlled by the British government, with far less rights in the case of EU migrants.[31] This more, not less, open door on migration, will almost certainly depress domestic wages, in line with traditional supply-side neo-liberal approaches to the labor market and to increased competitiveness, but in contrast to the initial expectations of Brexit.[32]

The same aim of increasing global competitiveness in line with the imperatives of neo-liberal globalization will produce a further liberalization of labor and environmental laws, finally freed from the checks and balances of European institutions, especially the European Court of Justice. An echo of this possibility can be identified in the decisions taken in the so-called Brexit bill by the newly elected Johnson administration after December 12, 2019.[33] Flexibility of labor markets will be facilitated by the loss of control of supranational institutions and will be justified as the only way to gain global market shares after leaving the EU trade area.[34]

This links to two further neo-liberal measures which could improve the attractiveness of the UK in the global environment and which have already been advocated by leading Tory politicians: tax cuts and reduction of state intervention in the economy.[35] In line with theories of the competitive state (Cerny 1995), attracting business in the age of globalization (especially when capital is very mobile, as in the case of financial capital), requires low taxes, a light-touch regulatory environment, the rule of law and political stability. The UK will need to be able to offer all this once outside the EU because it will no longer be the gateway to the largest regional trading bloc. It will therefore need to re-orientate the incentives it needs to offer foreign investors in a much more liberal way. However, lower taxes will reduce public spending and more spending for infrastructure will further decrease the share of public expenditure going to the welfare state, including the NHS, education and benefits. Again the lower strata of society will be the main losers in such a move, whereas the City of London will benefit not only from the new, more favorable regulatory environment, but also from the increase in the use of insurance services to substitute for the demise of the welfare state.

The direction of British economic structure change as a consequence of Brexit seems, therefore, unlikely to be towards social democracy, and even less, socialism, and more towards an exasperated form of neo-liberal globalization, the only one that, it is claimed, could guarantee some prosperity to the country outside the EU, and also the one that the City of London always favored to maintain its global competitiveness and its domestic hegemony.[36]

Indeed, the City is already positioning itself in this debate. The CityUK report published in July 2017 suggests that "Britain will lose its status as Europe's top financial centre unless it keeps borders open to specialist staff, improves infrastructure and expands links with emerging economies."[37]

8.4   CONCLUSION

Summing up, what really counts for the prosperity of the City is a relaxed regulatory environment which of course can be guaranteed by a friendly government post-Brexit.

However, this is a necessary but not sufficient condition for the City to maintain its hegemony both domestically and internationally in the globalization era.

The second vital condition is open access to markets globally. This could be jeopardized by Brexit as it is highly unlikely that the EU will grant the UK similar conditions of access to its markets as if it were still a member of the club. However, Brexit could also represent the catalyst for the adoption of ultra-liberal, Thatcher-style policies, ranging from a liberalization of labor and environmental laws, import tariffs and controls and low taxes, to the diversion of public funds from the welfare state to infrastructure.

As during Thatcher's monetarist era, deregulation, laissez-faire policies and policies favoring technological innovation will benefit the City of London and financial capital. This would enhance the capacity of the City to attract investment globally at the expense of the living and working conditions of the lower strata of society.

NOTES

1. "The 1979 Banking Act, the first attempt at statutory banking supervision in Britain, was prompted by (. . .) the EEC eager to harmonise the ground rules throughout the community in the interest of fair competition." See *The Economist* (1983), "Who polices the City?," July 2, p. 69.
2. The City Bullion Market, or London Gold Market, is the exclusive club of only five banks, Johnson Matthey, Mocatta & Goldsmith, Sharps Pixley, Rothschild and Samuel Montagu (a subsidiary of the Midland Bank), whose representatives meet every day of the week but Saturday and Sunday, at 10:30 am and 3:30 pm at the Rothschild's establishment, to fix the price of gold.
3. See "Report of the Committee set up to consider the System of Banking Supervision," London 1985.
4. The invisibles account comprises services, interest, profits and dividends (IPD) passing between the UK and other countries, and unrequired transfers to and from the government and the private sector. In 1990, services were 28% of total invisible credits, equally divided between financial and business on the one hand, and transport and travel on the other; IPD were 67% and transfers 5%.
5. The brokers were those Stock Exchange agents who operated in the interest and with the capital of their client. The jobbers operated with their capital and created the market for each kind of asset. The separation of the functions of broker and jobber, so distinctive a feature of the London market, dated only from 1908. Minimum commissions were introduced about 18 months later to defend "single capacity" by preventing the newly purified jobbers from directing business through complacent brokers to their erstwhile clients and counterparts on privileged terms. One rule could not survive without the other. See J. Hollis (1986), "A monopoly broken by a series of accidents," *The Times*, October 22, 1986, p. 18.
6. Namely, assistance in the issue and valuation of securities, distribution and sale, and sales management in the secondary market.
7. The Financial Services Act was passed by Parliament in October 1986.
8. The Act seeks to regulate all types of investment business. Schedule 1 to the Act covers five categories of business in relation to investments:
    (a) dealing in investments,
    (b) arranging deals in investments,
    (c) managing investments,
    (d) advising on investments,
    (e) operating collective investment schemes, such as unit trusts.
    "Investment" is widely defined in Schedule 1 to the Act, and includes:
    (a) securities,
    (b) options,
    (c) futures,
    (d) long term insurance contracts,

(e) contracts for differences.

Examples of these investments are:

(a) Securities: stocks and shares, bonds, debentures, certificates of deposit, government and local authorities bonds and units in unit trusts. The statutory definition of 'securities' is so wide that it was considered appropriate to make an express exemption for cheques and other bills of exchange, bank drafts, letters of credit and bank notes.

(b) Options: options to buy or sell an investment, sterling and foreign currency, gold silver and platinum or an option to buy or sell any such option.

(c) Futures: contracts for the sale of commodities and land where the price is agreed at the contract date and the subject matter of the contract is to be delivered at a future date. Contracts made for commercial purposes, not investment, are excluded.

(d) Long-term insurance contracts: long-term insurance business, as defined by the Insurance Companies Acts, but not personal health and injury insurance or term assurance (that is, life insurance which terminates on the expiry of ten years or earlier death).

(e) Contracts for differences: these are contracts under which a profit, or loss, arises by reason of currency exchange rates or price fluctuations in property of any kind, for instance, currency and interest rate swaps and index-linked National Savings Certificates.

See A. Laidlaw and G. Roberts (1990), *Law Relating to Banking Services*, London: The Chartered Institute of Bankers, pp. 97–107.

9. The SIB personnel were to be chosen among City operators and nominated jointly by the Trade Ministry and the Bank of England.

10. The SROs were the Trading Securities Association, TSA, created by the agreement between the Stock Exchange; SE, regulating the activity of securities and bonds operators, and the International Securities Regulatory Organisation, ISRO, representing the brokers acting in international financial markets, and, particularly, in the Euromarket; the Association of Futures Brokers and Dealers, AFBD, controlling futures and options markets; the Financial Intermediaries, Managers and Brokers Regulatory Association, FIM-BRA, representing a wide number of small, independent brokers acting primarily in the common funds and life-insurance sector; the Investment Management Regulatory Organisation, IMRO, grouping the operators managing the portfolios of institutional investors as banks, common funds, pension funds and insurance companies; the Life Insurance and Unit Trust Regulatory Organisation, LAUTRO, comprising insurance societies and investment funds. See Laidlaw and Roberts (1990), pp. 97–107.

11. See, at https://www.cityoflondon.gov.uk/about-the-city/how-we-make-decisions/Documents/implementing-markets-union.pdf (accessed April 28, 2016).

12. See, at https://www.cityoflondon.gov.uk/about-the-city/how-we-make-decisions/Documents/implementing-markets-union.pdf (accessed April 28, 2016).

13. *The Independent*: http://www.independent.co.uk/news/business/news/brexit-latest-news-deutsche-bank-london-frankfurt-uk-leave-eu-switch-a7826361.html (accessed July 26, 2017).

14. *The Independent*: http://www.independent.co.uk/news/business/news/brexit-latest-news-deutsche-bank-london-frankfurt-uk-leave-eu-switch-a7826361.html (accessed July 26, 2017).

15. *The Irish Times*: https://www.irishtimes.com/business/financial-services/brexit
    -a-dozen-london-firms-banks-moving-to-dublin-ida-says-1.3138874?mode=amp
    (accessed July 26, 2017).
16. *The Irish Times*: https://www.irishtimes.com/business/financial-services/brexit
    -a-dozen-london-firms-banks-moving-to-dublin-ida-says-1.3138874?mode=amp
    (accessed July 26, 2017).
17. *The Irish Times*: https://www.irishtimes.com/business/financial-services/brexit
    -a-dozen-london-firms-banks-moving-to-dublin-ida-says-1.3138874?mode=amp
    (accessed July 26, 2017).
18. *The Irish Times*: https://www.irishtimes.com/business/financial-services/brexit
    -a-dozen-london-firms-banks-moving-to-dublin-ida-says-1.3138874?mode=amp
    (accessed July 26, 2017).
19. See, at http://www.europarl.europa.eu/RegData/etudes/BRIE/2016/587384/IPOL
    _BRI%282016%29587384_EN.pdf (accessed December 21, 2017).
20. *The Finanser*: https://thefinanser.com/2017/07/fintech-6-5-billion-invested-first
    -half-2017.html/ (accessed August 1, 2017).
21. *The Finanser*: https://thefinanser.com/2017/07/fintech-6-5-billion-invested-first
    -half-2017.html/ (accessed August 1, 2017).
22. See https://thefintechtimes.com/category/fintech-london/ (accessed March 26,
    2019).
23. Reuters: http://uk.reuters.com/article/us-britain-eu-primary-dealers-idUKKBN1A
    B10U (accessed July 26, 2017).
24. Reuters: http://uk.reuters.com/article/us-britain-eu-primary-dealers-idUKKBN1A
    B10U (accessed July 26, 2017).
25. Reuters: http://uk.reuters.com/article/us-britain-eu-primary-dealers-idUKKBN1A
    B10U (accessed July 26, 2017).
26. Reuters: http://uk.reuters.com/article/us-britain-eu-primary-dealers-idUKKBN1A
    B10U (accessed July 26, 2017).
27. See http://www.bbc.com/news/uk-politics-40771900 (accessed August 1, 2017).
28. *The Independent*: http://www.independent.co.uk/voices/brexit-david-davis-free
    -trade-migration-labour-laws-low-taxes-a7845421.html (accessed August 1,
    2017).
29. *The Independent*: http://www.independent.co.uk/voices/brexit-david-davis-free
    -trade-migration-labour-laws-low-taxes-a7845421.html (accessed August 1,
    2017).
30. *The Independent*: http://www.independent.co.uk/voices/brexit-david-davis-free
    -trade-migration-labour-laws-low-taxes-a7845421.html (accessed August 1,
    2017).
31. *The Guardian*: https://www.theguardian.com/commentisfree/2017/sep/06/leak-eu
    -nationals-status-britain-brexit (accessed September 11, 2017).
32. *The Independent*: http://www.independent.co.uk/voices/brexit-david-davis-free
    -trade-migration-labour-laws-low-taxes-a7845421.html (accessed August 1,
    2017).
33. *The Mirror*: see, at https://apple.news/AxD5_NHQZSbiJSDqdzJytQA?fbclid
    =IwAR1l7V_fsSIO-ua1LDiY_Q0XKxUJv7kKLv-PoMTFwIUoZG7n
    _730Jw7EqVY (accessed on 23rd December, 2019); see also Science
    Business: available at: https://sciencebusiness.net/news/boris-johnson-vows
    -ditch-eu-rules-gm-crops?fbclid=IwAR1xRXR1ibjy3I9A8YIGXbJTC6M05
    NjAxvEgFoQ8AuGQDHo531qJZsZDPis (accessed December 23, 2019; and *The*

Guardian: https://www.theguardian.com/commentisfree/2017/sep/05/brexit-bill -government-negotiations-labour (accessed September 11, 2017).
34. *The Independent*: http://www.independent.co.uk/voices/brexit-david-davis-free -trade-migration-labour-laws-low-taxes-a7845421.html (accessed on 1st August, 2017).
35. *The Independent*: http://www.independent.co.uk/voices/brexit-david-davis-free -trade-migration-labour-laws-low-taxes-a7845421.html (accessed on 1st August, 2017).
36. *The Independent*: http://www.independent.co.uk/voices/brexit-david-davis-free -trade-migration-labour-laws-low-taxes-a7845421.html (accessed July 26, 2017).
37. The CityUK: see, https://www.thecityuk.com/research/a-vision-for-a-transformed -world-leading-industry/ (accessed August 1, 2017).

REFERENCES

Bank of England (1982), "Banking Act 1979: Annual Report by the Bank of England 1981–1982," *Bank of England, Reports and Accounts*, London: Hertford, p. 34.
Bank of England (1988), *Banking Act 1987*, London: Bank of England.
Cerny, P. (1995), "Globalization and the changing logic of collective action," *International Organization* 49(4): 595–625.
Cianferotti, S. (1993), *La regolamentazione e l'operativita' del sistema bancario e finanziario inglese (1930–1993)*, Firenze: Banca Toscana.
Coakley, J. and L. Harris (1983), *The City of Capital: London's Role as a Financial Centre*, Oxford: Basil Blackwell.
Financial Times (1985), "The standing of the City," *Financial Times*, December 19, p. 18.
Gowland, C. (1990), *The Regulation of the Financial Markets in the 1990s*, Cheltenham: Edward Elgar.
Johnson, C. (1989), "U.K. living on credit," *Lloyds Bank Economic Bulletin*, No. 131, November.
Johnson, C. (1990), "U.K. balancing acts collapses," *Lloyds Bank Economic Bulletin*, No. 142, October.
Lawson, N. (1992), *The View from No. 11*, London: Bantam Press.
Leigh-Pemberton, R. (1984), "Domestic financial markets: progress and problems", *Bank of England Quarterly Bulletin*, 24.
Lewis, D. (1987), "The Banking Bill: between Charybdis and Scylla," *The Journal of International Banking Law* 2: 51.
Longstreth, F. (1979), "The City, industry and the state". In C. Crouch (ed.), *State and Economy in Contemporary Capitalism*, London: Croom Helm, pp. 157–91.
Moran, M. (1991), *The Politics of Financial Services Revolution*, London: Macmillan.
O'Brien, L. (1973), "EEC regulations", *The Banker*, No. 123.
Ryder, F. R. (1979), *The Banking Act 1979*, London: Sweet and Maxwell, Introduction.
Skerrit, J. (1986), "A systems approach for the City revolution," *The Banker*, March 1986, p. 83.
Talani, L. S. (2012), *Globalization, Hegemony and the Future of the City of London*, London: Palgrave.

Talani, L. S. (2018), "'Pragmatic adaptation' and the future of the City of London: between globalization and Brexit," in Colin Hay and Daniel Bailey (eds), *Diverging Capitalism: Britain, the City of London and Europe*, London: Routledge, Chapter 3.

The Economist (1983), "Who polices the City?," July 2, 1983.

9. Brexit adds to Europe's need for economic rebalancing and technological impetus

Rémi Bourgeot

9.1   INTRODUCTION

The Brexit vote has prompted a debate about the United Kingdom's economic orientation, which, to some extent, echoes the European Union's own quest of economic rebalancing. The issue of reindustrialisation, despite being still insufficiently discussed, illustrates the rising awareness, across the globe, of the interlinkage between macro-financial imbalances and social malaise. The referendum's outcome has generally been attributed not only to political resentment towards the European Union, but also to the social anxiety that was exacerbated by the financial crisis and austerity policies.[1] Since then, the broad political pledge to reverse austerity has testified to the importance of these socio-economic factors,[2] which were not strictly linked to the issue of EU membership, in the case of the UK. Member states of the EU and the Eurozone in particular, whose economic conditions are more directly related to the bloc's economic approach, are, however, facing a similar trend of social discontent.

The relationship between the UK and the EU's remaining member states amounts to a kaleidoscope of divergence and similarities. European countries, including Britain, are both dealing with specific difficulties and a common trend of frustratingly slow economic growth, which stems from a pattern of weak productivity gains, amongst other factors. Modest productivity has been of particular concern to the UK since the global financial crisis, as, by some measures, the country's productivity level appears significantly lower than in other advanced economies, notably amongst its Western European peers. Despite the specificity of its exchange rate flexibility and the importance of its financial sector, Britain's overall productive dynamics, with a substantial external deficit, must be considered with respect to the particular system that has emerged in Europe from the turmoil of the global financial crisis and the euro crisis.

Divergences in competitiveness amongst members of the currency union, which were caused mostly by contrasting inflation rates, had dramatic consequences akin to a balance-of-payments crisis. After the crisis erupted, the impossibility of depreciation at the national level forced prices to adapt in a mechanism reminiscent of the classical gold standard. Most trade deficits were eventually suppressed, but at the cost of sluggish aggregate demand, high unemployment, depressed investment and disruptions in the social construct.

While fundamental doubts about the Eurozone took centre stage from 2010 onwards, the UK was generally assumed to follow a model of its own, and to deal with rather distinct issues. The proponents of a more redistributive approach did voice their opposition to spending cuts, very much like in the rest of Europe, but Britain's insertion in globalisation, at the centre of international financial flows, was seen as a given fact. In addition, the UK was able to reverse the damage of the global crisis on employment faster than many of its EU partners thanks in part to a more responsive monetary policy. While the country managed to restore jobs, from 2012, at a time when unemployment appeared stuck at dramatic levels in many continental countries, its productivity shortfall, however, seems to have worsened over the same period of time, as a result of particularly low investments.[3] A trade-off has emerged throughout Europe between investing in production means, in order to increase labour productivity and employ fewer people, on the one hand, and hiring more staff with stagnating productivity, on the other hand. The limitations of this binary approach point to the need for an economic vision that would take on board the economic and social potential of the current industrial revolution (robotics, artificial intelligence and 3D printing, amongst other technologies), in which Europe as a whole is lagging behind the United States and China.

At this point in Europe's economic path, increased divergence seems likely on several fronts, despite the common challenges facing domestic economies. While the British people voted to leave at least in part as a result of their social and economic anxiety, the referendum process was triggered, in the first place, by political circles which seemed little inclined to costly social policies.[4] Despite the reorientation in terms of social and infrastructure spending that Boris Johnson advocated during the 2019 general election campaign, the present interests of the services sector, especially finance, makes a great social and industrial turnaround rather unlikely. While London has been the EU's leading financial centre for decades, the UK might now, under these circumstances, resort to increased fiscal competition and to a model more resolutely based on offshore finance. The debate triggered by Brexit is of great importance to Europe as a whole, not only when it comes to preserving trade links with the UK, but as importantly in order to devise a more cohesive economic model within the European Union and in its neighbourhood, against the continual threat of non-cooperative policies and spiralling fragmentation.

The remainder of this chapter is structured as follows. Section 9.2 is concerned with the European context of large trade imbalances in which the UK's own external deficits have grown. Section 9.3 focuses on the internal devaluation sparked by the euro crisis. It shows to what extent divergence in terms of competitiveness within the Eurozone should be attributed to inflation differentials, and that the UK did not face such pressure to eventually adjust labour costs towards German standards as a result of the pound's depreciation during the global financial crisis. Section 9.4 reviews the reaction of the European Central Bank (ECB) and the Bank of England (BoE) in order to point out the limitations facing expansionary monetary policies which, after saving Europe from an even more prolonged downturn, have proved insufficient to solve underlying issues of productivity, modernisation, and social cohesion. Section 9.5 precisely points out the productivity and investment issue facing the British economy and the dilemma that has emerged in Europe more generally between employment and productivity since the global financial crisis. In this perspective, the conclusion (Section 9.6) addresses the need for a more sustainable and inclusive approach to technological modernisation.

9.2   REAL EXCHANGE RATES AND CURRENT ACCOUNT IMBALANCES IN THE EUROZONE AND THE UK

The array of arguments used in the UK and in the rest of Europe since the Brexit campaign have testified to the political complexity that typifies economic thinking in the EU and the difficulty to agree on a common approach to economic rebalancing. European officials have sometimes appeared perplexed by Britain's animosity towards a system which, in their view, follows "Anglo-Saxon" principles.[5] Meanwhile, a significant part of the Leave campaign has been led by Eurosceptics of the Conservative Party who are more supportive of free trade and unfettered globalisation than many of the political movements that invoke economic liberalism on the continent. A number of political leaders across northern Europe expressed their alarm at the prospect of losing a like-minded ally[6] in their struggle with the more statist inspiration of countries like France. Beyond the reference to general economic ideas, the public debate about Brexit, on both sides of the argument, has nevertheless been rather light on the actual European macro-financial context in which it is taking place.

The issue of the UK's current account deficit, which reached 5.8 per cent of GDP in 2016—before decreasing to about 4 per cent the following year—was sometimes dismissed as irrelevant to a modern economy focused on the services sector.[7] Yet, the combination of a large current-account deficit and roaring property prices, until the referendum, indicated a more pronounced level of economic imbalance than a large budget deficit alone. In Britain as on the continent, public accounts have nevertheless been the main focus of post-crisis policies, as the tremendous rise of deficits during the global financial crisis shocked policymakers. In the middle of the crisis, the UK reached a budget deficit above 10 per cent of GDP, which appeared closer to that of peripheral Eurozone countries under tremendous market pressure than of core countries.[8] Though particularly acrimonious, the Brexit debate barely touched on the broader issue of Europe's macro-financial imbalances.

The EU accounted in 2017 for 53 per cent of the UK's imports, or £341 billion, and 44 per cent, or £274 billion, of its exports. The UK's trade deficit with the EU reached £67 billion that year, or 3.3 per cent of its GDP, resulting from a deficit of £95 billion in goods and a surplus of 28 billion in services.[9] Meanwhile, it had a trade surplus of £41 billion with non-EU countries, resulting from an £83 billion surplus in services and a £42 billion deficit in goods. While the financial sector accounts for about 6.5 per cent of domestic output, it plays a key part in limiting the extent of the country's overall deficit.[10]

Britain's current-account deficit never reached highs of the same magnitude as in some peripheral Eurozone countries on the eve of the global financial crisis—nearly 10 per cent of GDP in the case of Spain, and a staggering 15 per cent in Greece (Figure 9.1). Nor is the structure of the British economy close to that of either country. The differences between the Spanish and the Greek economies are similarly substantial however. Large current-account imbalances have been a common feature of globalisation as it has unfolded over the past decades. These imbalances have nevertheless taken on a particular dimension within Europe. The combination of ambitious commercial integration and insufficient macro-economic coordination, with non-cooperative wage policies, sluggish productivity and exchange rate rigidity have all resulted in a particularly acute trend of economic divergence, of which current account imbalances are a revealing symptom, despite the variety of situations beneath that aggregate notion.

While imbalances within the Eurozone have been thoroughly commented on since the crisis, the UK's outsider status has often led observers to downplay its interconnection with the rest of Europe in terms of productive trends. Although the United Kingdom chose to remain outside the currency union, it did not, however, enjoy constant currency adjustments that would have guaranteed an overall external balance.

Despite legitimate mention across the globe, since the global financial crisis, of a "currency war" in which countries seek to depreciate their currencies on competitive grounds, many national governments rather tend to accept an overvalued currency with some enthusiasm in the first place, as this increases consumers' purchasing power for some time and encourages what appears to be an inalterable trend of financial influxes which benefit a number of eco-

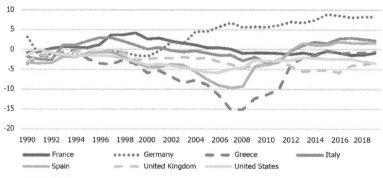

Source: IMF WEO.

Figure 9.1   Current account (% of GDP)

nomic sectors (Frieden 2016). In the UK, the City, which found its position reinforced by globalisation, had no particular interest in a fixed exchange rate of the currency union type and favoured more autonomous monetary policy and regulation (Talani 2016). This implies more pronounced movements in terms of real price competitiveness than in a fixed exchange rate setting, both in terms of real over-appreciation, on the one hand, and the possibility of a subsequent downward adjustment far less damaging than internal devaluation, on the other hand. As the City has the ability to benefit from exchange rate movements, a prolonged rise of the exchange rate, even if it becomes cut-off from real economic developments—as it did during the recovery—presents advantages in terms of funds inflows until an adjustment occurs, which can also be taken advantage of.

The pound's exchange rate versus the euro plunged during the global financial crisis, as the country was hit harder in the first years of the crisis than those European countries which do not have a similar focus on the financial sector and which did not exhibit a large external deficit. In the run-up to the Brexit referendum and in its aftermath, the exchange rate downward adjustment took place on a slightly different basis. The current account deficit did play a significant part in Britain's vulnerability to international flows, an issue which led Mark Carney, the BoE's governor, to describe the UK as depending on "the kindness of strangers".[11] But the depreciation was triggered, against this macro-financial background, by the uncertainty over the country's future relationship with the EU and the sustainability of its overall economic model.

Countries whose manufacturing sector is greatly integrated in global supply chains, like the UK, feel the effect of real exchange rate movements on their trade account mostly through the wage factor, whereas countries whose exports rely on smaller companies exporting their own products, like Italy for example, would be affected in a deeper fashion. In addition, many services are generally far less sensitive to international price variations than the real tradable sector, as their output is often attached to a specific territory. High-value-added financial services, on their side, rely more on the specificities of the architecture in which they are involved, especially if they are related to offshore financial activities—which makes the position of the UK financial sector rather particular in that respect. Although European economies all rely to a great extent on the services sector, the qualitative lines separating economic sectors have become increasingly blurred in modern value chains, and real exchange rates have turned out to have a significant impact on their overall competitiveness through labour costs. In the particular case of the Eurozone, the relevance of real exchange rate variations, i.e. variations of price indices in the context of the currency union, came back to haunt policy makers during the euro crisis, after this issue had been downplayed throughout the 2000s, in what appeared to be an integrated monetary construct.

9.3   LABOUR COSTS HAVE BEEN THE MAIN ADJUSTMENT VARIABLE IN EUROPE—WITH THE ADDITIONAL CONTRIBUTION OF THE POUND'S EXCHANGE RATE IN THE UK

The Eurozone's imbalances are key to understanding the European context around Brexit, and the type of vulnerability that the ensuing instability might aggravate in Europe (Chen et al. 2018; Luo 2017). Instability is inherent in a monetary union and can only be offset through close macroeconomic coordination and a damping mechanism based, for example, on fiscal transfers. The single currency tends to amplify divergence, as it precludes, by definition, any adjustment in terms of nominal exchange rates within the area. The underlying divergence can stem from various sources, either political or not. Most analysts have pointed to differences in terms of national economic policies, especially labour policies, since the euro's inception. Germany took steps from the early 2000s to pressure labour costs, in the context of the "Agenda 2010" strategy, while most other nations followed suit when they were struck by the crisis or later, as in the case of France, about 15 years after Germany's reforms. Differences in terms of inflation rates have turned out to be an even greater source of divergence in competitiveness, as countries with higher inflation levels have seen their prices rise compared to the core. This is precisely what happened to peripheral countries throughout the 2000s. Contrary to the most common interpretation, these countries did not experience any wage drift, as is clear from detailed unit labour costs (ULC) statistics, once inflation is properly taken into account (Bourgeot 2013; Talani 2015) (Figure 9.2). In most cases, despite property bubbles and spending sprees that fuelled current account deficits, real wages barely rose at all throughout the euro's first decade in these countries, and the same trend applied to productivity—a situation far from optimal of course. The divergence in competitiveness (in terms of nominal unit labour costs) resulted from Germany's wage policy and from the persistence of contrasting inflation rates across the Eurozone.

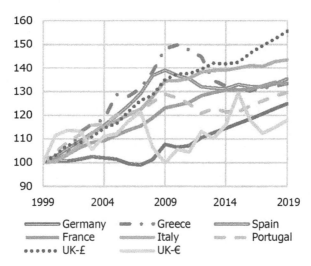

Source: Ameco, personal calculations.

Figure 9.2   Nominal unit labour costs (1999=100)

Over the 2000s, the United Kingdom followed a trend which was similar to that of Eurozone countries outside Germany, in terms of unit labour costs expressed in the national currency.[12] Nominal ULCs rose by about 35 per cent through the decade, while Germany's nominal ULCs stagnated, and even decreased at some point, until an 8 per cent rise took place from 2007 to 2009. Italy's nominal ULCs rose by the very same amount as Britain's until 2009 and actually followed the same trend until 2015. Spain's nominal ULCs rose at a slightly faster pace until 2009 before stalling as a result of the bursting of its housing bubble, and tremendous market pressure related to its banking crisis and its large external deficits. Italy was far less affected in the first place, as it had experienced neither a spectacular real-estate bubble nor the same kind of banking excesses centred on spiralling securitisation of the "subprime" type. Interestingly, if the pound's exchange rate versus the euro is taken into account, the UK can be considered to have been through a major adjustment in

terms of its nominal ULCs from 2007 to 2009. In this respect, it even fell back
to its 1999 level, hence joining Germany's longer-term trend. This nominal
exchange rate adjustment was followed by the halving of its current account
deficit, from almost 5 per cent of GDP in 2008 to 2.4 per cent in 2011. Italy's
current account deficit kept deteriorating significantly over the same period of
time, and only started to shrink from 2011, as a result of the euro crisis and the
fall of domestic demand, amidst a trend of collapsing credit.

Other non-euro countries followed a trend different from that of the UK.
Poland's nominal ULCs rose by little more than 15 per cent in the 2000s
(because of a large decrease in real unit labour costs earlier in the decade), at
a similar pace whether expressed in euros or in zlotys, despite some exchange
rate volatility in the meantime. Sweden provides a similar example, with
nominal ULCs rising by about 15 per cent in krona, and slightly less in euro.
In the Czech Republic and Slovakia on the other hand, nominal ULCs rose by
about 30 per cent in their respective korunas, but a massive increase in their
exchange rates led their ULCs expressed in euros to double, before stabilising
in the following years, both in the Czech Republic which retained its national
currency and in Slovakia which adopted the euro. This trend of overvaluation
led the Czech National Bank to subsequently follow the Swiss National Bank's
example in capping the appreciation of its currency during the Eurozone crisis.

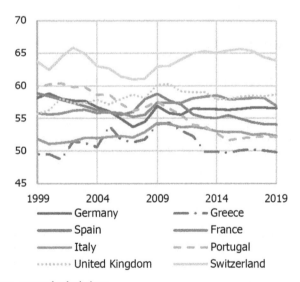

Source: Ameco, personal calculations.

Figure 9.3   *Wage share (% GDP)*

The study of the wage share[13] provides both an indication of the level of the wage bill compared to total output and the variation of the average wage relative to average labour productivity (in terms of output per employee) (Figure 9.3). The wage share rose by 5 per cent in the UK from 1999 to the onset of the global crisis in 2007, about the same amount as in Greece, while it stagnated in Italy, decreased slightly in France, decreased by about 5 per cent in Spain and Portugal, and by 7 per cent in Germany. Obviously, none of these countries can be considered to have experienced a wage drift, and several even experienced the opposite trend of falling wages compared to productivity. The UK experienced, over that period, a trend that was rather typical of European economies, with nominal unit labour costs rising mostly as a result of inflation, which accounted for about 20 percentage points of the 25 per cent rise from 1999 to 2007. In spite of a similar pattern of nominal ULCs rising mostly with inflation, peripheral countries were, in the absence of the kind of exchange rate adjustment that the pound sterling went through, wrongly considered to have experienced a dramatic wage drift.

Inflation rates did converge to some extent from the 1990s, but they remained unsurprisingly different across the currency area (Talani 2015), and the EU at large, throughout the 2000s—which means that prices actually diverged, although at a declining rate of divergence. Inflation rates have converged by and large since the crisis. This however has been achieved by suppressing demand and putting in place a generalised model of trade surpluses which is hardly sustainable for an economic area as a whole, especially since this shift does not rely so much on strong productivity gains as on depressed real labour costs. Austerity programmes have been a key part of this trend, in addition to the effects of mass unemployment. The United Kingdom's austerity programme was not of the same magnitude as the sudden adjustment experienced by peripheral Eurozone countries, but was still very significant in comparison to other large economies. However, the type of measures that were implemented varied greatly amongst countries. While the likes of France have mainly relied on tax hikes, the UK has focused more on spending cuts, notably in social programmes (Emmerson and Tetlow 2015).

9.4   MONETARY POLICY HELPED EUROPE DURING THE CRISIS BUT DOES LITTLE FOR IN-DEPTH REBALANCING

Against this background of fragmented macroeconomic policies, unconventional monetary policies have turned out to be the main tool available to keep European economies together and to somehow offset the effect of austerity policies and mass unemployment on aggregate demand. The Bank of England reacted early to the global crisis, along the same line as the Federal Reserve in the United States, with timely interest rate cuts from 5 per cent to 0.5 per cent, and an asset purchase programme that led the central bank to eventually hold £435 billion of British government bonds ($200 billion in 2009, £375 billion in 2012, and £435 billion with the round of quantitative easing put in place after the referendum).[14] The ECB took a considerably different approach in the first place, with rate hikes in the summer of 2008 to combat what Jean-Claude Trichet interpreted as inflationary pressures, and again in the summer of 2011 for the very same reason. Asset purchases remained limited under his presidency, and, because of their inadequate definition even more than their scale, they failed to deter market attacks on peripheral sovereign bonds.

After the ECB's Outright Monetary Transactions (OMT) programme, under Mario Draghi's innovative leadership, reduced peripheral bond yields tremendously, on mostly rhetorical grounds, the late implementation of quantitative easing (QE) in 2015, however, made it possible to partly offset, *ex post*, the deflationary context produced by austerity policies. In the UK, the BoE's approach was implemented in a timelier way, and was able to offset austerity policies, to some extent, while those were being implemented. The impact of its policies, notably on house and financial asset prices, was however criticised as feeding inequalities.[15] Beneath aggregate variables and the overall support to demand from monetary policy, large swathes of the UK are facing a social and economic situation that has little in common with the standards of the south east. The UK's economic model, with its flexibility, both supports high employment and high inequalities (Lavery et al. 2017),[16] notably in regional terms,[17] given the concentration of financial services in London. The UK stands out as the only G7 country where wealth inequalities have risen since the start of the century.[18]

In the Eurozone, the criticism of monetary action on social grounds has found far less support, despite a similar effect on asset and house prices, as the lack of significant monetary intervention for seven years after the start of the global crisis precisely made the case for central bank action in times of financial instability, in order to withstand a shock on funding channels and aggregate demand. Both the ECB and the BoE can be considered, in the end, to have followed the same type of strategy, from a market perspective, in order to ease funding conditions for governments and the private sector, and to preserve aggregate demand. The ECB was nevertheless able to achieve that aim only after years of political disagreement and prevarication, until it turned to a new consensus, which happens to be rather similar to that in place in other developed economies. While many commentators have lamented the European governments' inability to unite and work out a substantial solution to the ills of the currency union since the start of the euro crisis, the ECB eventually appeared as a rare symbol of unity and technical mastery. In the absence of a substantial agreement amongst European governments over a new model of cooperation, the ECB's expansionary monetary policies served not only to raise inflation closer to its 2 per cent target, but also as a palliative to the lack of political cohesion amongst member states.

A responsive monetary policy approach and the possibility of non-standard measures are undoubtedly needed to guarantee the sustainability of a currency union, and can notably offset the imbalances stemming, among other factors, from the unicity of interest rates policy against varied national backgrounds. A timely approach to central banking, although necessary, does not suffice however. Macroeconomic coordination as well as a stabilising mechanism are also necessary, especially in times of crisis. The lack of macroeconomic coordination could technically be solved, but European politics is found wanting in this respect. At a time when wage growth in Germany is indispensable to achieving rebalancing in the Eurozone, the political tools to encourage such a trend have become limited. And the German government's deleveraging strategy has, in addition, weighed on public investment, contributing significantly to the rise of the current account surplus to levels around 8 per cent of GDP.[19] This trend has led some German economists to advocate more domestic investments, especially in infrastructure, in addition to encouraging more pronounced wage hikes. The lack of investments in Germany is seen not only as fuelling trade imbalances, but also as capping the country's growth potential (Bach et al. 2013).

A usual response to the EU's woes on the part of individual member states consists in seeking to hastily develop partnerships in the rest of the world. After the euro crisis compelled many European countries into a severe adjustment, Germany's exports growth began to increasingly rely on non-European markets, thanks notably to the euro's weakened exchange rate. During the euro crisis, many German companies reoriented their exports towards China and other emerging markets, whose imbalances were often downplayed. Over the past few years, Britain has also seemed willing to give up on some of its industrial interests, beyond steel, in order to develop a special partnership with China—which, before the referendum, was considered as a way to further its role as Europe's main centre for renminbi trading and to attract related investment.

9.5 PRODUCTIVITY OR EMPLOYMENT: A NOXIOUS DILEMMA ENCOURAGING FISCAL COMPETITION

In the UK, as in the EU, the evolving consensus on the need for monetary action to support aggregate demand, when needed, and the search for global export markets and investment sources has somehow relegated policy action on more fundamental economic issues, especially on the productivity front.

While central banks' activism, both in the UK and in the Eurozone eventually, have succeeded in reviving final demand to some extent, slow labour productivity gains capped economic growth, and standardised structural reforms do not necessarily address the underlying issues. Despite country-specific recommendations in the European Semester and the more open perspective on competitiveness developed in the Europe 2020 strategy, a narrow definition still prevails (Bongardt and Torres 2019). Slow productivity growth is a general concern throughout not only Europe but the developed world, and even emerging markets, which, after reaching often far less than half of advanced economies' productivity levels, tend to face what has been described as the "middle-income trap".

The United Kingdom has not only experienced slow productivity growth throughout its recovery,[20] but it also stands out for its particularly low level of productivity compared to its western European peers, notably France, Italy and Germany. In addition to the difficulty in measuring productivity in modern economies, in the context of rising information and communication technologies (Syverson 2016), such comparisons necessarily rely on the notion of purchasing power parity (PPP), which remains prone to legitimate criticism. In terms of productivity expressed in PPP as output per worker, the UK stands at a level as low as 71 per cent of US levels, which compares to France at 88 per cent, Germany at 80 per cent, and Italy at 79 per cent (Figures 9.4 and 9.5).[21] The level of Japan's labour productivity, at 65 per cent of the US level, might also testify to the limitations of the measurement of productivity in PPP terms, especially while aggregating diverse sectors of the economy.

While the extent of the UK's lag in terms of productivity is hard to capture precisely, the very notion nonetheless tends to be backed by a pattern of low productive investments, and the development of low-paying jobs since the recession. In addition, productivity issues are linked to the weight of sectors that tend to employ workers in a low-productivity setting. It has been estimated that, in the UK, 66 per cent of employees are employed by corporations with below-average productivity, which compares to a 55 per cent level in Germany.[22]

Productivity growth has remained particularly low since the recovery, typically at less than 1 per cent per annum, and this slow growth has been more broad-based across sectors than in most other European economies.[23] Two types of trends have emerged in reaction to the global crisis. While most countries saw a dip in their productivity, as the fall in output was not matched by equivalent lay-offs, in Spain productivity soared by more than 2 per cent in the middle of the global financial crisis, after continuously declining until about 2006. The real estate boom translated into increased employment in low productivity activities, and the bursting of the bubble subsequently led to massive lay-offs that would push the unemployment rate above 25 per cent. The United

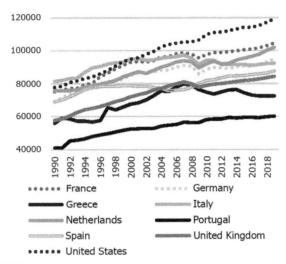

Source: IMF WEO.

Figure 9.4   *GDP per person employed (PPP), constant prices, 2011 US dollars*

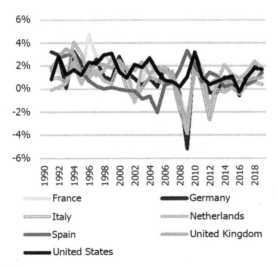

Source: IMF WEO.

Figure 9.5   *GDP per person employed (PPP), constant prices, 2011 US dollars, Y/Y change (%)*

States experienced a similar trend of rising productivity after the collapse of the housing bubble. Most European countries, however, saw their productivity fall, which was particularly acute in the case of Germany and the Netherlands, where social conventions led to minimise the impact of the crisis in terms of layoffs, even if this meant reducing employees' working hours.

While European countries are affected by a common trend of particularly weak productivity growth, it is quite notable that countries amongst the worst hit by the crisis have seen their productivity rise. Unlike Spain and Portugal, the sharp decline in Greek productivity, in addition to skyrocketing unemployment, testifies again to the failure of the economic remedy that has been imposed upon the country. While there seemed generally to be a trade-off between employment and productivity, Greece lost on both counts. Meanwhile, Italy, where the crisis has not been as severe as in other southern economies in the first place, experienced less extreme levels of unemployment than Spain, and saw its productivity rather decline, to reach the same levels in real terms as two decades ago.

Beyond the dramatic consequences of the global crisis and the ensuing euro crisis, the regime of slow productivity growth also points to sectoral speciali-sation. The extent of the UK's reliance of services limits the potential that can be found in the manufacturing sector. Manufacturing in the UK accounts for slightly less than 9 per cent of output, which compares with more than 20 per cent in Germany and 15 per cent in Italy.[24] Although a larger manufacturing sector does not constitute a systematic recipe for faster productivity growth, as exemplified by Italy's stagnating productivity, it nonetheless opens the way for such a development, in a pronounced way, under adequate policies.

While labour productivity growth in the services sector has varied greatly from one country to another, even the most pronounced progress in services productivity remains far smaller than what is usually seen in the manufacturing sector (Figures 9.6 and 9.7). Over the past 20 years, the United Kingdom led productivity growth in services, which overall rose by about 17 per cent, a pace similar to that of the United States, after a significant fall during the global crisis, especially as employment in the financial sector was hard to reduce as much as value added, for regulatory and technical reasons. This overall achievement pales, however, in comparison with the 50 per cent rise in manu-facturing productivity in the same country.

In addition, productivity in the services sector, especially in finance, is threat-ened by the changing relationship with the EU. London has been described by Mark Carney as "Europe's investment banker" (Carney 2017), accounting for "over half of debt and equity issuance by EU27 borrowers". The friendly regulatory environment that has been at the centre of the UK's approach in past decades since the Thatcher era, aimed in the first place to respond to the interest of the country's financial elite, should, however, make a "pragmatic

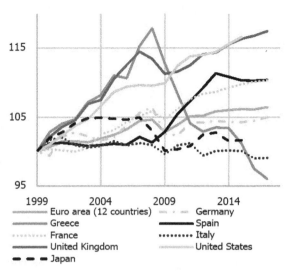

Source: Ameco, personal calculations.

Figure 9.6   *Gross value added (GVA) per person employed, services (1999=100)*

adaptation" likely, as explained by Leila Simona Talani in Chapter 8 of this book on the future of the City. The government's support to fintech provides an illustration of its effort to help combine the focus on services with productivity growth and to insert the British financial sector in global trends, from a more qualitative standpoint. Theresa May, during her time as prime minister, stressed the notion that the UK should be "unequivocally pro-business". In terms of taxation, she assured corporate leaders that "whatever [their] business, investing in a post-Brexit Britain will give [them] the lowest rate of corporation tax in the G20".[25] She went as far as to promise "big companies" to cut their corporate tax rate from 20 per cent to as low as 10 per cent, in case of a no-deal Brexit,[26] while more moderate proposals pointed to a rate closer to 17 per cent under a more positive scenario. Further illustrating his social turn, Boris Johnson announced his intention to drop any such plans, in order to fund increased social spending and to reverse austerity.[27]

The corporate tax rates mentioned before his successful attempt to appeal to more popular voters, compare with 33 per cent in France, about 30 per cent in Germany and Italy, 25 per cent in Spain, and as little as 12.5 per cent in Ireland.[28] The French and German authorities have also discussed plans to both

GVA per Person Employed, Manufacturing (1999=100)

━━━ Euro area (12 countries)	┄┄┄ Germany
·········· Greece	·········· Spain
┅┅┅┅┅ France	━━━ Italy
━━━ United Kingdom	━━━ United States
········· Japan	

Source: Ameco, personal calculations.

*Figure 9.7   Gross value added (GVA) per person employed,
manufacturing (1999=100)*

lower and harmonise corporate tax rates, but at significantly higher levels than what has been mentioned in the UK, typically around 25 per cent.[29]

Attracting, or retaining, large corporations through advantageous schemes would be an effective approach to preserving value-added and well-paying administrative jobs, in addition to the tax base. Yet these policies would not help to solve the country's underlying productivity issue, or to initiate a more social orientation of domestic policies. European governments could take advantage of Brexit to reach more ambitious integration goals that require more cohesion, on an array of issues (Bongardt and Torres 2016). Meanwhile, the threat of fiscal competition would undermine efforts to move towards a model of cooperation more focused on productivity growth, which requires a balanced environment for investments that should reward territories more on the basis of their productive potential than taxation schemes.

So far, the pattern of weak productivity has echoed investment trends. The severity of the crisis in peripheral Eurozone countries was illustrated by collapsing investments from about 30 per cent of GDP in Spain to about 20 per cent, from 25 per cent to less than 15 per cent in Greece, and in a less extreme fashion in Italy from about 22 per cent to 17 per cent of GDP (Figure

9.8). Total investments in the UK were, before the crisis, already below the European average, hovering around 17 per cent of GDP, and stabilised at an even lower level. EU membership has been central to the structure of investments in the UK (Dhingra et al. 2016), especially in terms of foreign direct investments, in the context of complex supply chains, which have exerted a profound effect on the insertion of the country in globalisation. The destabilisation of investment flows would further aggravate the consequences of their already insufficient overall levels in terms of the modernisation process and productivity enhancement. The prospect of this destabilisation is all the more daunting since trade statistics do not entirely reflect the complexity of investment and trade links amongst European countries, in terms of value added (Felbermayr et al. 2017). This situation appears particularly acute in the car sector, where global manufacturers have invested in the UK given its position in the EU, and where European companies provide more than half of the components used to assemble cars in the UK.[30]

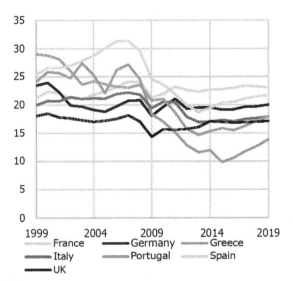

Source: IMF WEO.

Figure 9.8   Investment (% GDP)

The low and vulnerable levels of investments in Europe point to the lack of economic orientation aimed at modernising production tools, both in manufacturing and services. In the UK, investments are constrained by a low level of total savings, around 12 percent of GDP, while in other European

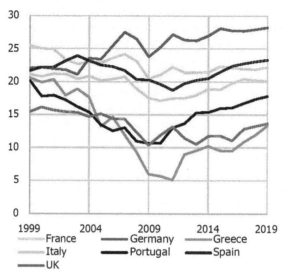

Source: IMF WEO.

Figure 9.9   Savings (% GDP)

countries, room for improvement in investments remains, especially in the case of Germany, with savings at about 27 percent of GDP, as a result both of an historical trend amongst German households, but also of the government's deleveraging strategy through lower public investments (Figure 9.9).

9.6   CONCLUSION: TECHNOLOGICAL UPGRADING IS KEY TO AVOIDING A NEW RACE TO THE BOTTOM

While debates over the management of the EU centre on institutional reform, even the stepwise approach advocated by some on a common budget and a deposit insurance scheme for the Eurozone has raised opposition amongst several member states. Since fiscal integration will remain limited in size and scope in the foreseeable future, the aim of economic policy coordination requires more attention than ever, in order to foster long-term stabilisation and real convergence amongst national productive bases, especially when it comes to embracing the ongoing technological revolution. Meanwhile, Brexit raises the prospect of further divergence, with a focus on fiscal competition rather than productivity enhancement, in particular where infrastructure and technology spending is needed.

The European Central Bank and the Bank of England have played a crucial part in steering the UK and the EU at large from the Great Recession that followed the global financial crisis. Though essential, however, monetary policy does not suffice either to create real convergence or long-term growth. Despite the recovery, growth has remained qualitatively fragile all over Europe, as productivity gains fell short of the levels needed to match the eventual effect of supportive monetary policies. Productivity growth during the crisis has been associated with massive layoffs in countries like Spain. On its side, the UK experienced strong employment growth after the recovery, but stagnating productivity. In order to tackle the productivity shortfall while creating new types of jobs, European policymakers will have to refocus their efforts on technological upgrading in tradable sectors, where productivity can be raised more efficiently than in low-paying services.

This does not imply seeking constant and massive trade surpluses at all costs, but rather developing the type of coordination that steers industrial competition towards modernisation. Although the economic model based on constant trade surpluses vis-à-vis the rest of the world is being generalised to the entire Eurozone (with a current account surplus above 3 per cent of GDP), this transition has relied more on a downward pressure on wages, investment and consumption than on productivity gains and technological catch-up. Meanwhile, the UK has gone through a prolonged period of large external deficits, which have magnified the threat from Brexit on its economic model.

A coordinated approach to investment is needed in order both to rebalance economic relations amongst economies, and to embark on a new wave of technological change. The industrial sector in most European countries is generally poorly automated and the area as a whole is just waking up to the strategic importance of artificial intelligence. At the same time, vast disparities persist among member states in terms of industrial sophistication and specialisation. The UK, France and the Eurozone's peripheral countries lag behind most other developed economies on the robotic front. Although robots are particularly suited for the car industry, which helped Germany given its specialization on the sector, the difference persists even when accounting for sector specialization. In addition, the replacement of obsolete systems follows a much slower pace in countries which are less automated.[31] While Germany's manufacturing sector has more than 309 industrial robots per 100,000 workers, Italy has 185, France about 132, and the UK a small 71, slightly lower than the world average.[32] This compares with 631 in South Korea (and an unemployment rate still below 4 per cent). Meanwhile, China is buying about a quarter of all robots produced worldwide.

Since the crisis, national economies have further diverged on the techno-logical front at a time when all European countries would have been expected to embrace the ongoing industrial revolution. European policymakers tend to focus more on structural reforms of the labour market than on the way robotics, artificial intelligence and 3D printing are starting to reshape the world economy, both in manufacturing and services. A coordinated shift from the current downward competition in terms of labour costs towards technology-based investment and competition would both help to address the roots of the productivity problem still facing Europe and to foster real con-vergence, at a time when Brexit and the outburst of populism throughout the continent point to the need for stronger and more inclusive growth.

NOTES

1. Thomas Fetzer, 'Had austerity not happened, leave support could have been up to 10% lower', LSE Blog, 2018, http://blogs.lse.ac.uk/politicsandpolicy/did-austerity-cause-brexit/; *New York Times*, 'In Britain, austerity is changing everything', 28 May 2018, https://www.nytimes.com/2018/05/28/world/europe/uk-austerity-poverty.html.
2. *Wall Street Journal*, 'Boris Johnson and the great realignment', 17 December 2019, see https://www.wsj.com/articles/boris-johnson-and-the-great-realignment-11576626535.
3. *Financial Times*, 'Manufacturing enjoys longest period of jobs growth for 40 years', 13 September 2018, https://www.ft.com/content/6e60e386-ab9a-11e8-89a1-e5de165fa619.
4. On the role of the 'liberal elite' within the Tory Party, see Piers Ludlow, 'Britain's liberal elite can't wash their hands of Brexit', October 2016, http://blogs.lse.ac.uk/europpblog/2016/10/27/an-elite-problem-too/.
5. See Reuters, 'Brexit would leave Europe less Liberal, less Atlanticist', 5 June 2016, see, at https://www.reuters.com/article/us-britain-eu-future-analysis-idUSKCN0YR0BH; Ulrich Speck, 'Why Britain is vital for the European Union', Carnegie Europe, 26 October 2012, http://carnegieeurope.eu/strategiceurope/?fa=49815.
6. See Leopold Traugott's blog post: 'How Brexit will affect Germany's role in the EU', May 2018, http://blogs.lse.ac.uk/europpblog/2018/05/18/how-brexit-will-affect-germanys-role-in-the-eu/.
7. For a brief account of the issue of the UK trade deficit with the EU and the histor-ical evolution of the debate, see Larry Elliott's column: 'Why the UK trade deficit with the EU is woeful and widening', *The Guardian*, 8 April 2018, https://www.theguardian.com/business/2018/apr/08/why-the-uk-trade-deficit-with-the-eu-is-woeful-and-widening.
8. Ameco, October 2018. The UK's public deficit reached 10.1 per cent of GDP in 2009, a level similar to that experienced by Spain (10.9), Portugal (11.2 the fol-lowing year), and to some extent Greece (15.1), while Italy's deficit reached 4.2 per cent of GDP in 2009, Germany 4.2 per cent in 2010, and France 7.1 per cent in 2009.

9. Statistics on UK–EU trade, UK Parliament, https://researchbriefings.parliament
    .uk/ResearchBriefing/Summary/CBP-7851.
10. Oliver Wyman, 'The impact of the UK's exit from the EU on the UK-based finan-
    cial services sector, 2016, https://www.oliverwyman.com/content/dam/oliver
    -wyman/global/en/2016/oct/OW%20report_Brexit%20impact%20on%20Uk
    -based%20FS.pdf.
11. Reuters, 'Bank of England says UK's reliance on kindness of strangers for finance
    is rising', 16 March 2018, https://www.reuters.com/article/us-britain-boe-banks/
    bank-of-england-says-uks-reliance-on-kindness-of-strangers-for-finance-is-rising
    -idUSKCN1GS12P.
12. The index of nominal unit labour costs can be defined as the nominal average
    wage relative to real productivity (per employee).
13. *Real* unit labour costs can be equivalently defined as the share of wages in GDP
    rather than as an index like nominal ULCs.
14. See 'Quantitative Easing' on the BoE's website, https://www.bankofengland.co
    .uk/monetary-policy/quantitative-easing.
15. *Financial Times*, 'Bank of England defends response to financial crisis after
    criticism', 10 April 2018, https://www.ft.com/content/4231c5a0-3caf-11e8-b9f9
    -de94fa33a81e.
16. For a measurement of inequalities in terms of the Gini index in OECD coun-
    tries, see https://read.oecd-ilibrary.org/social-issues-migration-health/income
    -inequality_9789264246010-en#page25.
17. See A. Haldane, 'The UK's productivity problem: hub no spokes', speech at the
    Academy of Social Sciences Annual Lecture, London, 28 June 2016.
18. *The Guardian*, 'UK only G7 country with wider inequality than at turn of
    century', 14 October 2014, https://www.theguardian.com/society/2014/oct/14/uk
    -inequality-wealth-credit-suisse.
19. International Monetary Fund (IMF) 'World Economic Outlook' database, October
    2018.
20. IMF Country Focus, 'UK economy must get more efficient', 14 February 2018,
    https://www.imf.org/en/News/Articles/2018/02/08/na021418-uk-economy-must
    -get-more-efficient.
21. Labour productivity per hours worked tends to indicate a similar pattern.
    Productivity per worker is used here in order to facilitate cross-country
    comparisons.
22. McKinsey, 'Productivity: the route to Brexit success', December 2016, https://
    www.mckinsey.com/featured-insights/europe/productivity-the-route-to-brexit
    -success.
23. J. Bughin, J. Dimson, V. Hunt, T. Allas, M. Krishnan, J. Mischke, L. Chambers
    and M. Canal, 'Solving the United Kingdom's productivity puzzle in a digital
    age', McKinsey Discussion Paper, September 2018, https://www.mckinsey.com/
    ~/media/mckinsey/featured%20insights/meeting%20societys%20expectations/
    solving%20the%20united%20kingdoms%20productivity%20puzzle%20in%20a
    %20digital%20age/mgi-productivity-in-the-uk-discussion-paper-september-2018
    .ashx.
24. European Commission's Ameco online database—data retrieved 12 November
    2019.
25. Politico.eu, 'Theresa May pledges lowest business tax rate in G20 post Brexit',
    26 September 2018, https://www.politico.eu/article/theresa-may-pledges-lowest
    -business-tax-rate-in-g20-post-brexit/.

26. *Sunday Times*, 'UK could slash corporation tax to 10 percent if EU blocks Brexit trade deal', 23 October 2016.
27. Reuters, 'UK's Johnson drops corporate tax cut plan in bid to woo voters', 18th November 2019, see, at https://www.reuters.com/article/us-britain-election -corporationtax/uks-johnson-drops-corporate-tax-cut-plan-in-bid-to-woo-voters -idUSKBN1XS1AR.
28. KPMG's database on corporate tax rates, https://home.kpmg.com/xx/en/home/ services/tax/tax-tools-and-resources/tax-rates-online/corporate-tax-rates-table .html (accessed 25 October 2018).
29. Reuters, 'Germany, France agree on harmonization of corporate tax systems', 20th June 2018,   see, at https://www.reuters.com/article/us-germany-france -tax-harmonisation/germany-france-agree-on-harmonization-of-corporate-tax -systems-idUSKBN1JG1RB.
30. *Financial Times*, 'Carmakers call for Brexit clarity', 5 October 2018, https://www .ft.com/content/fabfdd94-c884-11e8-ba8f-ee390057b8c9.
31. Reuters France, 'Des robots trop rares, trop vieux' ['Too expensive and too old robots'], 18th October 2012, see, at https://fr.reuters.com/article/topNews/ idFRPAE89H07S20121018.
32. International Federation of Robotics, https://ifr.org/ifr-press-releases/news/robot -density-rises-globally.

REFERENCES

Bach, S., G. Baldi, K. Bernoth, B. Bremer, B. Farkas, F. Fichtner, M. Fratzscher and M. Gornig (2013), 'Deutschland muss mehr in seine Zukunft investieren', DIW Wochenbericht 26/2013, DIW Berlin, https://www.diw.de/documents/ publikationen/73/diw_01.c.423520.de/13-26-1.pdf.
Bongardt, A. and F. Torres (2016), 'The political economy of Brexit: why making it easier to leave the club can allow for a better functioning EU', *Intereconomics* 51(4), pp. 214–19, https://archive.intereconomics.eu/year/2016/4/the-political-economy-of -brexit-why-making-it-easier-to-leave-the-club-could-improve-the-eu/.
Bongardt, A. and F. Torres (2019), 'The road towards a genuine economic and monetary union: more competitive and fairer', in Paolo Chiocchetti and Frédéric Allemand (eds), *Competitiveness and Solidarity in the European Union*, London: Routledge.
Bourgeot, R. (2013), 'Labour costs and crisis management in the Eurozone: a reinterpretation of divergences in competitiveness', Robert Schuman Foundation.
Carney, M. (2017), 'The high road to a responsible, open financial system', http://www .bankofengland.co.uk/publications/Documents/speeches/2017/speech973.pdf.
Chen, J., C. Ebeke, L. Lin, H. Qu and J. Siminitz (2018), 'The long-term impact of Brexit on the European Union', IMF, https://blogs.imf.org/2018/08/10/the-long -term-impact-of-brexit-on-the-european-union/.
Dhingra, S., G. Ottaviano, T. Sampson and J. Van Reenen (2016), 'The Impact of Brexit on foreign investment in the UK', Centre for Economic Performance (CEP), London School of Economics, http://cep.lse.ac.uk/pubs/download/brexit03.pdf.
Emmerson, C. and G. Tetlow (2015), 'Fiscal responses of six European countries to the Great Recession: a crisis wasted?', Institute for Fiscal Studies, https://www.ifs.org .uk/publications/8082.

Felbermayr, G., C. Fuest, J. Gröschl and D. Stöhlker (2017), 'Economic effects of Brexit on the European economy', EconPol Policy Report, Vol. 1, CesIfo, https://www.cesifo-group.de/DocDL/EconPol_Policy_Report_04_2017_Brexit.pdf.

Frieden, J. (2016), *Currency Politics: The Political Economy of Exchange Rate Policy*, Princeton, NJ: Princeton University Press.

Lavery, S., L. Quaglia and C. Dannreuther (2017), 'The political economy of Brexit and the UK's national business model', SPERI Paper No. 41, Sheffield Political Economy Research Institute, https://brussels.whiterose.ac.uk/wp-content/uploads/2017/05/SPERI-Paper-41-The-Political-Economy-of-Brexit-and-the-UK-s-National-Business-Model-PRINT-2.pdf.

Luo, C. M. (2017), 'Brexit and its implications for European integration', *European Review* 25(4), pp. 519–31.

Syverson, C. (2016), 'Challenges to mismeasurement explanations for the U.S. productivity slowdown', NBER Working Paper, https://www.nber.org/papers/w21974.

Talani, L. S. (2015), 'The origins of the euro-zone crisis: the EMU and the loss of competitiveness', at, https://www.eui.eu/Projects/PierreWernerChair/Documents/MIKE-ARTIS/MikeArtiscommemorationpaper.pdf.

Talani, L. S. (2016), 'Brexit: a real challenge for the future of the City', in *The Impact of Brexit on the City and the British Economic Model*, 'Diverging Capitalisms?' Series, Brief No. 1, Sheffield Political Economy Research Institute, www.policy-network.net/publications_download.aspx?ID=9408.

10. Brexit: what have we learnt?

Annette Bongardt, Leila Simona Talani and Francisco Torres

10.1 THE POLITICS AND ECONOMICS OF BREXIT

The chapters in this volume differ in their focus and approach but speak to each other across both parts of the book on the politics and economics of Brexit. The four chapters that comprise Part I, The Politics of Brexit, are concerned with what fundamentally motivated the UK's exit from the European Union (Bongardt and Torres; Di Quirico), which also includes the issue of sovereignty given the absence of a written UK constitution (Baroncelli and Rosini). Diodato and Giusti look at the narrative that underpinned Brexit in terms of its standing in the world once it had left the Union ('Global Britain').

Annette Bongardt and Francisco Torres (Chapter 2) argue that Brexit can be viewed as a logical consequence and culmination of the UK harbouring ever more divergent preferences from the EU. That divergence became incompatible and arguably unsustainable when EU integration deepened to Economic and Monetary Union but the UK was not prepared to go along with the requirements to make it function. There is hence political rationality behind the UK having triggered the EU's exit clause, Article 50 TEU. The authors discuss that the UK, however, found it unpalatable that, even as a third country to the EU, it still faces the same kind of dilemma as an EU member, namely that it has to make a choice as to the degree of proximity to the EU's internal market (by far its largest market), as any post-Brexit preferential trade agreement with the EU faces some trade-off between sovereignty and the available economic benefits. As for the EU, the UK's departure has on the one hand put in sharp focus the limits of differentiated integration and the need to face the question of the Union's optimum size, and has on the other hand also shed light on opportunities for the EU and important lessons for the sustainability of the club.

Roberto Di Quirico (Chapter 3) also argues that Brexit was not just an accident, resulting from an unexpected outcome of a populist referendum, but rather a real political option. His chapter shows that there was a long-term rationale for Brexit, already since the early years of the UK's membership in the EEC. The UK's approach to European further integration, which he characterizes as one of 'malign neglect', had become no longer sustainable when the UK had stayed out of EMU and economic governance advances, and had become ever more marginal in EU affairs and as a consequence also in its global role. In his view, at the time of the UK's June 2016 in–out referendum, the choice before the country was not between a mere in and out but between full integration or complete marginalisation in European affairs, and Brexit.

Stefania Baroncelli and Monica Rosini (Chapter 4) discuss another rationale for Brexit, the absence of a UK written constitution. They argue that the Brexit process challenges the principle of parliamentary sovereignty, which is the basic norm of the British constitutional system, in a number of ways. They examine three of those challenges, namely the use of a referendum to decide on the UK membership of the EU; the effects on executive-legislative relations; and the problems raised by the existence of devolved legislatures in Scotland, Wales and Northern Ireland. Analysing in particular judgements of the Courts, especially the Supreme Court, which seems ever more decisive for guiding the evolution of the UK form of state and government, they find that the principle of parliamentary sovereignty tends to resist these challenges and that tensions seem to pave the way for further developments.

Emilio Diodato and Serena Giusti (Chapter 5) focus on the prospects for the UK's foreign policy post Brexit, notably discussing the role of 'Global Britain' and pointing out its vagueness and its limits. In the authors' view, the departure of the UK from the EU will have dramatic implications for British foreign policy, given that the UK is no longer backed up by the European Union and its collective weight and standing. The authors employ discourse analysis of official speeches on the UK and EU membership, combining role theory and critical geopolitics to examine 'Global Britain'. They find that while losing influence in Europe, the UK is 'trudging through international politics', seeking a global role based on the revival of old narratives and their roots in the country's history, including the controversial empire era.

Part II of the book, The Economics of Brexit, comprises four chapters that examine different aspects of the UK's and/or EU's economic model. Pompeo Della Posta and Scheherazade S. Rehman (Chapter 6) begin by analysing the possible reasons for Brexit by tracking the performance of the UK economy and examining the social capital issues of increasing economic inequality and ethnic diversity up to (the referendum year) 2016. They observe that the increasing economic inequality and the fear by certain sectors of the population of the expected consequences of larger ethnic heterogeneity served as drivers for Brexit in that they created a fertile socio-economic ground for populism. The authors conclude, however, that Brexit is also due to the erosion of social capital, determined by a feeling of 'disconnectedness' as a common feature of the British population who voted leave, compelled to face on their own the negative consequences of globalisation and technological developments. In their opinion both the vote for Brexit and the subsequent political chaos are related to an actual reduction in, and in some cases a perception of, decreased social capital rather than hard economic factors.

Annette Bongardt (Chapter 7) focuses on the economic framework that EU membership provided as a possible motive for the UK's hesitations (until the December 2019 elections) over actually departing. Regardless of having voted for and triggered Brexit, the UK has found it difficult to actually exit the European Union. The chapter discusses the UK's Brexit dilemma in light of the benefits associated with the European single market cum regulation, examining the state of the internal market and the possibility of a truly single market in terms of market opening, regulation, and the institutional environment (including structural reform), as well as the single market as the EU's vehicle for (quality) growth and its governance. The chapter pinpoints the sources of the UK's ambivalent stance, discussing what the UK loses by giving preference to (regaining) sovereignty, from the point of view of the internal market's status quo and the possibility of pushing for a truly single market if it had remained in the EU (after all, the single market is work in progress), and considering what the country could or might have wanted to do in response. It concludes on the stark choices facing the country post Brexit.

Leila Simona Talani (Chapter 8) draws on a parallel between the monetarist approaches adopted by the British government in the 1980s and the UK responses to Brexit, which she argues will allow the City of London to thrive. She notes that the monetarism of former prime minister Margaret Thatcher responded to the needs and preferences of the British financial elite in light of the City's so-called 'revolution' of 1986–7, while deregulation practices ensuing from Brexit also meet the preferences of the British financial elite, especially at the dawn of a new innovation era. The chapter analyses the evolution of deregulation and innovation in the City of London during the Thatcher era and identifies those policies that will allow the City to thrive, noticing the similarities. Talani concludes that there is continuity between deregulation and innovation practices in the 1980s and the policy needs of the City after Brexit.

Rémi Bourgeot (Chapter 9) considers the challenges that are lying ahead in a context characterized by EU sluggish growth and productivity and a UK that may opt to increase its reliance on offshore finance and fiscal/regulatory competition. As he points out, the latter UK option risks aggravating the economic imbalances and inequalities that exacerbated the social malaise in the run-up to the Brexit vote. The author also defends that more cohesion is needed in the EU not only to address the consequences of Brexit and preserve ties, but also for the Union and the Eurozone to rebalance their model away from their short-term focus on current account surpluses and depressed labour cost. He holds that the ongoing industrial revolution offers opportunities to steer the EU and the UK towards a more efficient and inclusive growth model.

10.2   LESSONS LEARNT AND OUTLOOK

The chapters in this book have brought together both political and economic issues with the aim of disentangling matters with respect to possible drivers and implications of Brexit and to sharpen awareness of the relevance of certain issues within the context of the overall Brexit picture. A better understanding of the root causes and of the determinants of Brexit is also a precondition for assessing possible and/or likely further developments in the UK and the consequences of Brexit for the EU.

From the point of view of the politics of Brexit, there is political rationality in why the possibility of Brexit came up and why it happened (Bongardt and Torres, Chapter 2). And there are good reasons, above all economic, why the UK nevertheless dithered a long time over whether really to leave (Bongardt, Chapter 7). It is hence hardly surprising that any profound discussion of the UK's post-Brexit future has for most of the time been sidelined.

What stands out to start with is that the UK kept apart from other member states of the Union and that it often, and increasingly so, harboured different preferences from the EU club. British exceptionalism, or claims to it, is not a new feature. Misconceptions about the EU and about the UK's standing and role in the world date back a very long time and continue under the heading and narrative of 'Global Britain', as argued by Diodato and Giusti (Chapter 5). When the UK decided to join the EEC, it did so essentially motivated by economic reasons, with its empire falling apart and growth below the EEC's. Economic concerns overrode its previously dominant concerns with sovereignty. In light of the latter it had refrained from joining the EEC at its inception (the UK left the preparatory Spaak Committee in protest against supranational governance) and founded the European Free Trade Association (EFTA), a rival and intergovernmental club to the intrinsically political European integration project, with a narrow and tightly circumscribed purpose and scope (free trade zone).

After finally joining the EEC in 1973 and upon interacting with the club, one might have expected the country's preferences to converge with those of other member states and its negative attitude towards further integration – after all, the UK repeatedly subscribed to the objective of ever-closer union on the occasion of revisions of the founding treaties – to attenuate with inside experience and subside. Instead, the UK's attitude remained one of malign neglect, as put by Di Quirico (Chapter 3). This is not to say that the UK's role has not been important at times. Most notably, the single market of the EU would hardly have come into existence had it not been for the UK led by Prime Minister Margaret Thatcher (and its fit with supply side economics and liberalization).

Still, even with regard to the single market of the EU and despite its economic benefits, the UK came to dislike the EU regulatory model, displaying diverse and often divergent preferences, as explained by Bongardt in Chapter 7. This is true for the UK's financial sector, the City of London, as shown by Talani (Chapter 8). Della Posta and Rehman (Chapter 6) emphasize that the UK's socio-economic model was decisive for Brexit, not because of its economic growth performance but because of social capital issues (above all increasing economic in inequality). The EU has a tool, the Europe 2020 strategy, to address those issues but the coordination mode is soft and hence implementation depends on a member state's actions and its willingness and capacity (Bongardt, Chapter 7). The EU regulatory model also affords a significant degree of leeway in terms of regulation.

It was since the EU took a further step up the economic integration ladder at Maastricht, from a common market to Economic and Monetary Union, that the UK started to increasingly diverge and distance itself from the EU and that its position in the EU became incompatible, as argued by Bongardt and Torres (Chapter 2) and Di Quirico (Chapter 3). Above all, it was the fact that the UK opted out of monetary union that put it on collision course with a Union in which all members – present and future – committed to join the Eurozone at some point and where the only other country besides the UK that obtained a derogation, Denmark, shadows the euro area. UK preferences for a standalone economic union, meaning one that does not cater to the basic requirements for the good functioning and sustainability of the monetary union side of EMU, started to cause friction for the UK (different preferences for regulation) but became unsustainable for the EU political project. The UK had become the least integrated of all EU members when exiting the club (Chapter 2).

From an EU point of view, and as argued by Bongardt and Torres, Brexit came to illustrate that EU differentiated integration had reached its limits (Chapter 2). It was no longer possible to accommodate the UK without compromising the EU's political project and its essential values. The UK's idiosyncrasy, and especially its lack of a written constitution, made the task of integration – but also Brexit – difficult, as explained by Baroncelli and Rosini (Chapter 4). There is also the question whether the UK's preferences with regard to the socio-economic model of development – as discussed in Della Posta and Rehman (Chapter 6), Bourgeot (Chapter 9) and Bongardt (Chapter 7) – are not more aligned with many of its traditional allies (such as Canada or the USA, for instance with regard to labour and social standards) than with the EU's regulation-based model that envisages a social market economy (Chapter 7). As argued by Talani (Chapter 8), the City of London, which was able to carve out a regulatory space in line with its preferences in the single market while the UK was a EU member (unlikely to continue once the UK becomes a third country to the EU), is a case in point. The fact that the UK chose not to participate in many of the EU's most important institutions (above all EMU and Schengen but many others) not only meant that it set itself apart within the club but also that it thereby precluded its preferences to converge by way of shared experiences and lessons (as happened for instance in the Eurozone in the sovereign debt crisis). The UK's mixture of non-participation, boycott and veto in EU institutions in the end impeded the Union's ability to function.

In conclusion, there is political rationality for the UK's exit from the Union and for the Union, which is likely to work better without it. Brexit is no doubt a milestone – the UK is the first EU member country to have exited the club – but, in contrast to earlier expectations, the Union did not crumble and the political project neither dissolved nor was watered down. Rather, on the contrary, it emerged stronger throughout the withdrawal process, with the EU-27 united behind Brexit purpose and firm in defending the Union and its principles.

Of course, with Brexit settled, the EU and UK political games will go on in negotiations of the future bilateral relationship, which are bound to be complex and time-consuming (judging by the EU's experience with the Canada and Singapore free trade agreements). The UK might have become an EU outsider but it still has continued unfettered access to the EU single market until the end of 2020 under the transition period agreed under the Withdrawal Treaty. That might not be smooth sailing with regard to UK obligations. A foretaste was given recently by the UK's insufficient regard to its obligations (such as data protection and reciprocity) in its participation in the Schengen Information System. The UK could even have asked for a prolongation of one to two years of the transition period. Having curtailed the possibility of asking for prolongation by mid-2020, the UK government is hence letting wilfully loom another potential cliff-edge situation by 2021 that is to put pressure on the EU to give it an advantageous free trade agreement at unusual pace (another go at cherry-picking?). As a third country to the EU, the UK will face the hard choices and inherent trade-offs between available economic benefits and national sovereignty that arise in, and will define the depth and scope of, its bilateral future relationship with the Union.

How close the UK will stay to the single market remains to be seen. Note that a lot of UK trade is associated with global value chains or carried out intra-firm. This could be restructured in a way so as to avoid the imposition of export tariffs while keeping import tariffs low or at zero. For the UK, therefore, the issue of staying in the single market may not represent a major problem as far as trade in goods is concerned. As for trade in services, the political declaration to the withdrawal treaty already rules it out. For the EU, proximity to its single market is invariably conditioned by regulatory alignment. Still, some form of bilateral agreement, if bare-bones and incomplete, is very likely to be achieved by the deadline of 31 December 2020, which prioritizes sensitive issues (such as aviation, energy, pharmaceuticals and anti-terrorism) while other issues might be left to future discussions. Ultimately, the consequences of Brexit not only depend on the UK or the EU, but also on the direction of globalisation.

Index